Galen Grimes

SAMS
Teach Yourself

Upgrading and Fixing PCs

in 24 Hours

SECOND EDITION

SAMS

A Division of Macmillan USA
201 West 103rd St., Indianapolis, Indiana, 46290

Sams Teach Yourself Upgrading and Fixing PCs in 24 Hours, Second Edition

Copyright © 2000 by Sams Publishing

International Standard Book Number: 0-672-31881-4

Library of Congress Catalog Card Number: 99-069606

Printed in the United States of America

First Printing: March 2000

02 01 00   4   3   2

Trademarks

Warning and Disclaimer

ACQUISITIONS EDITOR
Betsy Brown

DEVELOPMENT EDITOR
Jon Steever

MANAGING EDITOR
Charlotte Clapp

SENIOR EDITOR
Karen A. Walsh

COPY EDITOR
Kim Cofer

INDEXER
Kevin Kent

PROOFREADERS
Tony Reitz
Matt Wynalda

TECHNICAL EDITOR
Dennis Teague

TEAM COORDINATOR
Amy Patton

INTERIOR DESIGN
Gary Adair

COVER DESIGN
Aren Howell

COPYWRITER
Eric Borgert

LAYOUT TECHNICIANS
Stacey Richwine-DeRome
Heather Hiatt Miller
Ayanna Lacey

Contents at a Glance

Table of Contents

About the Author

GALEN A. GRIMES has been working with computers since 1980 when he purchased his first PC, an Apple II+. Since then he has worked on PCs using DOS, Windows (3.1/95/NT 4.0), and UNIX, and has programmed in about a dozen different programming languages, including C/C++, Assembler, Pascal, BASIC, and xBase. Galen has a master's degree in Information Science from the University of Pittsburgh, and is currently on the faculty of Penn State University at its McKeesport campus teaching in the Department of Information Sciences and Technologies.

Although originally born and raised in Texas, Galen now makes his home in a quiet, heavily wooded section of Monroeville, PA, a suburb of Pittsburgh, with his wife Joanne and an assortment of deer, raccoon, squirrels, possums, groundhogs, chipmunks, and birds, which are all fed from their back door. Besides working with computers and surfing the Internet, Galen spends his time playing golf, bicycling, dabbling in amateur astronomy, gardening, cooking, and refining the art of "couch-potatoing." Each fall he and his wife Joanne are transformed into two of the most enthusiastic football fans for Penn State's Nittany Lions (see http://www.psu.edu/sports/).

Galen can be reached either by email at galen@felixnet.com or through his Web site at http://www.felixnet.com/.

Dedication

To Ross and Grant—I hope you know how fortunate you are to be exposed to computing at such a young age. I hope you make the most of it. Just remember: You can always call on me for help.

Acknowledgments

To everyone at Macmillan USA—especially Betsy Brown. Their work and ideas made a great contribution to this book.

Also my thanks go out to Jon Steever, Karen Walsh, Kim Cofer, Tony Reitz, and Matt Wynalda for the countless hours they slaved over the manuscript weeding out the errors, and for the countless suggestions they made, which ultimately helped produce a better product.

Tell Us What You Think!

As the reader of this book, *you* are our most important critic and commentator. We value your opinion and want to know what we're doing right, what we could do better, what areas you'd like to see us publish in, and any other words of wisdom you're willing to pass our way.

You can email or write me directly to let me know what you did or didn't like about this book—as well as what we can do to make our books stronger.

Please note that I cannot help you with technical problems related to the topic of this book, and that due to the high volume of mail I receive, I might not be able to reply to every message.

When you write, please be sure to include this book's title and author as well as your name and phone number. I will carefully review your comments and share them with the author and editors who worked on the book.

Email: `office_sams@mcp.com`
Mail: Mark Taber
            Associate Publisher
            Sams Publishing
            201 West 103rd Street
            Indianapolis, IN 46290 USA

Introduction

Upgrading is as American as apple pie and hot rods. In fact, the upgrade spirit we see today is most likely an offshoot of the hot rod craze that grew out of the 1950s. Back then there was a seemingly neverending contest to see who could make the hottest modifications to improve auto performance.

Despite the existence of a market seemingly flooded with commodity priced PCs, there are still a large number of savvy PC users who like to tinker under the hood of their PC and see what modifications they can make to improve computing performance.

Whether you place yourself within the ranks of the savvy PC user or the neophyte beginner, you don't have to sit on the sidelines any longer and nor do you have to wait to buy a new PC to see any type of performance gains.

Whether you merely want to add a bit more memory or want to make a wholesale upgrade of your motherboard, processor, and drive components, you now have the knowledge needed to feel comfortable tinkering under the hood of your PC.

It's now time to roll up your sleeves and start getting dirty.

PART I

Diagnosing Problems and Planning an Upgrade

Hour

HOUR 1

Making the Decision to Upgrade

It seems that a week hardly passes when news of a newer, faster, and more powerful PC isn't making headlines. Although most auto manufacturers have the luxury and breathing room of having to release new models only on a yearly basis, PC manufacturers sometimes appear to be releasing new models every quarter, if not sooner. It's no wonder PC users are confused and a bit apprehensive each time they go shopping for a new PC. The intense competition of the hot PC market is both a blessing and a curse for users. If you've been watching PC prices nose-dive, you are already aware of the consumer blessing this competition has produced. Users appear to be cursed, however, by being forced to play the "wait-and-see" game: "If I wait just a little longer before I purchase, I can get a faster, more powerful PC and pay less for it."

You do have an alternative to the wait-and-see game. Despite the downward trend of PC prices and the seeming glut of sub-$1000 PCs hitting the market, many users are opting instead to upgrade portions of their PC rather than purchase an entirely new PC. Although upgrading often will not exactly match the performance of a new PC, as you will see over the next 24 hours, selective upgrading of certain key components in your PC can substantially improve performance in the areas that matter most to you, depending on how you use your PC.

During this hour you will learn:

- When you should consider upgrading your PC and when you should forgo upgrading and purchase a new PC
- Which components in your PC can and should be upgraded and how to select the components to upgrade that will benefit you the most

When You Should Consider Upgrading Your PC

The first decision you are faced with is whether to upgrade or purchase a new PC. If you are still using a PC with a 486 processor (or heaven forbid, something older) the decision has already been made for you. Your old PC should be considered nothing more than an obsolete boat anchor or doorstop, and you should be concerned only with deciding how much you will spend on a new PC.

If you are still using a PC with a first generation Pentium processor, the decision may not seem so clear-cut (even though it really is). The early Pentium processors (that is, Pentiums with a clock speed of 100 MHz or less) are at least six years old and are not really capable of running the current batch of software at an acceptable performance level. But if you are still running Windows 3.1 and DOS 6.2x (or higher) and are content to perform some light word processing and spreadsheet tasks, and you occasionally want to browse a few Web sites on the Internet or play a few (older!) games, you may be able to squeeze another year or two out of that creaking old dinosaur.

 If you are still using Windows 3.1x, make sure you are using it with at least MS-DOS versions 6.2x or PC-DOS version 7.0. These versions of DOS offer you the best memory management operation with Windows, which in the long run will allow you the best level of performance.

Consider the fact that you have to look not only at how you are currently using your PC, but how you are likely to use it in the future. If you have not moved up to a new *32-bit* operating system such as Windows 98 or Windows 2000, you probably will in the next year because most major software manufacturers have long since ceased producing software that runs under Windows 3.1. Considering the speed of current processors, you should probably draw the line at a 200 MHz Pentium. If you are running anything slower, it's time to upgrade.

16-bit and *32-bit* are technical terms you will hear whenever the discussion turns to operating systems and/or programming, among other things. Quite simply, they refer to how computer instructions and data are processed by your computer, either in 16-bit units or in 32-bit units. Because a 32-bit unit is twice as large as a 16-bit unit, the assumption is that 32-bit programs and operating systems are twice as fast as their 16-bit counterparts. Twice as fast may be stretching it a bit, but the basic underlying assumption is generally true. 32-bit programs and operating systems are faster than 16-bit programs and operating systems.

What Components in My PC Are Upgradeable?

If you have browsed this book's Table of Contents, you already have an idea which components in your PC are upgradeable. If you haven't taken a quick look over the TOC, you may be surprised to learn that almost every component in your PC, including the processor, memory, video card, disk drives, and more, is a candidate to be upgraded.

Which components you decide to upgrade often will be determined by how you use your PC, but not always. Some upgrades make sense simply because the price of the particular component is too good to pass up. In the last few years, the price of hard disk drives has dropped dramatically. You can regularly see 10–12GB hard disk drives advertised for around $200. Remember the old saying, "…you can never have too much money or hard disk space."

If you're wondering where to start with your upgrading plans, Table 1.1 might give you some ideas on how to deal with some problems or issues you might already be facing.

TABLE 1.1   Quick Troubleshooting Table

Problem	Possible Upgrade Solution	Hour
PC locks up or can't load more than a few programs simultaneously	Add more memory	6

continues

TABLE 1.1 continued

Problem	Possible Upgrade Solution	Hour
Programs or files load very slowly from CD-ROM drive	Upgrade to faster CD-ROM drive	13
32-bit software won't install	Upgrade to 32-bit OS	23
Can't format larger hard disk drive	Upgrade your BIOS	10
Can't increase video resolution or number of colors displayed	Upgrade your video card	17
Repeatedly seeing "out of disk space" error message	Upgrade/add new hard disk drive	11
All PC operations run slower than expected	Upgrade your CPU	7
System clock losing correct time or has wrong time	Upgrade your BIOS	10

Upgrading Your Memory (RAM)

Your PC's memory typically is one of the easiest and least expensive components to upgrade (see Figure 1.1). Upgrading your PC's memory also has the added advantage of improving its performance. Sometimes the improvement in performance is large and other times it is small, but there is always an increase of some type.

NEW TERM   *RAM* and *memory* are often used interchangeably. RAM is short for Random Access Memory and is the electronic memory (chips) that your computer uses for running programs and storing temporary data. RAM is not the permanent storage area for files.

Not all memory performance improvements are readily apparent. For example, if you boost the memory above 16MB in a PC still running Windows 3.1, the performance improvements will not be very noticeable because Windows 3.1 cannot directly access more than 16MB of memory. The extra memory can be utilized for disk caching by the SmartDrive disk cache utility or used to create a RAM drive to improve the performance of the Windows

1

swap file. In case the terms are unfamiliar to you, a *disk cache* is a temporary holding area in memory for data that your computer might need to quickly access. A *swap file* is an area on your hard disk that Windows uses like memory when all of your RAM (electronic memory) is used up.

FIGURE 1.1

PC memory is probably the easiest of all upgrades you can make.

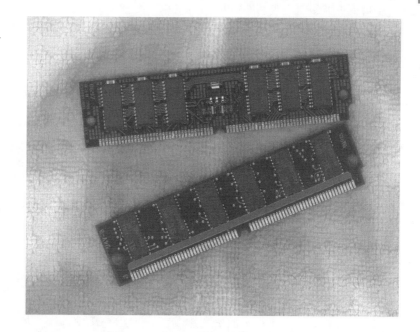

Memory upgrades are covered and explained in detail in Hour 6, "Upgrading Your PC's Memory."

Upgrading Your Processor

Because your processor is largely responsible for how fast your PC and your programs run, upgrading your processor will generally make most things run faster. But bear in mind that if you replace the Pentium 100 MHz processor in your PC with a 200 MHz Pentium processor, your computer will not necessarily operate as fast as a PC built "from the ground up" as a 200 MHz Pentium computer. It is not just the processor that determines how fast your PC operates. There are other technologies that come into play, and these differences also contribute to the computer's speed and performance.

NEW TERM *MHz* is the abbreviation for *megahertz* (millions of hertz per second) and is used as a measurement for the oscillating timing frequency used by processors. In simpler terms, it is an indication of the relative speed of a processor.

Upgrading your processor will generally yield some increase in performance. In Hour 7, "Upgrading Your CPU," I explain how you can determine if and when it is advisable to upgrade and how to select an upgrade processor.

Upgrading Your Hard Disk Drive

Upgrading your PC's hard disk drive (see Figure 1.2) is probably the second most common upgrade behind memory upgrades, largely because of the dramatic drop in hard disk pricing and the increase in available hard disk sizes.

FIGURE 1.2

You can never have too much disk storage space.

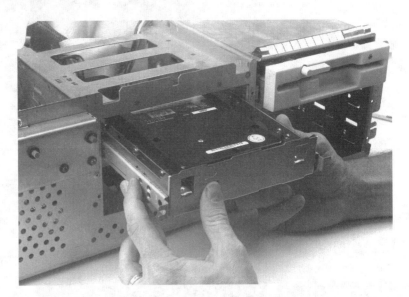

Upgrading a hard disk is also relatively easy. Although adding a larger hard disk drive might not seem like a significant performance improvement, consider your own habits in file creation and how often you acquire new programs you would like to try—especially if you regularly download shareware programs from the Internet.

If you once had or currently have a small hard disk, (small being defined as any hard disk 2.5GB or smaller), and you regularly find yourself deleting files to make room for new files or programs, you can appreciate the performance improvement offered by the addition of a larger hard disk.

Upgrading Your Video System

The majority of the time you choose to upgrade your video system, it will be for a specific application. For example, you might need a larger or higher resolution monitor (see Figure 1.3) to work with a specific application, such as graphic artistry or CAD (computer aided design). Many of the newer games also require better, faster video systems.

FIGURE 1.3
When purchasing a monitor, purchase as large as you can afford.

Even if you are not a graphic artist or CAD engineer, there are still good reasons to upgrade your video system. In Hours 17, "Upgrading Your Video Card," and 18, "Upgrading Your Video Monitor," I explain what benefits you gain from these types of upgrades.

Upgrading Other PC Components

The few components mentioned in this hour are not the only items in your PC that you can upgrade. In addition to memory, processors, hard disk drives, and video systems, you can also upgrade your floppy and CD-ROM drives, your PC's sound system, your modem, your computer's system board, chassis, power supply, and more.

In addition to upgrade information, I offer you some tips and helpful hints on how to diagnose and repair problems involving your hardware components and a few tips for generally improving your PC's overall performance. I even show you where you can get testing and performance monitoring software (see Figure 1.4), which provides before and after ratings on your components so that you can actually see the improvements your upgrades are producing.

FIGURE **1.4**

The Benchmark component of Norton Utilities is one of several performance monitoring programs you'll be introduced to.

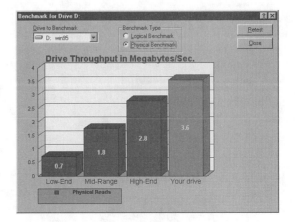

Lastly, I include an hour on upgrading your PC's operating system, if you haven't already done so, and why this can be one of the most important upgrades you can make. And if you are not a fan of Windows in its various incarnations, Hour 23, "Upgrading to a New Operating System," will also show you an alternative to Windows.

Summary

In the past hour, you learned what factors you need to consider when deciding whether to upgrade your PC. You also learned what components in your PC you can (or should) upgrade and what the pros and cons are of upgrading versus purchasing a new computer.

Q&A

Q With PC prices starting at the $400–$600 range, does it really make sense to upgrade a few components that can very quickly add up to $400?

A That depends on a number of factors: what kind of PC you're currently using, what you're using your computer for, how much money you have to spend, and how many computers you are thinking of upgrading. Keep in mind that PCs in the $400–$600 range are not top-of-the-line computers with all the latest technology. You're generally looking at PCs that are eight months to a year old, if not older. That's not to say these PCs aren't a bargain. If you're currently using a Pentium 100 with 16MB of RAM and a 550MB hard disk drive, spending $1000 to get a Pentium II Celleron at 300 MHz with 32MB of RAM and a 6GB hard disk drive is definitely a bargain.

Q **I've peeked inside my PC and it looks like I would need a degree in electrical engineering to start removing and replacing the components. Can a novice with little or no technical experience really upgrade PC components?**

A Absolutely. It may look complicated, but it really isn't. All you need is a basic understanding of what each component does plus a little patience and a screwdriver. All of the components that you will read about in this text are designed for end users to upgrade. You just have to know how to do it, which is explained in the next 23 hours.

1

Hour **2**

Understanding the Components in Your PC

Before you can begin upgrading the various components in your PC, it may help you to be able to identify each component and have a basic understanding of how each component functions.

During this hour you will learn:

- What precautions you need to take before working on your PC
- How to identify the various components inside your PC
- A basic understanding of the function of each component in your PC

Eliminating Potential Hazards

Before you go tinkering around inside your PC, you need to be aware of a few potential hazards that exist. Most of the potential problems you encounter can be far more damaging to your equipment than to you. Except for the power supply, the voltage inside your PC is far too low to be a serious hazard to you, but it can cause very serious damage to the sensitive electronic components.

This is one caution we cannot stress enough! The power supply in your PC is built using low release capacitors and contains more than enough wattage to kill you even after it is turned off and the plug is pulled. Absolutely, positively, DO NOT OPEN your power supply under any circumstances!

Although these precautions may seem obvious to anyone who works on any type of electrical equipment, they are nevertheless worth mentioning here:

- Unplug your PC before you begin any work on it that requires you to remove the cover. Too often many users are content with merely hitting the on/off switch, but on/off switches have been known to malfunction or stick. To be absolutely certain that no power is running through your system, unplug the power cord either from the back of your PC or from the wall receptacle.

- Ground yourself to release any possible static electricity. This is especially important during the winter months when hot, dry air increases the potential for static electricity. All electronic components in your PC can be damaged or destroyed by one good jolt. If you have a grounding wrist strap, attach it to your wrist. Otherwise, touch the metal case of your computer or the metal housing around the power supply to ground yourself. You can also touch a metal radiator pipe if you have one handy in your house or wherever you are working on your PC.

Static electricity is a bit harder to measure; however, to illustrate just how sensitive your PC's components are, the type of jolt you get from touching a doorknob after shuffling along a wool carpet in the winter is more than sufficient to destroy most components in your PC.

- Make sure that you have an uncluttered workspace. A large kitchen table is an excellent place to work, and because many kitchens have tile or linoleum floors, you can also guard against static electricity at the same time. Consider spreading a large towel under or near your PC to catch any small screws that you might drop while working on your computer. White or light colored towels make it easier to see small pieces.

Keep in mind, too, that some manufacturers will void your warranty if you open your case and go poking around inside your PC. Be sure you check your warranty before you begin laying out your grand upgrade plans.

Differentiating Between Desktop and Tower PCs

PCs come in two standard configurations—desktop models and towers. Figure 2.1 shows a typical desktop model PC, and Figure 2.2 illustrates a basic tower configuration.

FIGURE 2.1

A typical desktop model PC.

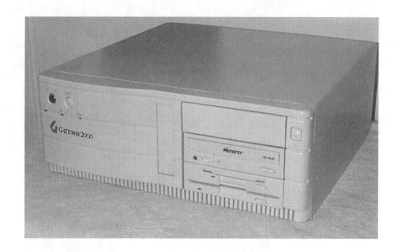

Desktop models may come in several sizes, often with names such as full-size, baby-AT, or slim-sized to denote some difference in relative size, but they all follow the same basic design layout, which is a PC laid out horizontally or flat on the desktop.

Tower models also come in a variety of sizes with corresponding names such as mini-tower, midsize-tower, full tower, and so on. If you look closely, you can see that the design of a tower is basically just a desktop model turned vertically or on its side. Turning a desktop on its side to produce a tower model does offer a few advantages. Towers generally take less real estate on your crowded desktop and larger tower models usually have additional space for more internal disk drives.

> Even before tower models were developed, PC users got the idea that PCs can work just as well vertically as they do horizontally. Some innovative entrepreneurs even began marketing stands for PCs so that you could turn a desktop vertically. If you are still using a desktop and you want to turn it on its side, go right ahead—just make sure it is stable.

FIGURE 2.2

A typical tower model PC.

Regardless of whether you have a desktop or a tower PC, looking from the front you will likely notice several similarities. The first thing you will notice is one or more drives that use some type of removal media such as a floppy disk drive, a CD-ROM drive, a DVD drive, a tape backup drive, or perhaps a removable media type hard disk drive. On the front of some PCs you may also find a reset button. A reset button generally is used to reboot your PC much the same as if you powered off and then powered on your PC—what's known as a "cold boot."

NEW TERM   You may have heard the terms *warm boot* and *cold boot*. The terms describe two methods of rebooting or restarting your PC. As the names imply, a *warm boot* is a reboot with the power on and a *cold boot* is a reboot with the power off. The difference between the two booting methods is more than just the presence of electrical power. A cold boot is a more thorough or complete boot-up process because it also releases any data that might still be in several system caches or memory holding areas. A cold boot runs a more thorough POST—the Power On Self Test. A warm boot is also less stressful on your electrical components.

Some PC manufacturers also place the on/off switch on the front of the PC to make it more convenient. Although this is just as common as placing the on/off switch on the back or the side of the PC, many experts consider it a mistake because it opens the PC to the risk of losing data if you accidentally hit the power switch and turn off your PC.

Identifying Your PC's External Connectors

Before you start poking around inside your PC you need to become familiar with the external connectors that are typically found on a PC. Most of these connectors are usually found on the back of your PC. (Figure 2.3 illustrates the typical array of external connectors.)

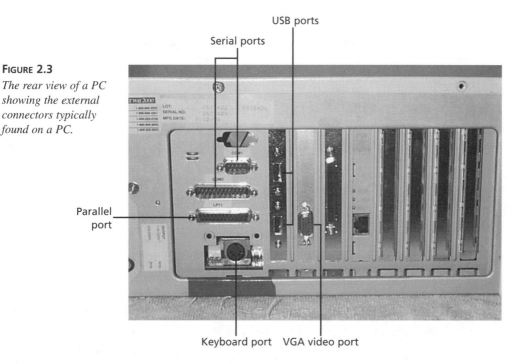

FIGURE 2.3
The rear view of a PC showing the external connectors typically found on a PC.

The following is a list of connectors you typically find on the back of a PC:

- *Serial port.* Used for connecting serial communication devices such as modems, printers, plotters, and so on. Serial ports can be either 9- or 25-pin D-shaped male connections. Typically you find two serial ports labeled 1 and 2 or A and B.

- *Parallel port.* Used for connecting parallel printers and some types of external removable media drives. Parallel ports are 25-pin D-shaped female connections.

Male and female connectors? For those of you who are not sure how to identify a male or a female connector, a male connector is one that protrudes and a female connector is one that surrounds or receives. If you are still not sure, ask your mother.

- *VGA video port.* This is what you plug your monitor into. It is a 15-pin D-shaped female connector.

- *Keyboard port.* Your keyboard is connected here by one of two types of keyboard connectors—the larger AT-style connector or the smaller PS/2-style din connector.

- *USB (Universal Serial Bus) port.* A 12Mbit/sec interface that supports up to 127 devices.

Identifying the Parts Inside Your PC

Before you begin working on your PC, it helps to be able to identify the basic components that you might need or want to upgrade or repair. Think of it this way: Before you attempt to do any routine maintenance on your car, you should be able to identify items such as an oil filter, a spark plug, and a radiator. The same principle applies to your PC. Before you start pulling out your hard disk drives or your memory SIMMs/DIMMs, you need to be able to locate and identify them.

Identifying the Main System Board

After you remove the cover of your PC and look inside (remember to unplug your PC and ground yourself), you can see the main system board, also known as the motherboard—an affectionate term that supposedly originated in the days of Apple II computers (see Figure 2.4).

The terms "main system board" and "motherboard" are often used inter-changeably and refer to the same component. Both are used in this book, so don't be confused.

FIGURE 2.4

A typical main system board.

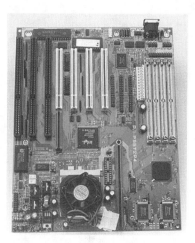

2

The main system board is usually mounted on the bottom of your PC if you have a desk-top model, or on one side of your PC if you have a tower model. The main system board can be thought of as a connection or communication terminal. Most of the other devices in your PC connect to it, either directly through one of the many connectors built in to the main system board or through an interface card that plugs into the main system board. (Main system boards come in a variety of sizes and shapes and are explained in greater detail in Hour 8, "Replacing Your Main System Board.")

Identifying the Microprocessor

The microprocessor, also referred to as the CPU or chip, is usually plugged into a socket or inserted into a slot on the main system board (see Figure 2.5) and is considered the brains of your PC. On some early model 486 computers, the CPU was soldered to the main system board.

Some computer manufacturers have been known to place microprocessors on interface cards that are plugged into the main system board, as opposed to placing the microprocessor directly on the main system board as do most manufacturers.

FIGURE 2.5

*A microprocessor
located on the main
system board.*

Most older microprocessors are roughly square in shape, as you can see in Figure 2.5.
Beginning with the Pentium II, Intel began housing their microprocessors in a container
that is a little smaller than a VHS tape cassette (see Figure 2.6).

FIGURE 2.6

*A Pentium II micro-
processor.*

Another difference you notice about the Pentium II is that the container that houses the
CPU is not plugged into a socket as all previous models of microprocessors were.
Pentium IIs and later manufactured Intel microprocessors are plugged into the main system board using a slot designed especially for the Pentium II. (In case you're interested,
the slot is called slot 1.)

The microprocessor executes the instructions written into the programs that you run on
your PC. Some examples of microprocessors are 80486 (also referred to simply as a
486), Pentium, Pentium Pro, Pentium II, and Celeron CPUs.

Sometimes you can't see your microprocessor because it is covered by a heat sink. A *heat sink* is used to help dissipate heat generated by your microprocessor and often looks like a black (or blue or silver) square or rectangle with a lot of small projections protruding from it.

2

When you hear a reference to the speed of particular PC, such as 100, 133, 166, 200, 233, 266, and so on, the speed reference is actually to the speed of the CPU.

Identifying Memory (RAM)

The memory in your computer (also called RAM, or Random Access Memory) is built in to modules called SIMMs (Single Inline Memory Modules). SIMMs are electronic modules about 10 1/2 centimeters long that sit in slots, usually located on your main system board (see Figure 2.7).

FIGURE 2.7
SIMMs in slots located on your main system board.

In some newer computers SIMMs have been replaced by DIMMs, which stands for Dual Inline Memory Modules. If you compare the two types of memory modules, you see that DIMMs look like oversized SIMMs (see Figure 2.8).

Even though memory (RAM) and hard disk space are both measured in megabytes (MB), don't confuse the two. Memory is used by your PC to run programs, and disk space is used to store files.

Identifying Disk Drives

Typically, PCs come equipped with two types of disk drives—floppy disk drives and hard disk drives. Both have changed considerably over the past ten years or so.

NEW TERM   To cover some general terminology and measurements, a *bit* is a plus or minus electrical charge (more commonly understood as 1 or 0). Eight bits equal one *byte*. A *kilobyte* (abbreviated KB) is 1024 bytes (2^{10} bytes). A *megabyte* (abbreviated MB) is one million bytes, and a *gigabyte* (GB) is a thousand megabytes or a billion bytes.

FIGURE 2.8

DIMMs are noticeably larger than SIMMs.

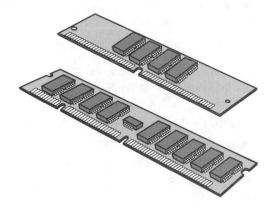

Originally, floppy disk drives were designed to accommodate 5 1/4-inch disks, and their capacity was only 160KB. Their capacity eventually grew to 1.2MB before they were gradually phased out and replaced by 3 1/2-inch drives. The 3 1/2-inch drive also went through its own evolutionary period, expanding from an original capacity of 720KB to its present storage capacity of 1.44MB.

Nowadays, virtually all PCs come equipped with a single 3 1/2-inch floppy disk drive (see Figure 2.9). However, a few manufacturers now offer you the option of including a Zip drive (see Hour 15, "Adding a Removable Media Drive") in addition to or even as a replacement for a 3 1/2-inch drive.

FIGURE 2.9

A 3 1/2-inch floppy drive in a PC.

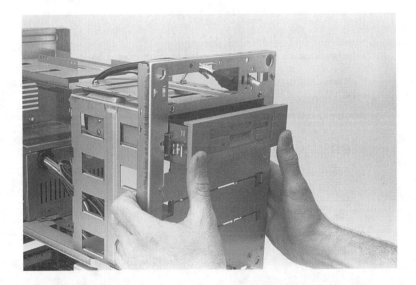

PCs have had hard disk drives ever since IBM shipped its first PC/XT model back in 1984 with a 10MB hard disk drive. Since then, hard disk drives have become faster, and their capacities have expanded beyond what anyone could have imagined back in 1984. Now it is difficult to purchase a PC with a hard disk drive smaller than 3–4GB (gigabytes). Although floppy disk drives are easy to identify (just look for the device into which you insert a floppy disk), to the uninitiated, a hard disk may not have any identifying labels or obvious clues. Hard disk drives can be placed almost anywhere inside your PC. Typically they have a black or silver case, are usually less than 1 inch thick, and have a gray ribbon cable attached to one end. They may be mounted inside a chassis or cage and are not visible from the outside of the PC (see Figure 2.10).

FIGURE 2.10
A typical hard disk drive inside a PC.

Identifying Interface Cards

Interface cards are electronic circuit cards that enable your PC to connect to or interface with another device. There are dozens, if not actually hundreds, of different types of interface cards that you can attach to your PC. To work with your PC, an interface card needs to be inserted into one of the slots located on your PC's main system board (see Figure 2.11).

Never remove or insert an interface card while your PC is on. You can seriously damage both the card and your main system board.

FIGURE 2.11

An interface card inserted into one of the slots on your main system board.

The most common type of interface card is a video display card, which enables a monitor to work with your PC. If you follow the cord that runs from your monitor to your PC, you see that it is plugged into a connector on an interface card. This is your video card.

On some PCs, the video card circuitry is built in to the main system board, eliminating the need for a separate video interface card.

Some other common types of interface cards that you are likely to find inside your PC are

- *Modem cards.* Used for communicating with other computers over telephone lines
- *SCSI (Small Computer System Interface) cards.* Used to attach SCSI devices such as scanners and external disk drives to your PC
- *Network interface cards.* Used to attached your PC to local area networks

Identifying the PC Power Supply

The last device inside your PC that you need to be able to identify is your PC's power supply. As the name implies, the power supply provides electrical power to the devices inside your PC. Transformer might be a more appropriate name because the power supply actually converts or transforms AC power into DC and steps down the voltage from 120 volts AC to 12.5 volts DC. The name power supply was tacked on originally, however, and has stuck through the years.

The power supply is easy to identify because the power cord plugs into the power supply from the outside of the PC. On the inside of the PC you should be able to see numerous cables running from the power supply to many of the devices in your PC, such as the main system board and the disk drives.

2

Summary

In the past hour you learned about the major components found in most PCs and learned how to identify them in your own PC.

Q&A

Q Is there a limit to the number of disk drives that you can attach to your PC? Can you mix IDE and SCSI drives?

A Most PCs can only accommodate 2 floppy disk drives because most PCs can only address floppy disk drives as either A or B. As for hard disk drives and removable media drives, you can theoretically attach up to 24 using SCSI—drives C through Z. You would probably encounter some practical obstacles such as available power and physical space, which would limit the number of physical drives to far less than 24. If you mix IDE and SCSI drives you will need to boot your PC from one of the installed IDE drives. SCSI drives cannot be made bootable if an IDE drive is also installed in your PC.

Q Do any PCs contain more than one CPU?

A Yes. Recently, some manufacturers have released PCs or workstations with two or four CPUs. These are usually positioned as high-end workstations and require an operating system capable of supporting more than one microprocessor. Windows NT 4.0, Windows 2000, and Linux all support multiple CPUs.

HOUR 3

Examining Your PC's System Configuration

In the last hour you learned how to visually identify most if not all the major components inside your PC. During this hour you will delve a bit deeper and learn how to examine the system configuration of your PC.

Learning about your PC's system configuration is important because when you upgrade a component you usually want to make sure that the configuration settings are the same. Also, when you add a new component, such as a CD-ROM drive, a removable media drive, or a second hard disk drive, you often need to make configuration changes, and you want to be sure you are not creating a conflict with an existing device.

Don't worry if some of the information mentioned in this hour seems a bit "techie," arcane, or unnecessary. Even if you don't need all the information for upgrading purposes, you might need it someday for troubleshooting.

During this hour you will learn:

- How to check your PC's system configuration
- How to examine the configuration of some of the devices installed in your PC
- What interrupts are and how they are used by your PC and its devices

Obtaining a Systems Configuration Program

Most computers sold in the last few years come with some type of diagnostics and configuration checking program that is capable of providing you with the configuration information you want to examine in this chapter. If, however, your computer did not ship with a configuration/diagnostics program, you can download one of several from the Internet.

Configuration, in the context used here, means how your PC is set up in terms of what communications ports it is using, what areas of memory are being used and how they are being used, what interrupts various devices are using, and so on. Basically, configuration means what devices are installed in your PC and how they are set up to work with each other.

One program you will likely want to keep a copy of is SysChk (http://www.syschk.com/) by Advanced Personal Systems (see Figure 3.1).

FIGURE 3.1

Advanced Personal Systems is the creator of the diagnostic program SysChk.

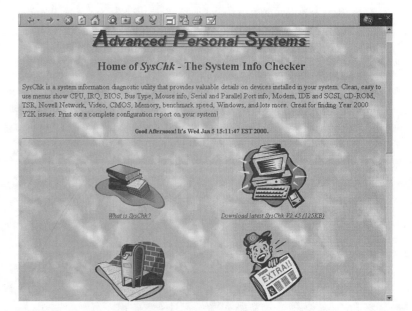

SysChk is an advanced analysis utility that enables you to examine the systems configuration of a PC. SysChk displays detailed information about the following components and systems:

- CPU and systems BIOS

NEW TERM *BIOS* is the acronym for Basic Input Output System and is a set of instructions built in to your computer to control how information and data flow in and out of your computer.

- Input and Output communications ports
- System interrupts and how they are used

NEW TERM An *interrupt* is short for *Interrupt ReQuest* (IRQ). Most PCs built in the last 10 years or so have a total of 16 Interrupts numbered 0 through 15. The original IBM PC had only eight. Interrupts are signals that various devices use to gain the attention of your CPU when they need processing time.

- Disk drives
- IDE/SCSI devices and configurations

NEW TERM *IDE* and *SCSI* are interfaces for connecting disk drives of various types to your PC. IDE stands for *Integrated Drive Electronics* and is an interface that enables up to two devices to be attached to each port. Originally IDE enabled data to pass to its connected devices at the rate of only 2 Mbits/sec, but newer Enhanced IDE Ultra ATA/66 interfaces and devices can transfer data at the rate of 66 Mbits/sec.

NEW TERM SCSI (pronounced "scuzzy") stands for *Small Computer System Interface* and enables you to connect up to seven devices to the interface. Since the original SCSI standard was released it has been updated several times and now includes SCSI-2 and SCSI-3, and can achieve data transfer speeds up to 80 MB/sec.

- Video information
- Memory usage and configuration
- Network information (if one is present)
- CMOS information

NEW TERM *CMOS* stands for *Complementary Metal-Oxide Semiconductor*, which is a type of memory that can hold its contents using a very low electrical current. CMOS memory is used to store the configuration information of your computer, and its electrical current is supplied by battery backup when your computer is turned off.

- Windows information (if a version is detected)

To Do: Downloading and Installing SysChk

Before you can use SysChk, you need to obtain a copy of the program. Follow these steps:

> If you are running Windows 95/98 or Windows 2000, you do not need to download a program such as SysChk. Windows 95/98 and Windows 2000 all come with utilities that analyze your PC's system configuration and produce a printout very similar to what you can get from SysChk. Later in this hour, I will show you how to obtain this information using Windows 95/98/2000.

1. Log on to the Internet and start your Web browser.

> If you do not have Internet access, you can still download the program. Most public libraries, colleges, and universities have Internet access PCs set up and available to the general public. You can use this publicly available Internet access to download the program.

2. Jump to the Advanced Personal Systems Web site at `http://www.syschk.com`.

3. Select the link to download the latest version of SysChk. The program begins downloading to your PC (see Figure 3.2).

FIGURE 3.2

Downloading the SysChk program.

4. The file you download, `syschk45.zip`, is in a compressed format and needs to be decompressed using a program that can decompress files in the ZIP file format.

> If you do not already have a copy of PkZip/PkUnzip or WinZip, you can download a copy from either `http://www.pkware.com` (PkUnzip) or `http://www.winzip.com` (WinZip). If you need to download a ZIP file decompression program, follow the instructions on installing the program.

> Anytime you encounter a file with the extension .zip, it means the file is in a compressed archive. The archive is compressed so that it takes up less storage space and downloads faster. To use the files stored in the archive, you need a program to decompress the archive. PkUnzip is a DOS-based program and WinZip is a Windows-based program.

5. Copy syschk45.zip into a temporary directory and then decompress the file. For the most effective use of SysChk, format a 3-1/2" floppy disk using the following command so that the disk will be bootable:

```
format a: /s
```

Then copy the files decompressed from syschk45.zip to the floppy disk.

> Using SysChk on a bootable disk is necessary if you are running Windows NT 4.0, Windows 2000, or another operating system that prevents direct access to your PC's hardware. Regardless of which operating system you use, you get a truer reading, especially on memory usage, if you run SysChk from a bootable floppy disk as opposed to using a DOS Window in one of the many flavors of Windows.

Using SysChk to Examine Your PC

Now that you have your SysChk boot disk ready, you can begin to examine the configuration setup of your PC.

To Do: Running SysChk

Follow these steps:

1. Place the boot disk you just made into your drive A.

2. Reboot your PC either by pressing the Ctrl+Alt+Del keys or by turning the power off and then back on again. If you are running Windows 95/98/NT, make sure you shut down your system properly first. If your PC prompts you to enter a date and time, merely press the Enter key at each prompt.

3. To start SysChk, type **syschk** and press the Enter key. In a few seconds the SysChk main screen appears displaying an overview of your system (see Figure 3.3).

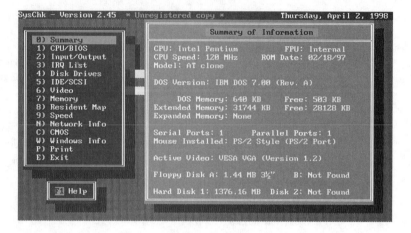

FIGURE 3.3

The opening screen of SysChk displaying an overview of your system.

As you can see on the Summary screen, SysChk displays a general overview of your system, providing information on the following:

- CPU type and speed
- Total memory and memory usage
- Serial and parallel ports installed
- Video mode
- Disk drives installed

To obtain more detailed information, select one of the items listed in the window on the left side of the screen. The detailed information about that component is then displayed in the window on the right side of the screen.

To Do: Examining Your Disk Drives

To show you how SysChk can display detailed information about the components and systems in your PC, let's use it to examine your disk drives.

1. Select 4) Disk Drives using the Up and Down arrow keys to highlight that selection. SysChk displays detailed information about the number and type of drives installed in your PC, beginning with the floppy disk drive (see Figure 3.4).

2. Use the Left and Right arrow keys to select Disk 1, the first physical hard disk drive in your PC. SysChk displays information about that hard disk drive (see Figure 3.5). If you have more than one physical hard disk drive, SysChk displays a second selection called Disk 2, and so on, for as many physical hard disk drives as there are installed in your PC.

▼ **FIGURE 3.4**

SysChk displaying information about the floppy disk drive installed in your PC.

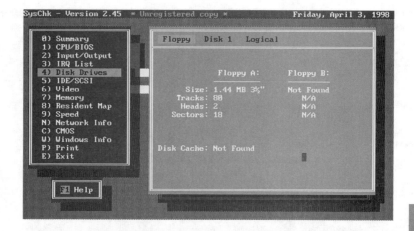

FIGURE 3.5

SysChk displaying information about your first physical hard disk drive.

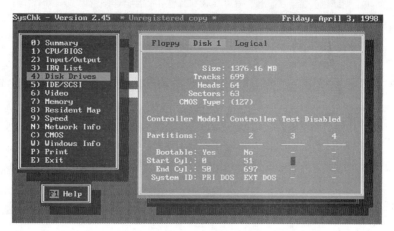

3. If your hard disk drive is partitioned into multiple logical drives, you can also display this information by selecting Logical (see Figure 3.6).

4. If you want to find out whether your hard drive is using an IDE or SCSI interface, select 5) IDE/SCSI. Next, select IDE 1 Info, and if your hard disk is IDE, SysChk displays IDE configuration information. If your hard disk is not IDE, SysChk does not display any information. If no information appears under IDE, select SCSI Info and see whether SysChk displays configuration information about your hard drive interface (see Figure 3.7).

▼ **FIGURE 3.6**

SysChk displaying logical information about the selected hard drive.

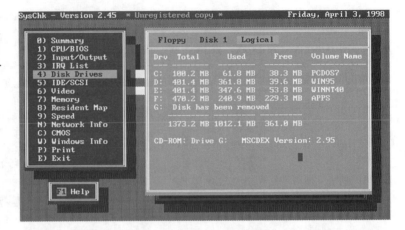

▲

FIGURE 3.7

SysChk displaying information about your hard drive interface.

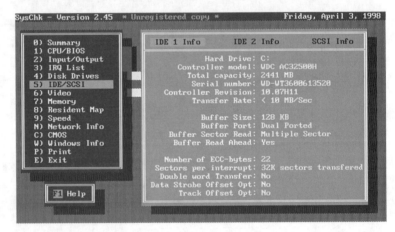

Using the Up/Down and Left/Right arrow keys, you can select all the components in your system and obtain detailed information about each one.

To Do: Printing Your Configuration Information

To Do

In addition to displaying information about your PC, SysChk can also produce a printed copy of the information it obtains.

1. Select P) Print and SysChk displays its print menu (see Figure 3.8).
2. Select one of the available options depending on whether you want to send the output to a printer or to a file.

▼

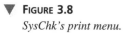

FIGURE 3.8

SysChk's print menu.

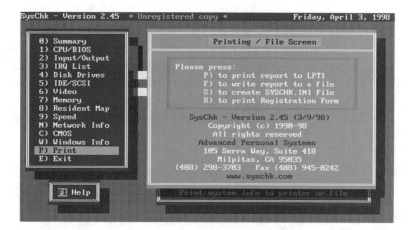

Make a hard copy printout of your system configuration and keep it in a safe place. This way you have a complete record of you PC's system information in the event that any or all of it has to be reentered into your PC.

Interrupt Conflicts

One of the most pressing problems you will encounter as you begin to upgrade different components in your PC is "interrupt conflicts." Most of the devices in your PC either directly or indirectly use an interrupt request, usually abbreviated IRQ, to communicate with the CPU. There are a total of 16 IRQs available in your PC (0 though 15) and about half are already assigned to specific devices (for example, keyboard, floppy drive, printer, and so on). The number of free IRQs available for you to use will vary according to what components are installed in your PC by the manufacturer.

Just remember, except for a few rare instances where IRQs can be shared by certain devices, the general rule is that each device needs to be assigned its own IRQ. When you have a conflict you will sometimes get some type of error message from Windows or your software that a conflict exists, but there is no guarantee that any warning will be issued. In some cases, the device simply won't work and you won't discover the conflict until you go looking for it. Be sure to thoroughly check your component documentation for assigning or changing IRQs and what to do if a conflict occurs. Your documentation will also specify what IRQs you can assign to a particular device.

Alternatives to SysChk

SysChk is not the only utility available that can analyze your PC. Another program (a trial version) you can download over the Internet is a program called SiSoft Sandra from SiSoftware, located at `http://www.sisoftware.demon.co.uk/` (see Figure 3.9). This is an excellent utility that provides you with more information about your PC than you'll ever need. The only drawback is that there is not a Windows NT or Windows 2000 version, yet.

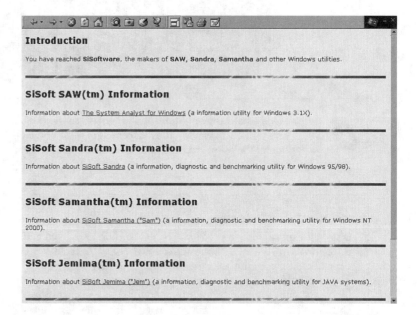

FIGURE 3.9

You can download a copy of SiSoft Sandra from the SiSoftware Web site.

Another utility program worth a preview is CheckIt by TouchStone Software at `http://www.touchstonesoftware.com/` (see Figure 3.10). CheckIt provides much of the same type of information as SysChk, but also is available in a Windows NT version.

You can also check a few other sites that offer PC systems utilities, such as CNET's Download.Com and Shareware.Com located at `http://www.download.com` (see Figure 3.11) and `http://www.shareware.com` (see Figure 3.12), respectively. To locate diagnostic utilities, search each site using the keyword "diagnostic."

If you are running Windows 95/98 or Windows 2000, you do not need to download a program such as SysChk. Windows 95/98 and Windows 2000 all come with utilities that analyze your PC's system configuration and produce a printout.

FIGURE 3.10

Another utility you can use to check your PC's configuration is CheckIt.

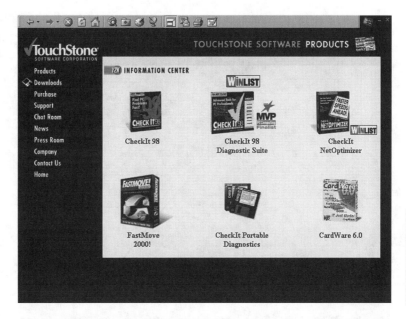

FIGURE 3.11

CNET's Download.Com Web site.

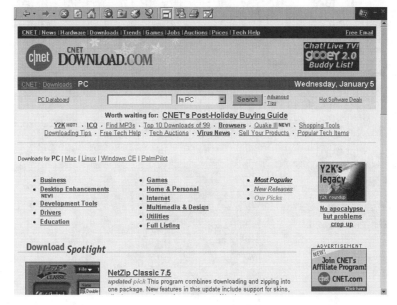

FIGURE 3.12

CNET's Shareware.Com Web site.

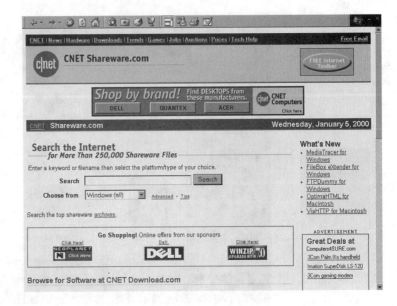

To Do: Using the Windows 98 Device Manager

Windows 95/98 is shipped with a utility called the Device Manager, which produces almost the same amount of information as you have seen SysChk and CheckIt produce. Use the Device Manager by following these steps:

1. From the Start menu, select Setting and then Control Panel to open the Windows 98 Control Panel.

2. Double-click the System icon to open the System Properties dialog box.

3. Select the Device Manager tab to access the Windows 98 Device Manager (see Figure 3.13).

FIGURE 3.13

The Windows 98 Device Manager.

▼   4. To the left of each device category you see a plus sign (+). The plus sign indicates that additional devices exist or additional information is available about that device category. Click the plus sign to display a listing of additional devices.

          5. Highlight one of the devices listed and then select the Properties button to see the

▲   type of information the Device Manager displays (see Figure 3.14).

FIGURE 3.14

The Device Manager displaying information about one of the devices installed in your PC.

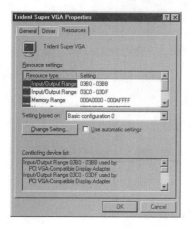

The Windows 98 Device Manager can also print the entire hardware configuration for you. At the main Device Manager screen, highlight Computer at the top of the device listing and then select the Print button.

To Do: Using the Windows 2000 Device Manager

Windows 2000 is also shipped with a Device Manager utility, which you can use to display much of the same information available from the Device Manager in Windows 98.

     1. From the Start menu, select Settings, Control Panel, and then select System. Double-click on the System icon to open the System Properties dialog box (see Figure 3.15).

     2. Select the Hardware tab and then under the Device Manager section select the Device Manager button to display the Windows 2000 Device Manager (see

▼   Figure 3.16).

▼ FIGURE 3.15

The Windows 2000 System Properties dialog box under Control Panel.

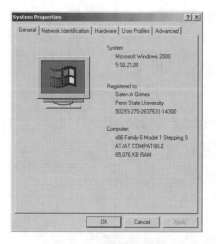

▲

FIGURE 3.16

The Windows 2000 Device Manager hardware configuration utility under Control Panel.

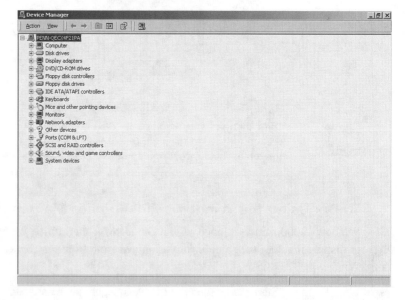

Just like SysChk, the Windows 98 and 2000 Device Managers can also make printouts for you of your hardware configuration.

Summary

In the past hour you learned how to use various utility programs to analyze the system configuration of your PC. You learned how to obtain a general-purpose analysis tool and how to use the tools that ship with Windows 98 and Windows 2000 Professional.

Q&A

Q You stated that there are only 16 IRQs (interrupts) available for use by devices installed in your PC. As I examine the information on IRQs in SysChk, however, it looks as though most of the IRQs are being used by the PC on devices that I did not install and that not many IRQs are left for me to use as additional devices. Is it possible or likely that I may run out of IRQs?

A It is not only possible, it has become a serious problem for a lot of users purchasing new PCs. You're right when you noticed that most of the IRQs are being used by devices you did not install and that when you start adding devices, IRQs can appear to be in short supply. Many users are now discovering that by adding a SCSI card, a sound card, an internal modem, a network card, and so on they are running out of IRQs. There are ways to juggle IRQs—you can turn off devices not being used and you can sometimes enable two devices to share an IRQ, provided they are not used simultaneously. In later chapters I point out tips on how to make the best use of your scarce IRQ resources.

Q If Windows 98 and Windows 2000 Professional both ship with utilities that can detect my PC's configuration, does that mean if I am running one of these two operating systems that I do not need a utility such as SysChk?

A After you gain some experience in diagnosing and troubleshooting problems in your PC and become more familiar with hardware configuration issues, you can probably abandon (or at least put it away on the shelf) a utility such as SysChk if you are running either Windows 98 or 2000. When you are just starting out, however, I would suggest that you use every systems analysis resource available. You may have noticed that the Utilities in 98 and 2000 aren't quite as thorough as SysChk or that the information is not presented in such a neat, easy-to-use package.

HOUR 4

PC Performance Monitoring and Diagnostic Tools

After you've made all of the changes and upgrades to your PC that you deem necessary, you might be curious to see how much improvement in performance your upgrades are making. In order to properly evaluate the upgrades you make, you need some type of hardware evaluation program, more commonly known as *performance monitoring* software.

Performance monitoring software enables you to take a set of base performance readings on your PC (before you begin making upgrades), and then as you make upgrades evaluate the (hopefully) improved performance in your PC.

This hour isn't just about testing your PC to see how much improvement you've gained from your upgrades. It also helps you locate a few tools that can help you diagnose any problems that might arise in your PC.

During this hour you will learn how to:

- Locate a few performance monitoring tools you can use to gauge the performance gains resulting from your upgrades
- Identify several diagnostic utilities to help you identify any problems that might develop with your PC

Performance Monitoring Programs

In Hour 3, "Examining Your PC's System Configuration," you learned about using diagnostic utilities to analyze your PC. In this chapter, you are introduced to a few additional utilities that you can use to analyze your PC, monitor your computer system's performance, and diagnose problems with your system.

Some of the utilities shown here are commercial products, whereas others are available free (or for a minimal shareware registration fee).

WinStone and WinBench

The WinBench and WinStone programs are the testing suites used by Ziff-Davis labs for all the product comparison testing they perform for the reviews they publish. WinBench and WinStone have no diagnostic functions but are two of the best performance testing programs you can acquire.

The suite of programs stress-tests your PC by simulating a series of real-world computational tasks, such as calculating a long and complex spreadsheet, reformatting and repaginating a long Word document, querying a large database, and performing a series of graphic-intensive display operations. You can select to run any one or all of the tests in the suite (see Figure 4.1).

In its first few incarnations, Ziff-Davis made these two utilities suites available for download. It wasn't long, though, before the programs were expanded and the total size of the two performance testing suites had evolved to well over 130MB; Ziff-Davis started distributing the two only on CD. The only cost for the CD plus shipping and handling was $6. Recently, Ziff-Davis began distributing a scaled-down version, which you can once again download from their site at `http://www.zdnet.com/zdbop/winbench/winbench.html`.

To order your copy of the WinBench and WinStone testing suite, go to `http://www.zdnet.com/zdbop/reqfrm.html` (see Figure 4.2).

FIGURE 4.1

*WinBench
performance-testing
a PC.*

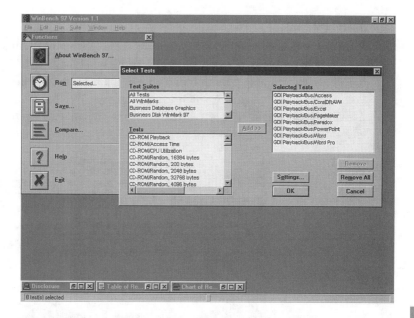

FIGURE 4.2

*You can order your
copy of the WinBench
and WinStone testing
suite from the Ziff-
Davis Web site.*

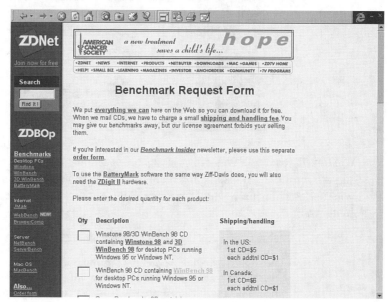

4

WinTune

WinTune is another popular Windows performance testing program and *Windows Magazine* has recently released its 1998 version, WinTune98. WinTune98 is somewhat unique among testing programs because there is a version you can download and run on your PC, or you can log on to the Internet, start your Web browser, and run WinTune98 over the Internet from *Windows Magazine*'s Web site at `http://wintune.winmag.com/` (see Figure 4.3).

FIGURE 4.3

Windows Magazine's WinTune98 Web page.

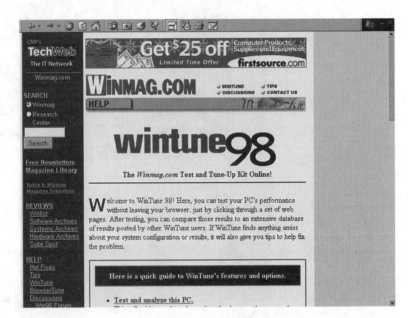

WinTune98 requires a Web browser capable of running ActiveX controls, which means that you must use Microsoft's Internet Explorer (version 3.0 or later) to run the program. WinTune98 will not run with Netscape and the ActiveX plug-in available for download on the Web.

> ActiveX controls are a potential security risk, and for this reason many users deactivate ActiveX controls when using Internet Explorer. If you have ActiveX controls turned off, you must reactivate them in order to run WinTune98.

WinTune98 performs a general systems analysis, a CPU performance test, a video system performance test, a memory test, a disk performance test, and finally sums up everything in a report summary (see Figure 4.4).

FIGURE 4.4

The WinTune98 testing summary, which is returned to you via your Web browser.

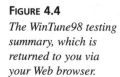
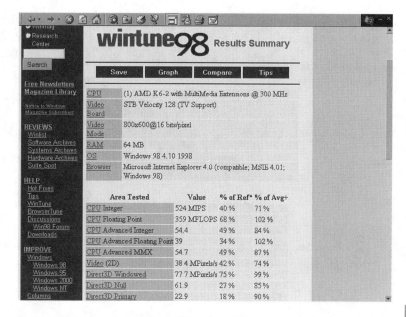

Norton Utilities System Information

One of the best known PC utilities, and one that has probably been around the longest, is the Norton Utilities (http://www.symantec.com/nu/index.html). Although its forté has been in the areas of diagnosing and repairing problems on your PC, it also includes a Systems Information section, which includes a few benchmarking tools (see Figures 4.5 and 4.6).

FIGURE 4.5

The Norton Utilities System Information benchmark for overall system performance.

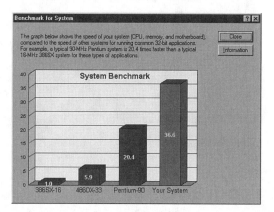

FIGURE 4.6

The Norton Utilities System Information benchmark for disk drive performance.

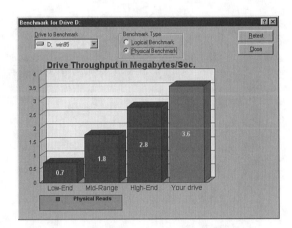

Later in this hour we delve into the "meat and potatoes" end of what the Norton Utilities are known for—namely their diagnostic and repair functions.

SiSoft Sandra

SiSoft Sandra (http://www.sisoftware.demon.co.uk/sandra/index.htm—$29 USD) was mentioned in Hour 3 as an excellent tool for identifying the components installed in your PC and identifying their configuration settings. The program also includes benchmarking tools you can use to check your PC's performance (see Figure 4.7).

FIGURE 4.7

SiSoft Sandra reporting performance results of a PC's hard disk drive.

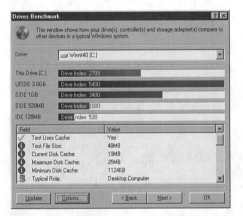

Diagnostic Programs

Just as numerous performance and benchmarking utilities are available to give you an assessment of your PC's level of performance, you can also find an abundant supply of available diagnostic tools. Many diagnostic utilities are designed to inform you when a problem has developed, and there are also a few that periodically check your system for potential problems.

AMIDiag

If your computer is using AMI (American Megatrends, Inc.) BIOS (see Hour 10, "Upgrading Your PC's BIOS"), there is a diagnostic program you can download and run to perform some rudimentary diagnostics tests (see Figure 4.8).

FIGURE 4.8

The AMIDiag diagnostics utility main menu.

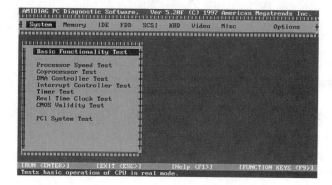

You can download a copy of AMIDiag at http://www.shareware.com (search on "diagnostics" or "amidiag"). If you want to purchase the full version, go to the AMI BIOS Web site at http://www.amibios.com.

The Norton Utilities

I mentioned earlier that besides including a performance monitor, the Norton Utilities also include a diagnostics application. Double-click the Norton System Doctor icon and you will see an application screen similar to one shown in Figure 4.9.

FIGURE 4.9

The diagnostics portion of the Norton Utilities, the Norton System Doctor.

The Norton System Doctor is a collection of monitoring utilities that you can set to monitor your PC's memory, disk drives, general systems operations, and Internet and network connections. For example, under the disk drive sensor section you can set the System Doctor to monitor general disk integrity, disk fragmentation, the physical disk surface, or

4

just the amount of free space available. Under the general system section, you can set System Doctor to monitor CPU utilization or check whether your anti-virus definitions are up-to-date. Under the memory section you can set System Doctor to monitor memory usage and alert you when you're running low on system memory, swap file space, or Windows system resources.

As you can see, the Norton System Doctor can be set to monitor much more than just the physical components in your PC. The aim of this diagnostics program is not just to monitor the health of your physical PC, but also the health of your overall system.

Norton Utilities makes versions of its utility suite for both Windows 95/98 and Windows NT. Because of the differences in how NT handles hardware access from 95/98, it is very important that you purchase the correct version for your system. Do not attempt to use the version designed for 95/98 on a computer running NT.

More Diagnostics Programs You Can Purchase

In addition to the programs already mentioned, here are a few other diagnostic programs you might want to consider trying/purchasing to help keep your system operating at peak performance levels:

- **CheckIt 98**—You can get more information about CheckIt 98 at `http://www.checkit.com/products/products.htm`.
- **PC Technician**—You can get more information about PC Technician at `http://www.windsortech.com`.
- **TuffTEST and TuffTEST-Pro**—Another PC diagnostic test worth kicking the tires on at `http://www.tufftest.com/` (see Figure 4.10).

Hard Disk Diagnostics

One area of PC operations that many users seem to eventually have problems with is the PC's hard disk drive. Years ago the saying was "… it's not *if* you will have hard disk problems, but *when* …" This seems almost passé now that hard disk technology has improved the reliability of hard disk drives to the point where most users never seem to experience a drive failure. Nevertheless, hard disk drives do still fail, and diagnostic programs are still designed to examine nothing but disk drives. One such program is Data Advisor from Ontrack Systems.

Ontrack Systems is primarily a data recovery company but produces Disk Advisor to help you avoid problems with your hard disk drive and hopefully avoid data loss. If you would like to download a copy of Data Advisor, go to the Ontrack Web site at `http://www.ontrack.com`.

Remember, one of the best ways to avoid hard disk drive disaster is to perform regular backups.

FIGURE 4.10

TuffTEST and TuffTEST-Pro are another set of PC diagnostic tools you might want to try.

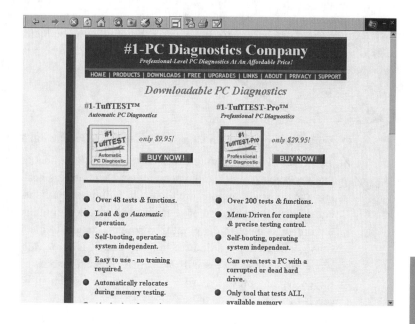

Not all problems are hardware related. There are viruses that can destroy your files and/or operating system and make it appear as though the hardware has developed a problem. Make sure you are running a good anti-virus program in addition to periodically checking your hardware. Make sure you also update the virus definition files regularly.

As you become more familiar with using diagnostic tools, you will also learn which problems require corrective action and which don't. Most of the programs mentioned in this chapter also usually explain these so-called "gray areas." This is to prevent you from needlessly spending time and money trying to correct a problem that is actually within the tolerances of normal operating parameters. If you are not in the habit of reading manuals, you should develop this habit when it comes to diagnostic utilities.

Summary

In the past hour, you learned about a few programs you can use to help you assess the performance gains in your PC when you upgrade one or more components. You also learned about diagnostics tools that you can use to help you identify problems when they develop and a few diagnostic programs that you can use to help you spot small problems before they become more serious.

Q&A

Q **What components in a PC are most likely to "wear out"?**

A Two types of wear seem to occur most often in PCs: heat and mechanical. Parts that undergo extremes in temperature changes, such as heat, seem to show more signs of wear and often exhibit a higher failure rate. This is why CPUs are all equipped with some type of heat sink and occasionally fans. But heat is not as big a problem as mechanical wear. Components subject to mechanical wear, such as drives, still seem to exhibit the highest rates of failure. Manufacturing improvements continue to increase the so-called "mean time between failure rates" for drives, but any part in your PC that undergoes movement is subject to the fastest levels of wear and thus failure.

Q **In the performance-testing program you demonstrated, I could see how fast each component operated but how do I know what the speeds really mean?**

A You have to remember that speed is relative. Is 60mph fast? For a two- or a four-legged animal running on level ground, it is, but for a car at the Indianapolis 500, it isn't. You may have noticed that in many of the performance testing programs, the speed of your component being measured was often compared against other similar components. Comparisons like this help, but the final determination of speed is going to be very subjective. It's going to boil down to what you think is fast. If it happens faster than you expect, you will consider it fast. But if you have to wait for something to happen, chances are you are not going to think it is happening very fast.

Q **Should I consider obtaining new diagnostic tools, or can I still use my old, trusty, reliable set that I have been happy with for the past few years?**

A By all means get new diagnostic tools. Older tools may not be able to properly analyze and test newer components in your PC and newer testing programs will most likely contain more precise testing utilities. Older tools are like older parts—they both need to be upgraded.

HOUR 5

The Tools of the Trade

In this hour you will learn what tools you need to upgrade and repair your PC. This section on tools is divided into two parts. The first part describes a simple set of hardware tools you will need to do most upgrades, and the second part lists a more advanced set of tools you should consider obtaining if you are inclined to pursue more complicated upgrades and repairs.

It also goes over a more detailed list of precautions you need to adhere to when working on your PC to make sure you don't cause any damage to yourself or your PC.

During this hour you will learn the following:

- What simple set of hardware tools you will need to perform simple upgrades and repairs
- What set of tools you will need to perform more advanced and complex upgrades and repairs
- What precautions you need to be aware of when you are working on your PC

A Simple Set of Tools

As you start to work on PCs, you'll quickly discover that you can perform about 90% of your upgrades and repairs with just a screwdriver. Make sure you have both a medium-sized flat-head screwdriver and a Philips screwdriver because some manufacturers favor one type of screw over the other. The exception here is Compaq. Since the first luggable Compaq was released in 1983, Compaq has used what are called Torx screws in all its systems (see Figure 5.1).

FIGURE 5.1

A Torx screwdriver—Compaq uses Torx screws in all its PCs.

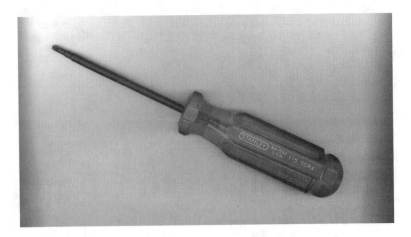

A Torx screw has a six-pointed, diamond shaped slot. Most of the screws in Compaq PCs can be removed with a T-15 size Torx screwdriver, but a few need a smaller size T-12 Torx screwdriver. You can pick up a set of Torx screwdrivers for a few dollars in most good hardware or home supply stores.

Jeweler Screwdrivers

Although many users get by for years with nothing more than a screwdriver for making simple repairs and upgrades, you may find that a few more tools make working on your PC a bit easier. Another inexpensive set of tools that you will sooner or later find almost indispensable is a set of jeweler screwdrivers (see Figure 5.2).

These are usually sold as a set of six miniature screwdrivers (three Philips and three flat-blade). You will find these screwdrivers extremely useful if you think you might be doing a lot of work on your PC.

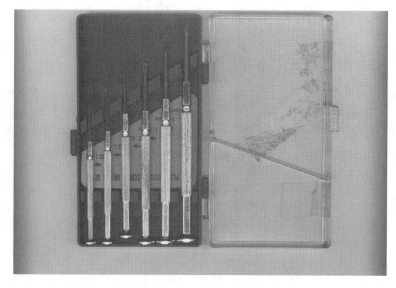

Computer Toolkit

Many computer stores also sell small computer toolkits for around $10–$20 with an assortment of PC-related tools (see Figure 5.3), some of which you may find useful and others of which you might not even be able to figure out what to use for.

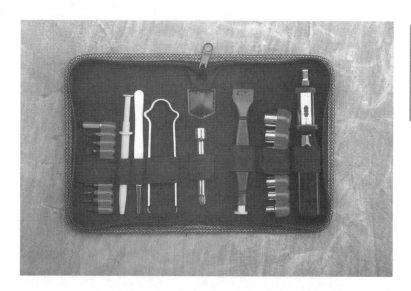

5

Three-Pronged Probe

One of the most useful tools you will run across in these types of toolkits is a device called a three-pronged probe (see Figure 5.4).

FIGURE 5.4

A three-pronged probe.

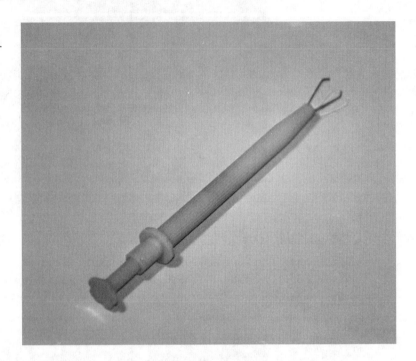

A three-pronged probe looks like a metal or plastic syringe with three moveable "fingers" where the syringe needle would normally be found. This is an invaluable tool for retrieving very small screws that you will invariably drop inside your PC. It's a lot easier and safer to retrieve the screw with a three-pronged probe as opposed to picking up your PC, turning it over, and shaking it until the lost screw comes tumbling out. A small pair of needle-nosed pliers or a small pair of surgical forceps, both sold in hobby and hardware stores, will work in place of the three-pronged probe, but you will likely find the probe easier to manipulate.

Don't attempt to substitute a magnetic probe for a three-pronged probe. Magnetic probes can damage components inside your PC.

Pencil and Paper

Two other tools you should make sure you have in your toolbox are a pencil and paper. Whenever you attempt to replace any component in your PC, you should always draw a diagram first, listing exactly where in your PC the component is being removed from and any cables or attachments connected to that component.

> Whenever you remove a cable from a component inside your PC, pay particular attention to the orientation of the cable. Several types of cables in your PC can be attached more than one way, which makes it extremely easy to accidentally install or replace a cable incorrectly.

While you have pencil and paper in hand, you should also get into the habit of keeping a log or journal of all changes you make to your PC. This log should include all changes made to your system as well as components you add. Be sure to include the date the change was made plus any specifications on the component you add.

Labels

You will also find small self-sticking labels, such as Avery or Brady labels, extremely useful when working on your PC. You should attach a numbered label (numbered 1, 2, 3, ...) to every wire or cable you remove, and mark on the diagram the corresponding numbered cable and its exact location inside your PC. This arrangement enables you to quickly and easily identify what each wire or cable is attached to.

Compressed Air

Finally, if you are like most PC users, you might open your PC once or twice a year, if that often. After 6–12 months or longer, you'll find a considerable amount of dust build-up in your system. A layer of dust in your PC causes more problems than merely one of aesthetics and a short bout of sneezing. A layer of dust can act as an insulating material, trapping heat that otherwise would be dissipated through the normal fan-controlled air circulation system. In short, the more dust you let accumulate in your PC, the quicker it will overheat, and overheating damages the components in your PC.

One of the best solutions for preventing dust build-up is to periodically take the cover off your PC and "blow it out" using compressed air. Compressed air canisters (see Figure 5.5) can be purchased from virtually any office supply store for a few dollars and should be part of every PC user's repair and maintenance toolbox.

5

FIGURE 5.5
A compressed air can-
ister, which you can
purchase in most office
supply stores.

If at all possible, take your PC outdoors before you "blow it out." Otherwise you'll end up making a bigger mess by merely shifting the dust from the inside of your PC to the outside of your PC and all over your desk and room. If you can't take your PC outside, at least move it off your desk and to a room where you can later vacuum the dust you blow out.

If you haven't already made your list of possible tools to purchase, here's a brief recap:

- PC toolkit
- Jeweler screwdrivers
- Three-pronged probe
- Pencil and paper
- Labels
- Compressed air

An Advanced Set of Tools

Unless you plan to become extremely involved in upgrading and repairing PCs, this section on advanced tools may seem overwhelming. But, read on. Although you may never get to apply this information to a hands-on situation, you may find it helpful the next time you have to take your PC in to a repair shop.

Soldering Iron

Very few computer experts recommend tinkering around inside your PC with a soldering iron, and with good reason. The individual components inside your PC, with very few exceptions, are meant to be replaced, not repaired. But keeping a soldering iron in your toolbox can be quite handy if you know how and when to use it (see Figure 5.6).

FIGURE 5.6

A typical electrical soldering iron.

I keep a soldering iron in my toolkit, but I will admit that I haven't had too much use for it lately. In the past, I mostly used it for fixing broken wires and creating custom serial cables for an assortment of serial printers. Hour 21, "Selecting and Installing a Printer," covers installing one or more printers to your PC. When you go shopping for a printer for your PC, one thing you will notice is that nearly 100% of the printers you see in computer stores come equipped with a parallel interface. Years ago this was not the case. In fact, I can remember when it was next to impossible to get a laser printer with anything but a serial cable. The problem was that there was nothing called a standard serial cable. Virtually every manufacturer came up with its own design for serial communications between a computer interface and a printer. This meant that if the printer manufacturer did not supply a cable for your particular computer, you were stuck with making your own. Making serial printer cables is not rocket science, but one tool you definitely need is a soldering iron.

Nowadays, I don't get too many calls to create custom serial cables for printers or too many other output devices. Most manufacturers wised up and realized that making serial cables was a dying art form and they stood a better chance of selling you a printer if you could also buy a standard cable and simply plug everything together yourself. I mostly use my soldering iron for simply repairing broken cables or cables chewed through by one of my cats.

5

Voltage Meter

Another somewhat uncommon tool I keep in my toolkit is a voltage meter (see
Figure 5.7).

FIGURE 5.7

A voltage meter.

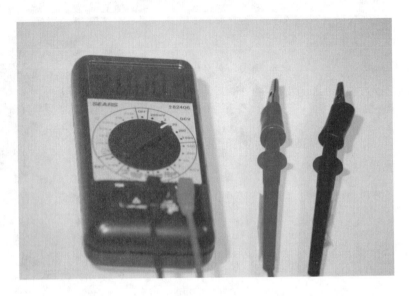

The primary function of a voltage meter is measuring the flow of current, and because
most of the current you encounter inside your PC is DC (direct current), make sure any
voltage meter you pick up can measure both AC and DC voltage. You'll use a voltage
meter mainly to diagnose problems with your power supply. Each of the 4-pin connectors sprouting out of your power supply should be delivering 5 volts of DC current. A
voltage meter can help you quickly determine if your power supply is failing or if one of
the connectors has developed a short circuit.

Although the primary function of a voltage meter is to test voltage, if you buy one in the
range of $30–$40 you'll wind up getting a few more useful functions that can be quite
helpful in diagnosing and troubleshooting PC problems.

Another use for a voltage meter is as a continuity tester. When used as a continuity tester,
you're more concerned with *if* a current is passing through an electrical circuit rather
than *how much* current is passing through the circuit. A good example here is in testing
cables. Using a continuity tester, you attach one cable from your tester to each pin on
your cable and test whether each pin (circuit) continues from one end of the cable to the
other. It helps to know the configuration of the cable, but even if you don't you can still
manage to test your cable using the trial-and-error method.

Safety Precautions When You Work on Your PC

Whenever you work on your PC, you need to put a number of safety precautions into practice, not only to protect your PC from possible damage, but also to protect yourself from possible harm. Neither working on PCs, nor PCs themselves, are inherently dangerous, but you need to be aware of some hidden risks.

Unplugging Your PC

This is the number one safety precaution you need to be aware of, and it cannot be repeated often enough. Either unplug your PC at the wall outlet or from the back of the PC. Don't merely rely on the on/off rocker switch because on/off rocker switches have been known to stick or malfunction. Besides risking a potentially lethal electrical shock, you can damage your PC and its internal components if you forget it is plugged in and try to remove an interface card or other electronic device while it is still receiving current. You could also accidentally drop a screwdriver or other metal tool on your main system board and cause a short, or worse.

> The only time you should ever work on your PC with the power on is when you are troubleshooting your power supply, and then be sure to exercise extreme caution.

Grounding Yourself to Prevent Static Electricity

Although not properly grounding yourself against static electricity is much more of a potential hazard to your PC than to yourself, don't underestimate this risk, especially during the cold winter months when circulating air in homes and offices tends to be drier than normal. Most of the sensitive electronic components in your PC (for example, microprocessors, memory, interface cards, and so on) can be seriously damaged or even destroyed by stray jolts of static electricity. Make sure you touch a metal object such as a desk, a chair, or a filing cabinet before you begin working on your PC, or use a grounding strap around one of your wrists (see Figure 5.8). Also, if possible, move your PC to a room that does not have a carpeted floor because most carpeting used in homes and offices contains synthetic fibers, which can increase the potential for static electric discharges. In addition, you might also consider investing $30–$49 dollars in a small room humidifier. Besides being healthier for your PC, it makes the environment a bit healthier for you as well.

5

FIGURE 5.8

A wrist grounding strap used to prevent static electric discharges.

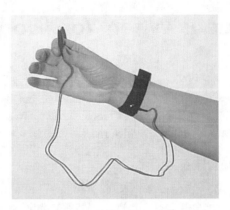

Keeping Magnets Away from PCs

Static electricity is not the only type of electrical charge you want to keep away from your PC. Magnetic charges can also damage some PC components such as disk drives. Make sure that any tools you use are not magnetized (for example, screwdrivers).

In Hour 20, "Upgrading or Adding a Sound System to Your PC," when we begin discussing upgrading your PC's sound system, you'll be presented with another little-known PC hazard that is worth mentioning here. In an attempt to cut costs, some PC owners have learned the hard way that you can't always use speakers from an old stereo with your PC. Stereo speakers are unshielded, meaning they can and often do give off strong magnetic charges that can distort the images on your screen or cause serious damage to PC monitors if placed within close proximity. Make sure you place nonshielded speakers at least 2–3 feet from your PC's monitor. How can you tell if a speaker is shielded or nonshielded? If the speaker was purchased for use on a stereo and not specifically for a PC sound system, consider the speaker a nonshielded speaker and keep it away from your monitor.

Summary

In the past hour you learned what tools you need to perform upgrades and repairs on your PC. You were given a list of simple tools you should include in your toolkit plus a few advanced tools you might want to consider including if you decide you want to do more complex diagnostics on your PC.

Q&A

Q Aren't some manufacturers producing PCs that you can take apart without the need for tools?

A Yes, sort of. Some manufacturers have been producing tool-less PCs that allow you to remove/replace most major components (disk drives, cards, and so on) but many of these are merely attached to an easily removable chassis. Often you will find that you still need tools to remove the component from the chassis. For the most part, these PCs are easier to work on but I have yet to see one that requires absolutely no tools.

Q Is there ever a time that I *should* open my PC to work on it with the power turned on?

A Yes, but only when you are testing the power supply.

5

PART II
Upgrading the Main System Components

Hour

HOUR 6

Upgrading Your PC's Memory

Upgrading the memory in your PC actually amounts to adding more memory to your PC. Unlike upgrading other components, such as your processor or CD-ROM drive, you rarely, if ever, remove the memory in your PC and replace it with better or faster memory. In fact, when you upgrade the memory in your PC, you have to be careful that you add memory that is identical to the memory already installed.

The only exception to this general premise is that you may opt to remove a memory module of one size and replace it with a memory module containing more memory. For example, if your PC contains four 4MB-memory modules, you may replace them with four 8MB-memory modules. Although this practice might at first seem wasteful, considering the southward direction of memory prices in the last few years and the performance gains from increasing memory in your PC, replacing smaller-sized memory modules with larger modules can actually make sound economic sense and at the same time increase the performance in your PC.

Upgrading your PC's memory probably gives you the most "bang for your buck" in terms of a how much a single upgrade can positively impact your PC's performance. Although upgrading the processor can affect the speed of most operations, upgrading the memory can extend the capability of your PC by enabling you to perform more tasks simultaneously, especially if you are running one of the more advanced operating systems such as Windows 98 or Windows 2000. Even if you are still running Windows 3.1 (please see Hour 23, "Upgrading to a New Operating System," if you are), a memory upgrade from 8MB to 16MB produces a dramatic boost in performance.

During this hour you will learn the following:

- How memory works in your PC
- The different types of memory you can put in your PC and how to select the right type
- How to install memory in your PC

Memory Is Like Money—More Is Better

Gather 10 PC experts in a room and you can probably get a consensus on the minimum amount of memory you should have for running various operating systems and environments. For Windows 3.1, most experts agree on 16MB; for Windows 95/98, they agree on at least 32MB, and for Windows 2000, no less than 64MB. In each case, although these amounts enable you to operate adequately, adding more memory actually improves performance. Adding more memory enables you to run more programs faster, open more files, and perform more tasks simultaneously.

Your PC uses memory as a temporary storage area for your microprocessor to perform calculations, store data, and store programs you want to run. Anything stored in memory, or RAM as it is called, remains there only as long as the power to your PC remains on, which is why RAM is also referred to a "volatile memory."

NEW TERM *RAM*, which is short for *Random Access Memory*, or simply called memory, is an electronic storage area used by your computer for data, information, and programs. RAM is where your computer moves information for rapid retrieval either before the information is saved to disk or as it retrieves previously saved information from disk. Your computer can access information in memory about 1000 times faster than from disk. Even though memory and disk storage both use the same reference designators for size (for example, KB for kilobytes, MB for megabytes, and GB for gigabytes), when the term memory is used it always refers to the volatile electronic area where information is stored temporarily. It does not refer to your permanent disk storage area, which should correctly be called disk space, disk storage space, or hard disk space.

A lot of memory installed in PCs for about the last five years has been in the form of SIMMs (Single Inline Memory Modules). See Figure 6.1.

FIGURE 6.1

A standard 72-pin SIMM.

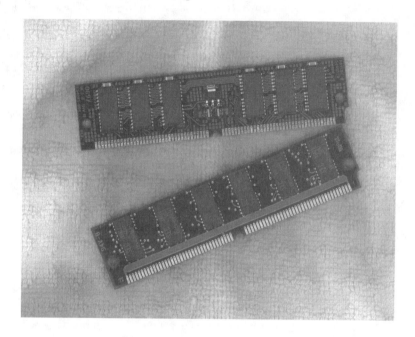

However, SIMMs have started being replaced in newer PCs with DIMMs (Dual Inline Memory Modules). See Figure 6.2.

FIGURE 6.2

A typical DIMM.

6

 While working on this book, one of my local computer stores ran a sale on memory. It was such a good sale that I decided it was time to follow some of my own advice. I decided to upgrade one of my older production PCs, an off-brand Pentium 166 MHz with 32MB of RAM. Because the Pentium takes memory SIMMs in pairs, I purchased two 32MB EDO SIMMs. The PC had four 8MB EDO SIMMs (one in each SIMM slot), so I removed two of the existing 8MB SIMMs and replaced them with the two new 32MB SIMMs, which gave me a grand total of 80MB RAM (32+32+8+8=80MB). This particular PC has Windows NT 4.0 installed, and NT 4.0 can literally use all of the RAM you can throw at it.

The upgrade proceeded without a hitch, and when I booted up the PC, my PC's BIOS and Windows NT immediately recognized the additional RAM and continued right along without ever skipping a beat. The performance with the additional RAM even surprised me!

Literally everything seemed to run faster. Programs started much quicker. Files loaded faster. Even connecting to the Internet and running my Web browser seemed to take less time and run faster.

There's no guarantee that your upgrade will enhance your performance as much as mine did. However, if you are running a PC with a 32-bit operating system such as Windows NT/2000 or Windows 95/98 that can utilize additional system RAM, then going from 32MB of RAM to 80MB will produce a change you will definitely notice.

Different Types of Memory

Memory modules that physically appear to be the same can differ dramatically in the actual speed of the memory and the type of memory used in the module. This is why it is very important to install only the exact type of memory designed for your PC. You can consult your PC's manufacturer or your user guide to determine the exact type of memory you can use in your system.

Here is a brief overview of some of the types of memory you may encounter:

- **DRAM (Dynamic RAM).** The most common type of memory used in PCs. It is also the slowest and cheapest type of memory still used in memory modules.

- **FPM DRAM (Fast Page Mode DRAM).** Another type of DRAM, which is slightly faster than standard DRAM.

- **EDO DRAM (Extended Data Out RAM).** Another type of Dynamic RAM used in memory modules. It is faster and more expensive than standard DRAM.

- **ECC EDO RAM (Error Correcting Code EDO RAM).** A very reliable and more expensive type of EDO RAM. Used primarily on network file servers and high-end workstations.

- **SDRAM (Synchronous DRAM).** A faster and more expensive type of DRAM used in processor cache memory and also appearing in faster, newer Pentium III–based PCs.

- **SGRAM (Synchronous Graphics RAM).** A type of synchronous DRAM used primarily in video graphics cards.

- **VRAM (Video RAM).** Another type of DRAM used on video cards. It is faster than standard DRAM.

> It's hard to definitively explain how much faster one type of memory is than another. In some cases it is next to impossible because manufacturers do not release the actual speeds of the types of memory they produce. You may see numbers such as 70ns or 60ns (ns=nanosecond=1/1000th of a second) used to represent SDRAM, DRAM, FPM DRAM, or EDO DRAM. After you start getting into SGRAM and VRAM, however, you usually won't see speeds listed, primarily because these types of memory aren't usually available for user upgrades. Also, because memory technology is constantly changing and improving, all these values may be superceded by a newer, faster memory type. In case you're interested, in the previous listing the memory types are listed in the order of their relative speeds.

Another method you can use to check the type of RAM used in your PC is to check one of several Web sites specializing in selling memory. Two that immediately come to mind are Kingston (`http://www.kingston.com/`) and Crucial (`http://www.crucial.com/`).

Both of these well-known sites offer online databases that you can access to find the exact type of memory used by your system (see Figure 6.3).

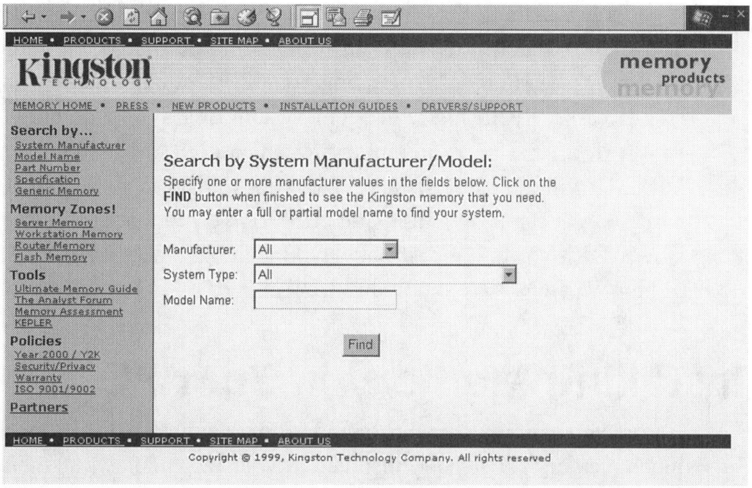

FIGURE 6.3

The Kingston memory identification system that you can access to identify the type of memory for your PC.

All you do is enter the manufacturer, system type, and model name and the database will identify the exact type of memory installed in your PC by the manufacturer. It also will usually supply information on types of memory you can use for upgrading and the maximum amount of memory your PC can accommodate (see Figure 6.4).

FIGURE 6.4

The Kingston memory type database displaying information on the type of memory used in an IBM PC.

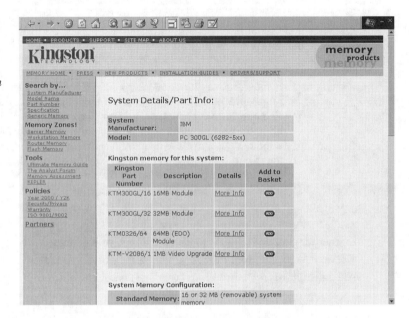

If the PC you are currently using has standard DRAM installed, you might be tempted to spend a few extra dollars to upgrade to FPM or EDO DRAM. Don't waste your money. The slight difference in speed probably won't be significant without also upgrading your processor (see Hour 7, "Upgrading Your CPU") and perhaps your main system board (see Hour 8, "Replacing Your Main System Board"). Although you won't see any significant performance boost in replacing standard DRAM with faster FPM DRAM or EDO DRAM, trying to cut costs and save a few dollars by replacing EDO DRAM with standard DRAM can have a dramatic effect on performance, albeit the wrong way. Using slower DRAM can noticeably degrade your PC's performance. This is a classic example of being "penny-wise and pound-foolish."

Installing Memory in Your PC

Before you can finalize your memory upgrade plan, you first need to determine how much memory is currently installed in your PC and how the memory is installed. How the memory is installed in your PC means how many SIMMs or DIMMs are physically installed and in what configurations. Many older Pentium PCs probably have 4MB, 8MB, or 16MB SIMMs. SIMMs are installed in what are called SIMM slots and the usual configuration is to have four SIMM slots in a row on your main system board (see Figure 6.5).

FIGURE 6.5

The usual configuration of four SIMM slots on a main system board.

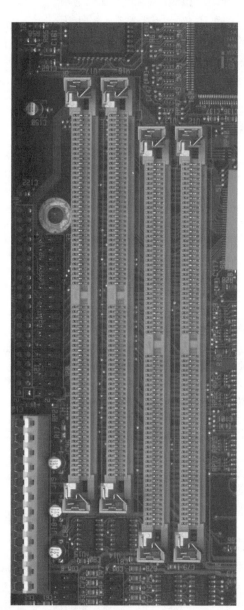

6

Memory for 486-based Computers

If you are still holding on to an old 486-based PC, you can mix SIMMs of different memory sizes. For example, you can have two 4MB SIMMs and one 8MB SIMM installed for a total of 16MB of RAM (4+4+8=16).

Most Pentium-based systems need to install SIMMs in pairs, meaning you never see the preceding configuration of two 4MB SIMMs and one 8MB SIMM because this totals three physical SIMMs in the PC. You have either a total of two or a total of four SIMMs installed. Check your manufacturer's documentation for the types of SIMMs and possible physical combinations of SIMMs you can install in your PC.

> Another consideration when installing memory SIMMs in older 486-based PCs is whether the SIMMs are parity or non-parity. A parity SIMM uses an additional memory chip for error-checking the data held in memory. As the process for making memory chips improved, the need for a parity chip was no longer needed, but some manufacturers of early model 486 PCs used both parity and non-parity SIMMs. If your PC uses parity SIMMs, any additional SIMMs you install must also be parity SIMMs.

Memory for Pentium-Class Computers

Early model Pentium-class PCs used the same 72-pin SIMMs as 486-based PCs, except that there was no parity versus non-parity issue. Many Pentium-class PCs also replaced standard DRAM SIMMs with faster FPM or EDO DRAM, providing still another boost in performance. Unlike the SIMMs used in 486-based PCs, the SIMMs in Pentium-class PCs have to be installed in pairs. For example, if you have a Pentium-class PC with two 8MB SIMMs installed in two of the four SIMM slots, to upgrade or add more memory you have to install two more (a pair) SIMMs to fill the remaining two empty SIMM slots. You cannot add just one additional SIMM.

In later model Pentium Pro, Pentium II, and Pentium III PCs, SIMMs were replaced by DIMMs. One DIMM is the functional equivalent of two SIMMs, which is why in Pentium Pro, Pentium II, and Pentium III PCs you sometimes see only two or three DIMM slots instead of the usual four SIMM slots and why you can install a single DIMM.

Installing SIMMs

Before you begin to install additional SIMMs in your PC, take a minute and look closely at how the SIMMs are installed in your computer. At each end of the SIMM there is a small clip holding the SIMM in place. Notice too that the ends of the SIMMs are not the same. One end of your SIMM is square and the other end looks like it has a small rounded notch removed. When you insert a new SIMM in your computer, make sure you align the squared end and the notched end the same as your existing SIMMs. You will also notice, printed on your main system board, that the SIMM slots are numbered, usually 0 through 3 (not 1 through 4) or 0 through 7 (not 1 through 8). Always fill the lowest number empty slot. For example, if you have SIMMs installed in slots 0 and 1, the next SIMM would be installed in slot 2.

To Do: Installing SIMMs in Your PC

To install memory SIMMs in your computer:

1. Turn off the power to your PC and unplug the power cord.

> Make absolutely certain the power is turned off! If you attempt to install SIMMs in your PC with the power on, you are guaranteed to destroy the SIMMs and possibly also your motherboard! Remember too that all memory is susceptible to static electricity, so be sure to take proper precautions to reduce static.

2. Hold the SIMM by the top edge and gently insert the SIMM into the next empty SIMM slot at an angle (see Figure 6.6). Make sure the SIMM is seated firmly into the slot (and that both sides are evenly seated in the slot).

FIGURE 6.6

Inserting a new SIMM into an empty SIMM slot.

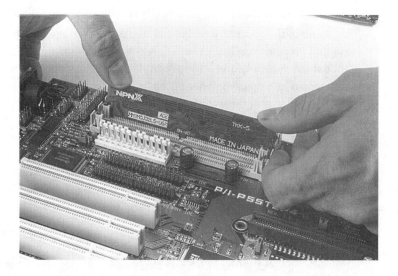

6

▼

▼ 3. Apply even pressure on the SIMM and gently push the top edge of the SIMM down so that the new SIMM is inserted into the slot at the same angle as the existing SIMMs (see Figure 6.7). On some PCs the SIMMs may be seated straight rather than at an angle. You should hear a slight snap as the SIMM clips grasp the newly inserted SIMM. If your clips are plastic, be very careful not to accidentally break or bend them.

FIGURE 6.7
A newly inserted SIMM in a SIMM slot.

4. Repeat steps 2 and 3 for all the SIMMs you have to install in your PC.

5. Replace the cover to your PC and turn on your computer. Depending on the age of the computer you have, your PC may work with the newly installed memory without any further action on your part. If you get an error message indicating that the amount of memory in your PC has changed, you may have to start your PC's hardware setup program (see Hour 3, "Examining Your PC's System Configuration") to change the amount of installed memory in your PC's CMOS memory. Essentially, you are changing the amount of memory from the amount you had before you installed the additional SIMM(s) to the amount of memory now installed in your PC. After you make the change, be sure to save the new CMOS settings you make, and then reboot your PC. Your PC now recognizes the memory you installed and
▲ makes the memory available for use by your programs.

Installing DIMMs

DIMMs are actually easier to install than SIMMs. DIMMs install in slots similar to SIMMs except that DIMMs are not angled in the slots. DIMMs insert straight down into the slots. Unlike the clips for SIMMs, the clips for DIMMs fold inward when the DIMM is inserted and fold outward when the DIMM is removed (see Figure 6.8). The pressure of the DIMM forces the clips inward to hold the DIMM in place. To remove a DIMM, you simply press outward (and downward) on the clips and the DIMM pops up.

FIGURE 6.8

A DIMM inserted into a DIMM slot.

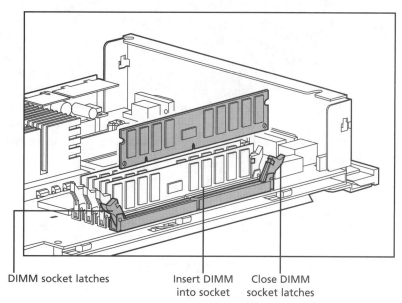

DIMM socket latches   Insert DIMM   Close DIMM
into socket   socket latches

Stretching Your Memory a Little Farther

Upgrading the memory in your PC is definitely one way to improve performance in your PC, but you also want to make sure you are using your memory wisely. Here are a few tips you can put to good use to help stretch your memory as far as possible:

- If you are still running DOS/Windows 3.1, make sure you have upgraded the version of DOS you have operating under Windows 3.1 to at least 6.2x if you are using MS-DOS. If you are running IBM's PC DOS, make sure you are using version 7.0. These versions provide the best memory management.

- If you are still running DOS/Windows 3.1, make sure you are making all your memory available to Windows. In your CONFIG.SYS file, make sure you are loading the EMM386.EXE driver with the NOEMS option to turn off Expanded memory and use as much available memory for extended memory, which Windows 3.1 can use. (Windows 3.1 cannot use expanded memory.) The line to load the EMM386.EXE driver should look something like this:

```
device=c:\dos\emm386.exe noems
```

6

- If you are still running DOS/Windows 3.1, consider upgrading to Windows 95/98 or Windows 2000. If your PC has the horsepower to run these 32-bit operating systems, they do a much better job at managing memory than the DOS/Windows 3.1 combination.

- Whatever version of Windows you are running, don't automatically start every program you think you might need. Even though Windows 95/98/NT/2000 do a much better job of managing memory than Windows 3.1, opening unnecessary programs wastes systems resources and degrades performance. If there are programs starting that you did not set to start, you can check your startup folders or AUTOEXEC.BAT file to remove the programs. To remove programs from your startup folder, simply drag the icon out and place it into another folder. To remove programs from your AUTOEXEC.BAT file, either delete the command line, which starts the program, or place REM at the beginning of the line and turn the command line into a remark.

- If you are running Windows 95/98, make sure you have the system set to enable Windows to manage your virtual memory settings (see Figure 6.9). Even if you are experienced in working with virtual memory or received advice from your office guru on how to set virtual memory in Windows 95/98, leave this setting to the default value.

FIGURE 6.9

The correct way to set virtual memory in Windows 95.

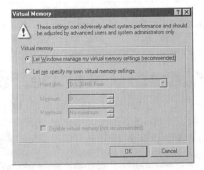

- If you are using any type of disk compression software, turn it off. These were advisable years ago before hard disk prices did a nosedive. Now these programs do little more than waste systems resources and degrade system performance.

- If you are running Windows 2000, make the following change in virtual memory (RAM paging memory) to improve performance: Make the initial value and maximum value of your paging file the same (see Figure 6.10). If you make the maximum size larger than initial size, NT will waste resources adjusting the size up and down, and this adjustment can affect performance.

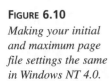

FIGURE 6.10

Making your initial and maximum page file settings the same in Windows NT 4.0.

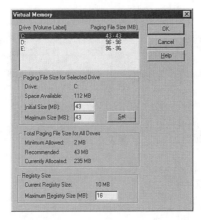

Summary

In the past hour you learned about the various types of memory used in PCs, how to identify the memory installed in your PC, how to identify the type of memory needed for your upgrade, and how to upgrade or add memory in your PC. You also learned some tips on how to better manage your PC's memory depending on which operating system you are running on your PC.

Q&A

Q If synchronous RAM is so much faster than DRAM, why isn't it used in SIMMs and DIMMs?

A It is, but not with all systems. In the past it was too expensive. But as RAM manufacturing techniques continued to improve, the costs came down enough to use SDRAM with Intel's fastest CPUs, beginning with its 400 MHz Pentium II processors and on up to its current level of Pentium III processors.

Q Why do most PC manufacturers limit the number of DIMM slots on main system boards to three?

A Most likely because of space limitations. A main system board is only so big. As they got smaller, and with everything else they have to place on a board, the manufacturers decided to restrict the number of DIMM slots to (usually) three. You usually don't see those limitations on main system boards used in file servers because the memory requirements on file servers are considerably higher than on PCs.

6

HOUR **7**

Upgrading Your CPU

You learned in the last hour that upgrading your PC's memory is the first part of the performance upgrade equation. Upgrading your computer's CPU (central processing unit, also called the processor or microprocessor) is the other half of the coin if you want to beef up your PC's performance. Your computer's CPU is the brain inside your PC. The CPU processes the instructions in your programs and operating system and is the single most important factor in improving your PC's raw computing speed.

When a computer manufacturer designs a new model PC, 9 times out of 10 the design decision is influenced by the release of a new CPU. In the past few years, it seems that new CPUs are coming off the drawing board at a record pace, fueling what seems like a constant bombardment of new model PCs.

Although this seemingly never-ending introduction of new model PCs and new CPUs has produced a certain anxiety among computer buyers, it has also produced a cottage industry for upgrading PCs, and one of the first components most users think of upgrading in their PC is the CPU.

In this hour you will learn the following:

- The basic differences between the various microprocessors available for your PC
- How to identify the type and speed of the CPU installed in your PC
- How to select and install a new CPU in your PC

Understanding Processors

In the last few years, PCs have come to be identified by the type and speed of the CPU installed. For example, most of you have heard someone describe their PC by saying they have a "Pentium 300," or they have a "Celeron 433." What they're referring to is the type of CPU installed in their PC and the *clock speed* of the CPU.

New Term   *Clock speed* is a measurement of how fast—its maximum speed—a particular CPU is set to operate. The speed is the measurement in megahertz (abbreviated MHz) of an oscillating timing crystal used to control how fast the CPU can perform internal operations. Maximum implies that there is also a minimum speed, which is no longer the case. It was true with some early 286 and 386 processors that you could adjust the speed (although why anyone would ever want to use anything but the maximum speed is beyond me). Since the 486, however, the stated clock speed is the speed at which the CPU should be operating, according to the manufacturer. Later in this hour, you will see that is not always the case.

Intel Corporation (www.intel.com) makes most of the processors found in PCs today. The following sections discuss the processors Intel has made for PCs starting with the 486.

The 486 Series

Intel released the 486 (officially the 80486) in 1989. The first release was the 486SX chip running at 25MHz. The 486SX was the original replacement for the aging 386 chip. The original 486SX did not include a math coprocessor, but Intel subsequently released the 486DX, which did include a math coprocessor.

New Term   A *math coprocessor* is a portion of a CPU that contains instructions for processing floating point mathematics. The addition of a math coprocessor enables your computer to process floating point calculations very quickly. Without a math coprocessor, floating point calculations must be converted to the slower form of integer math. Since the 486 CPU, the math coprocessor component has been incorporated into the processor. Prior to the 486, a math coprocessor was a separate chip, usually with the designation x87 (for example, 80287, 80387, and so on).

Intel produced 486 chips ranging in speeds from 25MHz to 100MHz. In the past when you upgraded from a 486 CPU, your upgrade path extended only to the next level of Intel's processors, the first generation Pentium class processor or one of its counterparts from either AMD or Cyrix.

The Pentium Series

Despite a succession of chips with numerical designations (for example, 186, 286, 386, 486), Intel chose not to call its next generation CPU the 586, but opted for the name Pentium because its legal department advised that numeric designations could not be copyrighted or trademarked. Intel released the first Pentium CPU in 1993. The original Pentium was developed to operate at a speed of 60MHz and delivered about twice the performance of a 486 operating at about the same speed (in megahertz).

The Pentium Pro Series

Intel replaced the Pentium chip with the Pentium Pro, a processor optimized to run 32-bit applications. The Pentium Pro runs nearly twice as fast as the original Pentium when running 32-bit applications, but drops in performance when running 16-bit applications.

The Pentium Pro is physically larger than the original Pentium (see Figure 7.1), which necessitated that PC manufacturers redesign their main system boards to accommodate the larger sized chip. This change in size also means that an upgrade to a Pentium Pro from either a Pentium or a 486 requires a motherboard upgrade (see Hour 8, "Replacing Your Main System Board").

FIGURE 7.1

A Pentium and Pentium Pro showing the difference in size.

The Pentium II Series

The Pentium II processor is essentially a Pentium Pro with MMX. Intel developed MMX (Multi-Media eXtensions) as a series of instructions built in to the processor to enhance audio and video functions. The original Pentium II was released in May of 1997 with a

7

clock speed of 233MHz. Intel later released versions with clock speeds of 266MHz, 300MHz, and in 1998 speeds of 333MHz, 350MHz, 400MHz, and 450MHz.

Intel made another design change when it created the Pentium II processor. Intel designed the chip on a type of bus card that requires a special slot, termed slot 1 on the main system board for the chip (see Figure 7.2).

FIGURE 7.2

A Pentium II CPU, which gets inserted into a "slot 1" slot on a main system board.

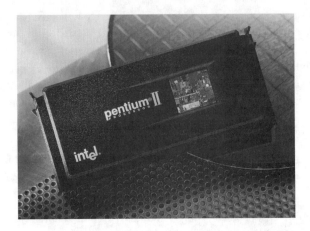

Because of this design change, there is no upgrade path to the Pentium II chip from any other Intel designed CPU. The only upgrade options are from a slower clock speed Pentium II to a faster clock speed Pentium II. Even these types of upgrades are limited because of changes in the other supporting chips used in the main system board. In preliminary tests, the difference in performance between a 300MHz Pentium II and a 400MHz Pentium II was only 17 percent. The difference in performance between a 350MHz and 400MHz Pentium II was only 7 percent.

The Pentium III Series

In February, 1999, Intel released the Pentium III processor running at a speed of 450MHz. Within a few months Intel released Pentium IIIs running at speeds up to 650MHz and hinted that it probably would not stop until the Pentium III hit 1000MHz. The Pentium III (as was the Pentium II) also was released in a "Xeon" version, which was mainly designed for the increased demands of a file server.

The AMD Series of CPUs

Although Intel still controls the lion's share of the PC processor market, it is not the only game in town. One competitor that many PC users have turned to for CPU upgrades is Advanced Micro Devices, Inc., more simply known as AMD. AMD can be found on the Web at http://www.amd.com.

AMD was founded in 1969 and today is the largest competitor producing Intel-compatible processors. AMD is especially popular among the upgrade crowd because its CPUs perform as well as Intel's. AMD's K5 series of processors directly competes against Intel's Pentium and Pentium Pro series and its K6 and K7 series are competitive with Intel's Pentium II and Pentium III series. Another factor that makes AMD's earlier model CPUs attractive is that they are pin for pin compatible with most main system board sockets used by Intel's 486 and Pentium series processors. This means that if you currently have a 486 or low-end Pentium and you want to upgrade to a Pentium Pro or Pentium II level processor, AMD's K5 and K6 chips will more than likely fit into your existing main system board CPU socket. AMD made a dramatic design change when it introduced its K7 series of processors. Even though the K7 looks very similar to Intel's Pentium II and Pentium III series processors, the K7 will not fit into a Slot 1 motherboard. The AMD K7 requires a motherboard with a proprietary slot designed to accommodate the K7.

The Cyrix Series of CPUs

Still another alternative to Intel is Cyrix Corporation, a division of National Semiconductor. You can find Cyrix on the Web at `http://www.cyrix.com`.

Cyrix also makes socket-compatible processors that can replace or upgrade from Intel's Pentium and Pentium Pro series processors. Unfortunately, Cyrix has not kept pace in the neck-and-neck race between Intel and AMD and at last report produced a processor with a top clock speed of 433MHz.

Identifying Your CPU

Before you can upgrade your CPU, you need to correctly identify the CPU that is installed in your PC. In addition to identifying the CPU, you also need to know the clock speed of your CPU. After you identify the CPU in your PC, you can decide which CPUs lie along your upgrade path.

After you take the cover off (make sure you exercise all cautions mentioned in Hours 2, "Understanding the Components in Your PC," and 5, "The Tools of the Trade"), look for what is probably the largest chip in your computer. On many computers the processor is in a plastic holder called a *ZIF* socket (see Figure 7.3).

New Term *ZIF* stands for *Zero Insertion Force*. One common problem in inserting chips is the possibility of bending or breaking the pins when you push (or jam) the pins of the chip into very tight socket holes. In a ZIF socket you don't have to push the pins of the chip into a socket. Instead, you merely place the pins into oversized socket holes and move a lever that "grabs" and locks the pins and holds the chip in the socket.

7

FIGURE 7.3

An empty ZIF socket.

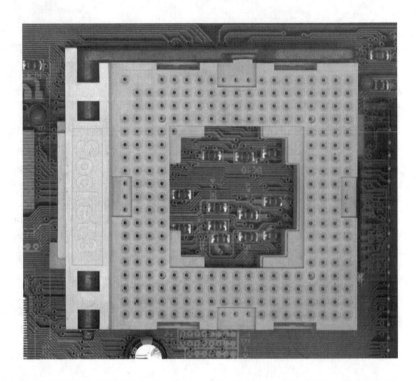

If you discover that your CPU is soldered to your main system board and your motherboard does not include an empty upgrade socket, replace the cover and forget about upgrading. If you want a faster PC, you have to purchase a newer PC or replace the main system board (see Hour 8).

Don't be surprised if you remove the cover and don't see anything that looks like a CPU. On some smaller systems, it is common to have disk drive housings covering your CPU. If this is the case, you have to also remove your disk drives to gain access to your CPU. Just pay careful attention to anything you remove (make a diagram if it helps you remember), and be sure to replace any components and cables exactly the same way you removed them.

After you've located your CPU, the first thing you need to look for is any writing on the CPU identifying what type it is. You are looking for information identifying the CPU as a 486 or Pentium and information displaying its speed.

A heat sink and/or a fan covers many processors. A heat sink is nothing more than a metal attachment, often black, silver, or blue in color, which has several dozen fins or projectiles. These are used to help dissipate the heat that processors give off. If you can't see anything identifying the processor type and speed, go back to Hour 3, "Examining Your PC's System Configuration," pull out SysChk (or one of the other utilities mentioned), and use it to identify your CPU.

You need to know exactly what type of processor is installed in your PC to purchase an upgrade. This information enables you to make sure you purchase a faster upgrade processor and an upgrade CPU that is compatible with your computer system.

In choosing an upgrade processor, most experts recommend/suggest the "100 percent rule," which simply states that you should upgrade to a processor that is roughly 100 percent faster than what you currently own. For example, if you currently have a 166MHz Pentium, you should not consider upgrading to anything less than a 300MHz (or the next highest speed chip such as a 333MHz) processor.

Besides speed, there are also slight voltage differences between some processors. If you know exactly what type of processor is currently installed in your PC, the company you purchased the upgrade from will be able to sell you an upgrade processor that will be guaranteed to operate correctly in your PC. When ordering an upgrade processor, be sure to also get the make and model of the PC you are upgrading and the BIOS manufacturer and BIOS date. BIOS information can also be obtained using SysChk.

Besides power consumption differences, Intel has also made changes in the socket design and number of pins in its processor chips, even in chips within the same family. For example, the earliest model Pentiums, the 60MHz and 66MHz models, cannot be upgraded to the faster Pentiums in the 75–200MHz range because the pin design was changed from 273 pins to 320 pins (and later 321 pins).

7

PC Bottlenecks

Everyone knows what a bottleneck is. It is a narrowed portion of a bottle that restricts the flow of whatever is in the bottle. Well, PCs can also have bottlenecks. When you upgrade your CPU, the CPU may not provide as much performance improvement as you might expect because of a bottleneck in your CPU.

Your PC was designed around the original CPU. When you upgrade the CPU, you may have a faster processor, but you still have all the remaining equipment, which was designed to work with the original, slower CPU. In other words, even though the upgrade processor processes data faster than the original CPU in your PC, the upgrade processor is slowed down by the speed of your other components, which do not operate at the same speed as your new CPU.

Does this mean that it is a waste of money to upgrade your CPU? No, because a faster CPU results in faster performance. But just keep in mind that the new CPU is working through a bottleneck—your older system.

Keep in mind that virtually any device in your PC that operates at a certain speed can become a potential bottleneck when you start upgrading components such memory (Hour 6, "Upgrading Your PC's Memory"), hard disks (Hour 11, "Replacing, Upgrading, or Adding a Hard Disk Drive"), CD-ROM drives (Hour 13, "Upgrading or Adding a CD-ROM Drive"), video cards (Hour 17, "Upgrading Your Video Card"), and so on.

Removing and Installing a CPU

If your main system board (your motherboard) is equipped with a ZIF socket, and almost all socket 7 motherboards (see Hour 8 for an explanation of socket 7 motherboards) are so equipped, removing the current processor is a snap.

If you are replacing a CPU in a plug-in card, skip to "To Do: Removing a CPU in a Plug-in Card from a Slot-1 Slot."

To Do: Removing a CPU from a ZIF Socket

To remove a processor from a ZIF socket:

1. Swing the lever out slightly to unlock it, and then swing back the ZIF socket lever to release tension on the pins.
2. Gently lift out the processor.

If your motherboard does not have a ZIF socket, you can still remove your processor with a minimal amount of effort. Many companies that sell upgrade processors include a processor extraction tool with the upgrade. Several types of processor extraction tools are available. Figure 7.4 shows you two types.

Figure 7.4

Two types of processor extraction tools.

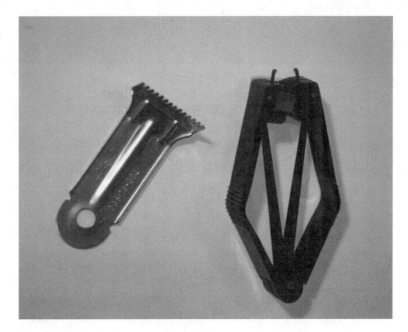

To Do: Removing a CPU Using a Processor Extraction Tool

To remove the processor using the extraction tool:

1. Follow the instructions that come with the processor extraction tool you purchase. If you purchase the large tweezer-like model, open its jaws wide enough to allow you to gently insert each of the two prongs under the sides of the CPU, and then gently squeeze the sides where the tool is its widest. This squeezing action gently lifts the CPU up and out of its socket. If you purchase the small pry bar type, gently insert it under each of the four sides of the processor and gently press down on the extraction tool. The tool is designed so that this downward pressure lifts up on the processor.

2. If your instructions call for you to repeat step 1, do so as many times as is necessary until you can gently lift the processor out of the socket. Remember to take your time. You don't need to hurry to remove a processor.

▼ To Do

▲

7

If your upgrade processor is not shipped with an extraction tool, run down to the local computer store and purchase one. The tool costs only a dollar or two and is well worth the investment because it (almost) guarantees that you will safely remove the processor without damaging it or your system board.

As you remove your old processor, note that one corner of the processor is notched and/or has a marking dot (see Figure 7.5).

FIGURE 7.5
Each CPU has a notched corner to properly line up the CPU with the socket.

Note that the notched corner of the processor is lined up with a similarly notched corner of the socket. When you insert the upgrade processor, you must make sure that the notched corners (or the dot) line up exactly as they do with the old processor.

 If the notch on the upgrade processor is not lined up exactly with the notch on the socket, your PC will not operate correctly and you could damage the upgrade processor and possibly also your motherboard.

Make sure you are grounded before you remove the upgrade processor from its container.

To Do: Inserting the New Processor

To insert the upgrade processor in your PC:

1. Locate the notch on your upgrade processor and on the processor socket.

2. Line up the notches and carefully insert the upgrade processor into the socket. If you have a ZIF socket, simply move the locking lever back to the lock position. If you do not have a ZIF socket, make sure all the pins on the CPU are lined up with the holes in the socket, and then gently apply pressure to the center of the processor until it is firmly seated in the socket.

   Check to make sure no pins are bent. If you see any bent pins, use your processor extraction tool to remove the CPU. Then, using a pair of needle-nose pliers, very carefully straighten any bent pins and try again to insert the CPU into the socket.

To Do: Removing a CPU in a Plug-in Card from a Slot-1 Slot

If you are upgrading an Intel-based CPU installed in a plug-in card, the task is almost as easy as replacing a CPU into a ZIF socket.

To remove a CPU in a plug-in card:

1. The CPU plug-in card is held in place by two clips on either side of the card in a cardholder. The holder supports the card vertically into Slot-1. Flip the clips outward, releasing the card.

2. Gently lift the card up and out of the slot.

To Do: Inserting a CPU Plug-in Card into a Slot-1 Slot

To insert the replacement CPU card into a Slot-1 slot:

1. Read over the instructions accompanying your replacement CPU. The instructions will illustrate how to properly align the new CPU plug-in card into Slot-1. Insert the CPU plug-in card into the holder and gently, but firmly, insert the plug-in card into the slot.

2. Flip the two clips (on either side of the holder) back to the upright position to hold the plug-in card securely into the slot.

If you are currently using a PC with an Intel CPU in a plug-in card and are considering upgrading to AMD's new Athlon CPUs, *Don't*! While the Athlon CPU's plug-in card will fit into a motherboard designed with a slot-1 CPU slot, the Athlon CPU is "electrically" incompatible. The Athlon requires a different motherboard, which uses what is called a "Slot-A" slot.

7

On many PCs, your new processor should be recognized and configured automatically to operate in your PC. If your PC displays an error message when turned on, run your computer's hardware Setup program as you did in Hour 5, "The Tools of the Trade," to configure your CMOS settings in your PC with your upgrade processor. Be sure to check your PC's instruction manual to see whether you need to set a jumper on the motherboard.

Overclocking

In the last few years some very industrious upgraders have discovered another way to get more megahertz out of their CPUs. The process is called overclocking.

Overclocking is simply running the CPU at a slightly faster speed than the speed certified by the manufacturer. When manufacturers test and certify their CPUs, many times they rate the CPU at a speed slower than the maximum the CPU is capable of running. In effect, they build in a little cushion to make sure that the CPU will perform at the stated speed. The key to overclocking is to adjust the CPU frequency/bus frequency ratio on your motherboard to a higher setting than is specified for your particular CPU. The CPU frequency/bus frequency ratio is often expressed as a timing setting such as 2x, 2.5x, 3x, 3.5x, 4x, and so on. To overclock your CPU, simply set the ratio to the next higher setting, if your CPU is not currently using the top setting.

> **Overclock at your own risk!!!** Even though many overclockers swear that this practice is perfectly safe, overclocking is not supported by any CPU manufacturer, and there is a potential for damaging or destroying your CPU and motherboard by overclocking. If you are curious about overclocking your CPU, check out several sites that explain this practice in more detail, such as `http://www.sysopt.com/overfaq.html`.

Summary

In the past hour you learned the evolutionary history of the Intel line of processors beginning with the 486. You learned what upgrade paths exist for the various processors and that you do not have to stick solely with CPUs made by Intel.

Q&A

Q What are the advantages and disadvantages of upgrading with an AMD processor as opposed to an Intel processor?

A The major advantages are cost and a longer upgrade path. AMD processors are a lot less expensive than Intel processors and still use the same socket as the original

Pentium processor, which enables you to upgrade to a Pentium Pro or Pentium II level (equivalent) CPU without having to also upgrade your motherboard. The major disadvantage is that it is not always possible to directly compare the performance of AMD processors to Intel processors. One method of determining computing performance is by comparing the speed of the CPU, but part of performance is affected by the speed and efficiency of the motherboard housing the CPU. Because an Intel Pentium II level CPU is using a totally different type of motherboard than an AMD Pentium II level processor, it's hard to make a direct comparison between the CPUs, even when they are rated at the same speed.

Q **How compatible are processors made by Cyrix and AMD with Intel CPUs?**

A I have not heard of a single case of a program running on an Intel processor that does not also run on processors by AMD and Cyrix.

7

HOUR **8**

Replacing Your Main System Board

Many computer experts believe that main system boards are better candidates for being replaced rather than upgraded. The reason for this belief is that any time you upgrade your main system board significantly, you most likely need to upgrade several other components in your PC as well. The CPU, memory, and possibly several of the interface cards in your PC will probably need to be upgraded to match the performance gains offered by the new system board. Rather than replace this much of your PC, in many cases it is cheaper to forgo the main system board upgrade and just purchase a new PC.

For most users, the only financially justifiable reason for replacing a main system board is if the one currently in your PC is damaged, and you replace the board with one identical or similar to your current board. You might also consider upgrading your motherboard if you are considering upgrading your CPU to the new AMD K7 (Athalon) CPU. It requires a motherboard with a special slot to accommodate this chip. Regardless of your reason for replacing your main system board, in this hour you will learn all you need to know to accomplish this sometimes tricky procedure.

During this hour you will learn the following:

- How to identify the type and size of your current system board
- How to choose a replacement system board
- How to remove your current system board and replace it with a new board

Are You Upgrading or Replacing?

As I said earlier, most experts believe that if you upgrade your main system board to a model that is a significant advancement over the one presently installed in your PC, it is likely that you may have to replace other components as well. For this reason, it is usually a better choice financially to forgo the upgrade and purchase a new PC, especially because the prices of new PCs have been dropping continually over the last few years.

 Main system boards are also referred to by the somewhat less technical name "motherboard." The two terms are used interchangeably in this chapter.

Here's an example to illustrate this point. Suppose that you have a PC with a 486 CPU installed. You may have an early model 486 system board that has a rather slow bus speed and can only work with slower memory.

NEW TERM The bus in your PC is the connecting electronic pipeline among your processor, memory, and the PC's peripherals, such as drives and interface cards. *Bus speed* refers to how fast data and instructions are able to move among the CPU, memory, and your PC's peripherals. Part of the bus speed is controlled by how wide the bus is and the speed of the bus. *Bus width* refers to how many bits of data can be passed at one time—8 bits, 16 bits, or 32 bits. Obviously, a bus that can pass data 32 bits at a time can operate faster than a bus that can pass data only 8 bits at a time.

If you purchase a system board that improves significantly on both of these performance inhibitors, you may quickly discover that you've only traded one performance bottleneck for another. Your system board may be faster, but now your old memory and CPU are slowing down your performance. You may also discover that your old 486 system board had VESA local bus expansion slots for many of your interface cards (see Figure 8.1) and your new system board has PCI bus expansion slots (see Figure 8.2).

The change from VESA local bus to PCI means that some of your interface cards will not fit in your new system board and you will have to replace them in addition to purchasing a faster CPU and faster memory. Whereas you may have thought you would be spending only $150–$200 for a new main system board, now you've discovered that your tab is almost $1000:

System board	$150.00
32MB of memory	100.00
Pentium 200MHz	400.00
Replacement PCI cards	300.00
TOTAL	950.00

FIGURE 8.1

VESA local bus expansion slots on a main system board.

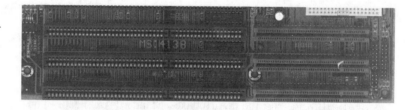

FIGURE 8.2

PCI bus expansion slots on a main system board.

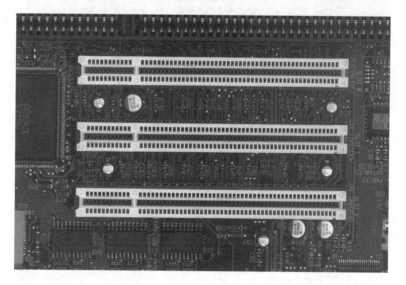

For $950 you've purchased only a new system board, memory, CPU, and maybe two replacement interface cards. Check the advertising supplements in your Sunday newspaper and you'll see several companies willing to sell you a complete, new PC for around $800–$900, and they'll probably toss in several hundred dollars worth of bundled software to sweeten the deal.

Although it may seem impractical to ever purchase a more advanced main system board, many so-called power users routinely purchase them as the basis for building a custom-designed PC. If you ever decide to build your own custom-designed PC, the information in this hour will be instrumental in helping you do that.

How System Boards Have Changed

Main system boards have undergone dramatic changes since IBM released its first PC back in 1981. Most of the major changes and advances seen in system board design have resulted from changes or advancements in bus design, chipsets, and processors. Here is a brief overview of the six major bus designs that have been incorporated into PCs since 1981:

- *8-bit (or "original IBM PC") bus.* The original 8-bit bus design used in IBM PCs, XTs, and early PC-compatible computers.
- *16-bit ISA bus.* The first 16-bit bus was essentially a 16-bit upgrade of the original IBM PC bus; the ISA (Industry Standard Architecture) bus was used originally in the IBM AT computer and AT-compatible computers.
- *Micro Channel Architecture bus.* IBM's proprietary 32-bit bus; used in its PS/2 computer line. No manufacturer other than IBM ever used this bus design because other manufacturers did not want to pay license fees to IBM.
- *EISA bus.* The computer industry's response to IBM's proprietary MCA bus; used mainly in network file servers manufactured by Compaq; EISA stands for Extended Industry Standard Architecture. In addition to the EISA bus cards, you can also use ISA bus cards.
- *VESA local bus.* The first 32-bit bus design used in 486 computers that was fast enough to support graphical environments.
- *PCI bus.* Designed to overcome many of the speed limitations of the VESA local bus to support the higher bus speeds required by the Pentium processor line.

The 486-based PCs used both VESA local bus and PCI bus system boards. The first 486-based PCs were created using the VESA local bus design, but later were switched to the more advanced PCI bus. Pentium-based PCs have mainly used system boards with a PCI bus.

 Compaq did create some Pentium-based file servers with EISA bus system boards.

8

If you have a 486-based PC, you can easily tell whether the main system board is VESA or PCI. The easiest way to distinguish the two types of main system boards is by their specialized type of expansion slots. Look back at Figures 8.1 and 8.2 and you see a VESA local bus type slot and a PCI bus slot.

Bus design changes are not the only factors that have affected system board design changes. Main system boards have also undergone changes in their physical size and shape. Since the first 486-based PC rolled down the assembly line, system boards have come in one of six basic sizes: standard AT, baby AT, LPX, ATX, and NLX. In the last year or so some manufacturers have also started shipping what is called a "baby ATX" motherboard.

Before you can select a replacement system board, you need to make sure you can correctly identify the board currently installed in your PC.

The Standard AT System Board

This type motherboard is so called because it roughly matches the size of the motherboard used in the original IBM AT computer—12 inches wide by 13.8 inches in depth. By today's standards, this is a very large board and fits only into full-sized desktop and tower computer cases (see Hour 9, "Upgrading Your PC's Case and Power Supply"). Most system board manufacturers have all but abandoned this size motherboard in favor of the smaller designs.

The Baby AT System Board

The baby AT system board, as you might guess, is a scaled down version of the standard AT sized motherboard. The miniaturization is due to advancements in technology that enable many of the components on motherboards to be reduced. Figure 8.3 illustrates the basic layout of the baby AT motherboard.

Figure 8.4 shows you the difference in size between the standard AT sized motherboard on the left and the baby AT sized motherboard on the right (see Figure 8.4).

The LPX Motherboard

The LPX (and also the "mini-LPX") motherboard is easily identified by a unique design element not present in any other motherboard design. The LPX motherboard (see Figure 8.5) has a riser card inserted into a slot on the main portion of the board. The riser card contains slots into which your interface cards are inserted. The LPX design was developed by Western Digital and is still used in PCs manufactured by IBM, Compaq, and Gateway.

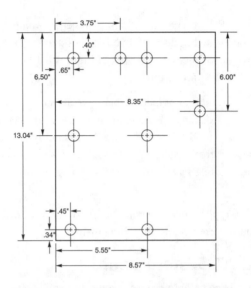

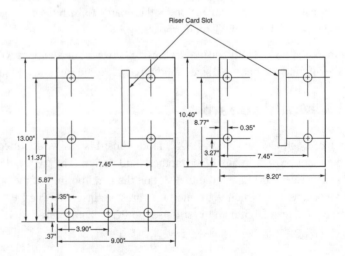

You may encounter two problems with an LPX motherboard: Because of the use of the riser card, they generally have less potential for expandability because they have fewer expansion slots. The other problem is that you may have difficulty finding a replacement motherboard except from the manufacturers who generally charge more for replacement boards than a third-party vendor.

The ATX Motherboard

The ATX motherboard, designed by Intel in 1995, is sort of a hybrid baby AT and LPX model, which at first appears to be turned sideways. This is the design used in many of the PCs manufactured in the last 2 to 3 years and is considered by some to be the de facto standard design. The design of the ATX enables PC manufacturers to produce fewer crowded and congested hardware configurations, making access to components you might want to upgrade easier. Figure 8.6 shows the basic design of the ATX motherboard.

FIGURE 8.6

The ATX motherboard layout showing location of PC features.

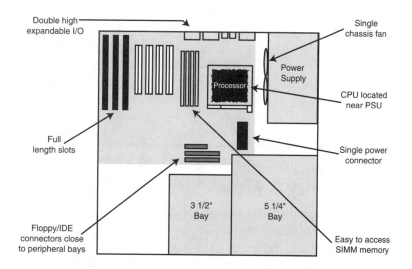

Be aware that because of the layout and positioning of components on the ATX motherboard, such as the location of the power connectors, mouse connectors, and keyboard, the ATX motherboard will not fit in cases designed for either the standard AT or baby AT motherboards.

The baby ATX motherboard is simply a scaled down version of the standard ATX motherboard designed to fit into a baby ATX style case (see Hour 9).

The NLX Motherboard

The NLX motherboard design is fairly new and was designed specifically for computers using the Pentium II processor. The NLX design contains many of the best features of both the ATX and LPX (see Figure 8.7).

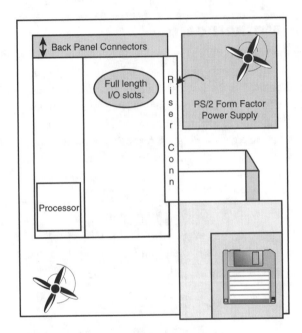

FIGURE 8.7

The basic layout of the NLX motherboard.

Installing a New System Board

Regardless of which motherboard size or style you purchase, replacing your existing system board requires careful planning. Although replacing a motherboard may at first appear to be a major technological undertaking, in reality all you need is a little bit of planning and a bit more patience (and of course a screwdriver or two) to get the job accomplished successfully.

Remember to unplug your PC and ground yourself before you remove the PC's cover. Make sure you carefully remove each component from your existing motherboard and make sure that you place all the components on a safe surface, such as an uncluttered tabletop, where they cannot be damaged physically or by static electricity.

To Do: Removing Your Old Motherboard

Follow these steps to remove your old motherboard:

1. The very first task you need to perform is to make a diagram of all the connections (ribbon cables, jumpers, thin-wire cables, interface cards, and so on). Pay particular

▼ attention to the orientation of each connector, especially those connectors that can be attached more than one way, such as ribbon cables. Notice that most ribbon cables have a red strip on one edge of the cable. This red strip is used to orient the first pin—called pin 1—to its correct position with the connecting plug. Be sure to label or identify each connecting device attached to your motherboard.

2. Read and reread any and all instructions that come with your new motherboard. There might be steps you need to take either before or after you install the new motherboard, such as moving jumpers.

3. Examine your existing motherboard in its case to see exactly how it is attached to the case. Notice the number and position of screws and nonmetallic connectors and supports.

4. Remove all interface cards from your motherboard by first removing the retaining screw and then gently lifting the card out of its slot. Sometimes, you may need to gently rock the cards to get them out. If any cables are attached to any of the interface cards, carefully remove and label each of the cables.

5. Carefully remove the memory SIMMs and/or DIMMs and the processor installed in your computer. If it is awkward to remove these now, you can wait until you have removed the motherboard from the case to remove the processor and memory SIMMs.

6. Remove any cables attached to your motherboard and label them one at a time. Note the orientation of the power cables connected to your motherboard. The power cables are the two multi-wire, multi-colored cables running from the power supply to the motherboard.

One way to easily remember how to reattach the power cables from your motherboard (on all but ATX motherboards) to the power supply is that the black wires are always on the inside edges of the two connectors next to each other.

7. When all components and connectors have been removed from your motherboard, remove the screws and standoff connectors (the small plastic supports) holding your motherboard in its case. Carefully remove the motherboard from its case. Note the orientation of your motherboard to its case. If you still need to remove the
▲ CPU and memory, do so and carefully put them in a safe place.

Now that you have your old motherboard out of the PC's case, half of your job is done. To install your replacement motherboard, you merely have to follow the exact same steps as to remove your old motherboard, only in reverse order.

To Do: Replacing the Motherboard in Your PC

▼ To Do

Here's what you need to do to replace the motherboard in your PC:

1. You might find it easier if you insert the CPU and memory into the new motherboard before you place it back into your PC's case. If you need to, review Hours 6, "Upgrading Your PC's Memory," and 7, "Upgrading Your CPU," on how to insert SIMMs/DIMMs, and CPUs.

2. Place the new motherboard in your case, paying attention to any possible changes in the standoff connectors and connecting screws. Be sure to use all your screws to allow for proper grounding.

3. Replace the power connectors according to the diagram you made when you removed your old motherboard.

4. Replace your interface cards. On some older motherboards users occasionally had problems with interface cards being placed over processors, but new motherboard designs, such as the ATX motherboard, rearranged the placement of CPUs and cards to avoid this problem. The biggest problem you can encounter with replacing all your cards is making sure that the new motherboard has the same number of expansion slots as your old motherboard. Be sure to reconnect any cables that were attached to the cards.

5. Perform any setup operations dictated by the instructions included with your new motherboard.

▲

When you have reattached everything to your new motherboard that was removed from your old motherboard, you are ready to turn on your PC and test your handiwork. If your PC fails to start or displays any errors, note the error and check the instructions that came with your new motherboard. Recheck your work. When you have corrected the problem causing the error, retest your PC.

Summary

In the past hour you learned about the various types of main system boards used in PCs, how to identify the various types of system boards, what criteria you use in deciding if you want to upgrade your system board, and how to remove and install a system board.

Q&A

Q Where did the term "motherboard" originate?

A The term actually predates the original IBM PC and goes back to the Apple II computer. As the story is told, when the Apple II came out it had more of a home/hobbyist image as opposed to a corporate/business image. Someone decided that the term "main system board" seemed rather harsh and cold and did not keep with the "softer, gentler" image Apple was trying to project. So, in an attempt to soften the terminology, someone started calling the system board a "motherboard" and the term has just held on.

Q All of the motherboards mentioned are one-piece boards. Did manufacturers ever make multi-piece motherboards?

A Yes, but they mainly consisted of proprietary designs and were never standardized. Occasionally you will still see these multi-piece designs, but they are rare.

HOUR 9

Upgrading Your PC's Case and Power Supply

Upgrading your PC's case and power supply may seem like a fairly inconsequential upgrade, but believe me, there is a method to this madness. As you begin to upgrade or, more specifically, add components to your PC such as additional hard disk drives, CD-ROM drives, removable media drives, and so on, you are adding components that require both space and electrical power. Look ahead to the many chapters on adding some type of disk drive and you will see how often I mention that if you have an empty drive bay…yada yada yada…. Well, not too many PCs leave the factory with four or five empty drive bays. And if you have been giving some thought to adding a CD-ROM drive, a Zip drive, and a second hard disk drive, you might be stopped dead in your tracks when you discover that you have only one empty drive bay left in your PC (if that).

As for electrical power, too many PC users have learned the hard way that as you continue to add components, you cannot just keep adding Y-connectors (see Hour 11, "Replacing, Upgrading, or Adding a Hard Disk Drive") and expect everything to function properly.

Upgrading your PC's case and power supply may seem like major surgery, but it is something the average PC user can easily accomplish with just a screwdriver, a little time, and a little patience.

During this hour you will learn:

- What features to look for in selecting a new case or power supply
- The different types of PC cases available
- What steps you need to follow to transfer your motherboard and peripherals from your existing case into a new case

Deciding to Upgrade Your Case and Power Supply

When you purchased your current PC, you probably thought it came in a perfectly adequate case. Everything was neatly arranged and the drives, motherboard, interface cards, and so on all fit together in a nice, neat, orderly package. So, why would you want to pull everything out and stuff all your components into a new box? Well stop for a moment, remove your PC's cover, and take a long, hard look inside your PC and see how much room there is for adding any extra drives or other components. Can you add one or two more hard disk drives? Can you add an internal Zip or Jaz drive? Can you add a CD-ROM drive (if you don't already have one)? Can you add a DVD drive? Can you add a tape drive?

For whatever reason (often to keep costs down), some manufacturers use a fairly small case when they design and manufacture their PCs. Whether the reason is to keep the package that you place on your desk as small as possible, or whether it is to keep their costs down by keeping their package (and packaging) smaller, the end result is that you have a PC that may not be as expandable as you'd like.

Although most PCs can very easily be upgraded into a new case, some PCs, because of their proprietary design, cannot be upgraded simply because their manufacturers used a nonstandard motherboard and case design. If you open your PC and see a motherboard that does not seem to fit the designs mentioned in this chapter (or in Hour 8, "Replacing Your Main System Board"), the chances are good that your system cannot easily be upgraded, and you should not even attempt to upgrade to a new case unless you also consider upgrading your motherboard as well.

The obvious answer to the need for more room is simply to swap your existing case for a new one. If you read Hour 8, you're already aware of what it takes to replace the motherboard in your PC, and as I said before, any average PC user can replace a case with just a screwdriver, a little time, and a little patience. Well, now you have to follow the same procedure, but reverse the process. To replace your case, instead of placing a new motherboard in your existing case, you are placing your existing motherboard into a new case. To save yourself some time, remember that you probably don't have to remove the processor and memory from your motherboard when removing it from one case and placing it into another.

9

What to Look for When Shopping for a New Case

Although not exactly like buying a new car, you want to look for certain features when shopping for a new case. Some of the features in a new case that definitely make your life easier and your upgrades smoother include

- *Multiple drive bays.* The main reason you are purchasing a new case is probably to add additional drives (hard disk drives, CD-ROM drives, DVD drives, removable media drives, and so on), so make sure your new case has more drive bays than you currently need so that you have room to expand (see Figure 9.1). Most cases have a mixture of 3-1/2 inch and 5-1/4 inch drive bays. The 3-1/2 inch drive bays are used to add additional hard disk drives, and the 5-1/4 inch bays are used for CD-ROM and removable media drives. If, however, you run out of 3-1/2 inch bays with the proper mounting hardware, you can place a hard disk drive into a 5-1/2 inch drive bay. Keep in mind, too, that some replacement cases may only come with one or two 3-1/2 inch drive bays.

If you have SCSI hard disks, CD-ROM drives, or removable media drives in your PC, it is possible to purchase a separate case that only houses your SCSI drives. These SCSI cases include their own power supply and fans and are a good way to remove some of the devices responsible for the heat buildup inside your PC. You will need to purchase a new cable for your SCSI chain because the cable you have now only works inside your PC. If you do decide to pursue this option, and you plan to retain some devices inside your PC as well, make sure your SCSI card supports both external and internal devices simultaneously. Some SCSI cards don't.

FIGURE 9.1

A computer case with extra drive bays.

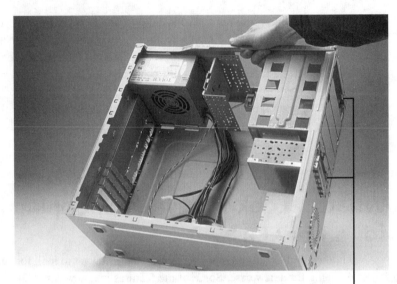

Extra drive bays

- *Multiple fans.* Keep in mind that as you add additional drives and other components into your PC, you also add more devices that produce heat. Look for cases with at least two fans to help disperse the extra heat buildup, in addition to the fan on the power supply. If possible, try to find a case with large fans.

- *Large power supply.* In this case, large means wattage, not physical girth. Try to get a power supply in the range of 250–400 watts. Keep in mind that those additional drives you plan to add all require power to operate.

- *Extra power connectors.* Although extra power connectors are not essential, having a few extra saves you a trip to the local computer store to purchase Y-connectors (see Figure 9.2).

- *Sturdy construction.* If you purchase locally, rather than through the mail, examine the case before you buy it (be sure to examine the actual case you purchase, not just a display model). Try to get a case that seems like it is constructed with heavier gauge steel rather than a flimsy type of sheet metal. Look to see whether the seams are even and that all seams meet with no gaps. Check to see that the cover or door fits securely and is easy to open or remove. If you purchase your case by mail order, try talking to several computer consultants in your area to see whether they can recommend one or more brands for you to purchase.

- *Front panel indicators and controls.* Many cases come equipped with several front panel indicators and controls. Although not all are essential, some can come in handy. The essential controls include a reset button, an on/off switch (this prevents you from having to reach around back to turn on your PC), and a drive activity indicator light. Make sure instructions are included with your case to let you know how to connect the front panel controls and indicators to your motherboard. If your existing case has front panel indicators and controls, make note of how and where these are connected to your motherboard.

FIGURE 9.2

You can supplement extra power connectors with a few Y-connectors.

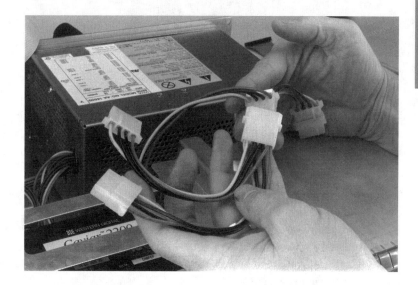

- *Removable mounting plate and drive bays.* A removable mounting plate (see Figure 9.3) makes it easier to install and access your motherboard. Removable drive bays, both internal and external, make it easier to install and access any drives that you install in your PC.

 External drive bays hold drives that are physically accessible to you, such as floppy disk and CD-ROM drives. Internal drive bays are bays holding drives that you don't need to physically access, such as hard disk drives.

Cases (which are also referred to as chassis), just like PCs, can be purchased as either desktop or tower models and come in a variety of sizes. Desktop case sizes are usually referred to as standard, baby AT, and slimline. Desktop cases usually don't offer you as much expansion space as do tower cases. Just make sure the case you purchase is designed for your type of motherboard (see Hour 8).

FIGURE 9.3

A removable mounting plate makes it easy to access your mother-board.

Tower cases usually have a larger variety of available sizes, such as mini-tower, medium, large tower, server-size, and super-sized. Usually the difference in sizes is due to the number of drive bays and the size (wattage) of the power supply.

Desktop units have the advantage of occupying a smaller piece of your office real estate and are generally less expensive than tower cases. Tower cases, on the other hand, offer more room for expansion and can be placed on the floor next to your desk so that they don't take up any valuable desktop space. When you place a tower on the floor next to your desk, you likely have to purchase expansion cables (that is, longer cables) for your monitor and keyboard.

Upgrading Your Case

There are no hard and fast rules for upgrading your PC's case except that you should be patient and methodical, and should make note of anything you remove or disconnect. However, here are a few suggestions you might want to follow after you unplug the power cord, ground yourself, and remove the cover from your existing PC case.

> Grounding yourself is extremely important to prevent damage from static electricity, but be sure to exercise the same caution with each component that you remove from your PC. Make sure to place your drives, SIMMs, and your CPU someplace where they are not subject to damage by static electricity.

To Do: Upgrading Your PC's Case

The following is one method you can use to replace your existing case with a newer model:

1. Make sure you diagram the location of every component before you move or remove anything. This includes drives, cables, power connectors, and any miscellaneous items installed in your PC. Note also how any mounting hardware is installed.

2. Carefully remove your interface cards first. If any cables are attached to any of the cards, remove the cables before you attempt to remove the cards. One at a time, remove the screw securing the card in place, and lift the card out of its slot. Place each card in a safe location so that they are not damaged.

3. Next, remove your disk drives and ribbon cables. Again, you should note how they are connected and which cables are connected to each drive. Also remove any mounting hardware used to support your disk drives. Carefully note how the mounting hardware is installed and where all mounting screws are installed.

4. Next, remove your memory SIMMs (or DIMMs) and CPU. When removing the SIMMs/DIMMs, be careful not to damage the SIMMs, DIMMs, or the clips holding them into each slot (see Figures 9.4 and 9.5). If your CPU is inserted into a ZIF socket (see Figure 9.6), remove the fan and/or heat sink if there is one, unclip the latch, lift it up to release tension on the pins of the CPU, and lift your CPU out of the socket. This step is often done by users as a means of making sure that the CPU and memory SIMMs are not accidentally damaged. If you feel comfortable leaving the CPU and SIMMs in place, do so.

FIGURE 9.4

Clips used to secure SIMMs in their slots.

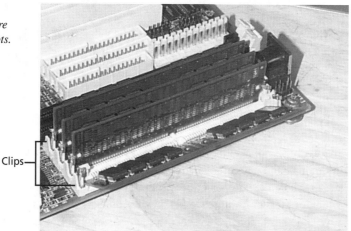

Clips—

▼

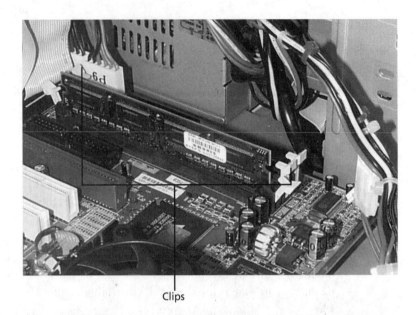

FIGURE 9.5
Clips used to secure DIMMs in their slots.

Clips

FIGURE 9.6
A ZIF socket securing a CPU on a motherboard.

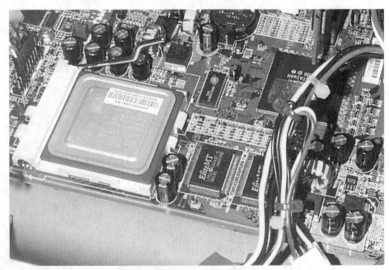

5. After every component has been removed from your case and motherboard, stop for a minute and note the remaining cables attached to your motherboard. Note in particular how the two power cables are attached to your motherboard's power connectors. In most cases, the two black wires on each power connector (if you have an AT style motherboard) are next to each other (see Figure 9.7). Check to see whether your PC follows this convention. If it does not, make note of how the

power cables are attached to the motherboard. Also note whether your disk drive ribbon cables are attached to connectors on your motherboard. If they are, note the direction and position of the red edge of the ribbon cable. Note, too, whether a series of smaller cables and wires are attached to your motherboard from your case's front panel. These are for your front panel indicator connections and controls. Finally, note the placement of screws and standouts (plastic supports) for your motherboard. Remove all screws, making sure not to accidentally damage your motherboard with the tip of the screwdriver, and then remove your motherboard and put it in a safe place.

9

▲

FIGURE 9.7

The two black wires on the power supply connectors (on an AT style motherboard) are usually next to each other, as shown here.

You don't normally remove the power supply because almost all new cases come with power supplies already installed.

To install your motherboard and components into the new case, simply follow the previous five steps in reverse order, making sure you pay close attention to your diagrams and notes. Just be patient, take your time, and you should have no trouble installing the motherboard and components into your new case.

When you have double-checked every connection and diagram you've made, plug in your PC and hit the power switch. Your PC should boot up just like before. If your PC does not boot, unplug the electrical cable. First check your power connectors to your motherboard to make sure they are properly positioned and then check to make sure your SIMMs (or DIMMs) and CPU are all properly seated. In most PCs, these are usually the components that, if not properly installed, keep your PC from booting.

Power Supplies

When you purchase a new case, it usually comes equipped with a power supply, but you can also purchase power supplies separately. The two main reasons for purchasing a separate power supply are as follows:

- Your existing power supply fails.
- You want to add additional devices to your PC, and your existing power supply does not output sufficient wattage. Older PCs with only a few internal devices have been shipped with smaller wattage power supplies. If your power supply is in the 75–125W range, you should consider replacing it for this reason.

The most important factor to consider when purchasing a new power supply is whether it fits in your existing case. If you do not purchase a new power supply from the same company that supplied your original power supply, it probably is a good idea to remove the power supply you are replacing and take it with you to your local computer store. This way you can compare the new power supply to the old one, check for size, and make sure that the power connection cables, mounting screws, and off/on switch are all in the same relative positions.

One caution that cannot be repeated too often is the importance of making sure to reconnect the power supply cables to your motherboard properly. Make sure you note how the power supply cables (on an AT style motherboard) are connected before you remove them. In most cases the two black cables (on an AT style motherboard) are next to each other when the two connectors are plugged into the motherboard. If you accidentally reverse these connectors you can fry your motherboard. On an ATX style motherboard there is only one connector, which can only fit one way.

You can easily remove your existing power supply with just a screwdriver and a little patience. Remember to label each cable you remove and, most importantly, make sure you unplug the power supply before you begin removing it from your case. Be careful that you only remove the screws holding the power supply in the case and do not accidentally remove the screws from the power supply itself.

Don't even think about trying to open a failed power supply to attempt repairing it. First, they usually aren't worth repairing; a new power supply can be purchased for around $20–$30. Second, power supplies are all manufactured with slow discharge capacitors, which can carry a considerable (and dangerous) charge even after they are unplugged.

Summary

In the past hour, you learned about upgrading your PC's case and power supply. You learned both what criteria are important in selecting a new case and a few tips on how and where to purchase one. You also learned step-by-step how to remove the components in your existing PC and how to reinstall them into your new case.

Q&A

9

Q Is heat buildup really a problem with PCs nowadays? I thought all the solid state electronics and miniaturization eliminated most of the previous heat buildup problems.

A You're right when you say that solid state electronics and miniaturization have reduced a lot of the heat buildup problems, but when you start adding multiple hard disk drives, tape drives, Zip drives, and so on, you are also adding more heat sources in your PC. Take a look at your PC, and if you have almost anything newer than a 486/33, chances are you see a heat sink glued to the top. Heat dissipation has been one major concern with all the processor manufacturers because, as they keep adding transistors to CPUs (1–5 million or more depending on the type you have), CPUs keep getting hotter. Compare the heat sink on the top of a 200MHz Pentium Pro to the heat sink on the top of a 486/66. The Pentium Pro heat sink isn't larger just so that it fits the top of the CPU. You may have noticed, too, that some PC manufacturers also place an auxiliary fan on top of the CPU in addition to the heat sink. Heat buildup is still a problem, which is why it pays to make sure that any new case you purchase has a minimum of two large fans. One of the often unmentioned advantages of the SCSI interface is that it enables you to remove some of these heat-producing components (hard disk drives, CD-ROM drives, Zip and Jaz drives, and so on) outside of your PC into one or more separate cases.

Q The fan in my case seems adequate for removing any heat buildup. Do I really also need a fan mounted on my CPU as well?

A Yes! Definitely! As CPUs get faster they get hotter as well. Not only do you need a fan on your CPU, but you should also make sure your CPU has a heat sink installed as well. The fan/heat sink on the CPU will help dissipate any heat buildup and the fan, or fans, inside your case will help dissipate any heat buildup in your case, which could damage components other than your CPU.

Q Does it make a difference whether you operate your PC with the top off? I've seen some PCs with warning labels saying not to, but the PC seems to operate just the same with the top on or off.

A Operating your PC with the top or cover on or off gets back to the problem of heat dissipation. Your PC case is designed with a certain airflow pattern in mind, and when you remove the top or cover, you disrupt its airflow. It's okay to operate your PC for a few minutes with the cover removed, but you should not make a habit of operating your PC for any length of time with the cover off.

Hour **10**

Upgrading Your PC's BIOS

In the past, upgrading your PC's BIOS ranked right up there in importance with getting your shoes resoled. But that all changed around the latter part of 1997. Word began to spread about something called the "millennium bug", and soon, just about everyone with a PC began scrambling to see whether his or her PC could tell the difference between the years 1900 and 2000. As we all know now, the so-called "millennium bug" was not really a bug; it was just another example of human shortsightedness. Regardless of what you want to call it, it was a real problem, and it was something of which every PC user needed to be aware.

Of course, the millennium bug was not the only reason you should have considered for upgrading your BIOS. Some PCs need a BIOS upgrade in order to accept an upgrade processor. Some PCs need a BIOS upgrade to recognize a hard disk of more than 500MB. And some PCs need a BIOS upgrade in order to work with a removable media drive or some other new technology that will soon be coming down the pike.

So where does this fit in with upgrading your PC's BIOS? Well in this hour you will find out, and you will learn:

- What your PC's BIOS is and what it does
- Why your PC's BIOS affected your PC's capability to function correctly past December 31, 1999
- How to locate a BIOS upgrade for your PC
- How to install a BIOS upgrade on your PC

What Is the BIOS?

The next time you turn on your PC, pay close attention to the information displayed onscreen. The *BIOS*, which stands for *Basic Input Output System*, is software, or more correctly called *firmware*. It enables your computer to boot and your processor to access the hardware devices such as the hard disk drive, video card, system clock, and other peripherals. The BIOS also controls the POST (the Power On Self-Test), the diagnostic and initialization program, which runs every time you turn on your computer.

NEW TERM *Firmware* is essentially software that has been embedded into certain chips in your computer and that runs automatically without intervention on your part. The distinction is usually made between programs that you can easily change, erase, and delete—software—and programs that you cannot easily alter—firmware.

Every BIOS is specific to a certain type of motherboard, so even if you notice that the BIOS in your computer is made by the same company that manufactures the BIOS in your neighbor's computer, it doesn't necessarily mean that the BIOS in one is identical to the other. If the two of you have different makes of PC, you can almost guarantee that the BIOSes are different in each.

The BIOS in various computers varies in size and functionality somewhat, but a core portion is about 64KB in size in every computer that claims to be "IBM PC compatible."

Why You Need to Upgrade Your BIOS

Your BIOS was made about the same time as your computer, and although it may have served you well so far, many things have undoubtedly changed since your computer was manufactured. New types of peripherals have been invented, disk drives have gotten larger, and new types of video cards with higher resolutions have been created, among other things. In short, the BIOS in your computer has remained static while the rest of the computer industry has continued at its usual hectic, dynamic pace. For example, the

BIOS in some early model 486 computers was designed while most hard disk drives were still around 200–400MB in size. When users of these computers attempted to install larger hard disk drives—in the 2–4GB range—they discovered that their computers could not recognize more than the first 528MB of their new multi-gigabyte hard disk drives. The reason behind this problem is that the BIOS in their computers is not able to understand *Logical Block Addressing* (LBA). In simpler terms, it means the BIOS cannot address all the storage space on the hard disk drive beyond the first 528MB because that is as high as it can count. The answer to this problem is simply to upgrade the BIOS. If you find that no BIOS upgrade is available for your PC (another hint that it's time to purchase a new PC instead of upgrading your current model) sometimes you can solve the LBA problem by applying a software patch.

Year 2000 BIOS Concerns

Probably the most famous BIOS problem discovered to date is the year 2000 problem, more commonly referred to as the Y2K (Y=year, 2K=2000) problem. Your computer has an internal timer, which does nothing but measure the passage of time. Your computer has a battery backup, which you earlier learned holds information in your CMOS memory. The battery backup also supplies power to your computer's timer, or system clock. The BIOS translates information from the timer into a readable date and time. If your computer contains a BIOS that uses four digits for the year portion of the date, then one second past 11:59:59 p.m. on December 31, 1999 correctly became 12:00:00 a.m. January 1, 2000. If, however, the BIOS in your computer only used two digits for the year portion of the date, it thought 1 second past 11:59:59 p.m. on December 31, 1999 was 12:00:00 a.m. on January 1, 1900. Computer programs that also use two digits for the year did, and continue to do, the same thing. Again, the solution for your computer (not your software) is to upgrade the BIOS.

Testing Your Computer's BIOS for Y2K Compliance

If it isn't already readily apparent, you can perform two simple tests to determine your computer's BIOS for Y2K compliance. The first is simply a real-time transition test.

To Do: Y2K Real-Time Transition Test

The following is a simple real-time transition test you can perform to check your PC's BIOS for Y2K compliance:

1. At a DOS or system prompt, enter the command **date** and then press Enter.

   This displays the current system date on your computer and prompts you to enter a new date.

2. Enter **12-31-99** and then press Enter.

▼ 3. Now enter **time** and press Enter.

This displays the current system time on your computer and prompts you to enter a new system time.

4. Enter **23:59:30** and press Enter.

> The vast majority of computers use military time clocks, so to set the time for 11:59 p.m. you have to enter it as 23:59.

5. Wait about a minute and then reenter the **date** command. If your computer displays Saturday January 1, 2000 as the date (see Figure 10.1), it passes the first of the two tests, the real-time transition to year 2000. If your computer displays the date as Monday January 1, 1900, however, your computer's BIOS is using two digits for the year portion of the date instead of four digits.

▲

> The BIOS in many computers also does not display a date in the year 1900. Instead, those computers default to a date beginning somewhere around January 1, 1980.

FIGURE 10.1

Computer correctly displaying January 1, 2000 as the date.

```
C:\>date
Current date is Thu 05-07-1998
Enter new date (mm-dd-yy): 12-31-99

C:\>time
Current time is  2:51:26.55p
Enter new time: 23:59:45

C:\>date
Current date is Sat 01-01-2000
Enter new date (mm-dd-yy):

C:\>
```

To Do: Performing the Retention of BIOS Date After Rebooting Test

The second BIOS test that you can perform to test Y2K compliance is a test to see whether your BIOS retains a date into the year 2000 after you reboot your computer. Take these steps:

1. If your computer successfully passed the previous Y2K BIOS test and displays the date as Saturday, January 1, 2000, press Ctrl+Alt+Del to reboot your PC.

▼

If you are using Windows 95/98/NT/2000, execute the proper shutdown procedure before pressing Ctrl+Alt+Del to reboot.

2. Go back to a DOS or system prompt and reenter the **date** command and then press Enter.

   If your computer retains the date of January 1, 2000 after rebooting, your computer passes the second test, retention of the BIOS date after rebooting.

▲

Although the Y2K problem is probably the most pervasive reason most users upgrade the BIOS in their computer, as you have seen, it is not the only reason. If you attempt any of the upgrades mentioned in this text and run into a problem with your computer not recognizing the device or component that you are attempting to install, you should suspect a BIOS problem and consider a BIOS upgrade for your computer if one is available.

10

Don't attempt a BIOS upgrade just for the heck of it. BIOS upgrades are serious undertakings and you should only perform a BIOS upgrade when you are absolutely certain you need the upgrade. In most cases, you can consult with the computer's manufacturer to determine whether you need to upgrade your computer's BIOS.

How Do I Upgrade My BIOS?

Early 486 model computers had chips on the motherboard that stored the BIOS routines and that had to be physically replaced in order to upgrade the BIOS (see Figure 10.2).

Later model 486 computers, however, and all computers since the first Pentium models have what is called *flash BIOS*, which means you can run a program on a floppy disk to upgrade your BIOS, which is then stored in *EEPROM* chips, and no physical replacement of chips is necessary.

NEW TERM *EEPROM* stands for *Electrically Erasable Programmable Read Only Memory* and is a special type of chip used to store your BIOS programs. Under normal circumstances, the programs stored in EEPROM chips are stored permanently. You can, however, use special programs to update and replace the programs stored in EEPROMs. This is what happens when you upgrade flash BIOS.

FIGURE 10.2
BIOS chips on an older 486 mother-board.

Determining If You Need to Upgrade Your BIOS

If you install a new peripheral and it doesn't work and you have checked every part of the installation procedure and everything checks out OK, chances are you need to upgrade your BIOS. In most cases, this problem surfaces when you attempt to install not just a new peripheral but a new type of peripheral.

Also, if you receive notice from your dealer or from your PC's manufacturer that there is a defect in your current BIOS and they recommend that you upgrade, it is time to upgrade.

Establishing the Type of BIOS You Have

If you have a Pentium or later processor in your computer, you can rest assured you have a flash BIOS. If you have a 486 processor, your chances are 50–50 that you have a flash BIOS (if you are still using a 486-based PC, forget the BIOS upgrade and just purchase a new PC; you're long overdue for one).

If you still have your original documentation, which lists the type of BIOS in your PC, the documentation also likely indicates whom to contact about upgrading your BIOS.

If you don't still have the original documentation that came with your PC, there is another method to determine the type of BIOS in your PC. Turn on your PC and write down all the BIOS information displayed when your computer boots. The BIOS information is usually displayed in the upper-left corner of your screen just after your PC completes the POST (Power On Self Test). Look for the name of a company and a number that looks like some sort of serial number. That number is the BIOS version (see Figure 10.3).

FIGURE 10.3

The BIOS version appearing onscreen after POST.

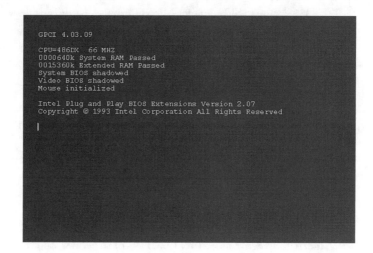

You can also check your CMOS settings using one of the systems checking utilities mentioned in Hour 3, "Examining Your PC's System Configuration," for BIOS information (see Figure 10.4).

FIGURE 10.4

SiSoft Sandra displaying BIOS information.

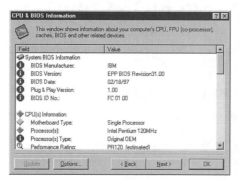

After you have the BIOS information about your PC, you can contact your PC's manufacturer to find out what type of BIOS you have. Be sure to also have the model of your computer when you contact the manufacturer, or check the manufacturer's Web site.

Different Methods for Upgrading Your BIOS

If you do not have flash BIOS, and you insist on retaining and upgrading your old 486, you can contact your PC's manufacturer about ordering a new set of BIOS chips. You can also contact one of two BIOS upgrade companies, Micro Firmware, Inc. and Microid Research (Unicore Software). Micro Firmware can be reached at 800-767-5465 or 405-321-8333. You can also contact Micro Firmware at `http://www.firmware.com`. Microid Research can be reached at 800-800-BIOS and 508-686-6468. Microid's Web site is located at `http://www.unicore.com`, or MR. BIOS at `http://www.mrbios.com`, or try `http://www.sysopt.com/bios.html`.

If you do have flash BIOS in your PC, and you have Internet access, you can most likely download the program to update your PC from a variety of sources. Look at the Web site run by your PC's manufacturer. Most computer manufacturers run a Web site and provide BIOS and other upgrades and updates for their customers. If your PC's manufacturer does not maintain a Web site, you can look on the Web sites run by several of the leading BIOS manufacturers. The following is a short list:

- **Award**—`http://www.award.com`
- **Phoenix**—`http://www.ptltd.com`
- **American Megatrends, Inc. (AMI)**— `http://www.megatrends.com`

You can also check the company from whom you purchased your PC if you did not purchase directly from the manufacturer.

Installing Upgrade BIOS Chips

If you order BIOS upgrade chips for a computer that does not have flash BIOS (in my opinion, throwing good money after bad, but that's another story), it's very easy to install the chips yourself.

To Do: Installing BIOS Upgrade Chips

To install BIOS upgrade chips onto your PC's motherboard, follow these steps:

1. Turn off and unplug your PC.
2. Discharge any static electricity by first touching the exterior of the your PC's case, and then remove the cover from your PC.
3. Examine the new BIOS upgrade chips you ordered. Notice the size of the chips, their markings or labels, and most importantly, look for a notch or dot in one end of the chips (see Figure 10.5).

▼ **FIGURE 10.5**

A notch on one end of the BIOS chip indicates the chip's proper orientation.

10

4. Now look on your motherboard and find chips that look similar to the chips you ordered. If you're not sure, check your PC's documentation for the exact location of your computer's BIOS chips. Record which direction the orientation notch is positioned.

5. Before you remove a chip, check your instructions to see in what order you need to replace the chips. You want to make sure you install the replacement chips (if there is more than one chip) in the correct socket.

6. The chips you ordered should have been shipped with a tool resembling a large set of tweezers with the tips turned inward. This tool is a chip extractor, or chip puller. You should have also received instructions on how to use the chip extractor to remove your old BIOS chips. If the instructions are not included, simply place each of the turned in tips under the ends (length-wise) of the chips and gently lift upward, rocking back and forth, until the chip lifts out of its socket. Repeat this procedure for all your old BIOS chips. If a chip extractor did not come with your new BIOS chips, a trip to your local computer store can usually remedy this oversight.

If you don't have a chip extractor you can also remove your chips by gently prying them out using a small flat-blade screwdriver. Just make sure to pry one side and then the other, a little at a time, until each chip is loosened enough to remove. Keep in mind, however, that a chip extractor is the safest and preferred method for removing chips.

▼

7. As per your instructions, replace your old chips with the new chips you ordered. Make sure you insert the chips with the orientation notch facing in the same direction as the chips you just removed. Be very careful not to accidentally bend any of the pins on the chips as you insert them into their sockets. If the pins are spread too far apart, place the chip on its side on a hard surface such as a tabletop and gently roll the pins until they are a little closer. By placing the chip on its side and rolling it, you make sure that you bend all the pins together.

8. Double check your work to make sure that the new chips are properly installed in the socket, that they are oriented properly, and that no pins are bent. When everything looks okay, turn on your PC. If the new BIOS chips are properly installed, your PC should boot as before.

▲

Upgrading Flash BIOS

Upgrading a PC with flash BIOS is a snap. If you ordered the BIOS upgrade program from the manufacturer or your dealer, the program should come on a bootable disk. If you downloaded the BIOS upgrade program from the manufacturer's bulletin board or Web site, follow the instructions to create a bootable upgrade disk.

To Do: Upgrading Flash BIOS

To upgrade your flash BIOS with a bootable upgrade disk:

1. Turn off your PC.

2. Place your BIOS upgrade disk into your floppy disk drive and turn on your PC.

3. The bootable disk should automatically start the upgrade program and upgrade your flash BIOS. Watch your screen for any prompts asking you to enter any information about your PC. The entire upgrade procedure should take about 1–3 minutes.

> Make sure you do not reboot or turn off your PC while you are upgrading your flash BIOS. You can permanently damage the BIOS, and your computer, if you do.

▲
4. When the upgrade is completed, remove the upgrade disk and reboot your PC.

Summary

In this hour, you learned about some of the functions of your computer's BIOS, and some of the operations that can go wrong when your BIOS does not function with your computer or its devices. You also learned what you need to do to identify the type of BIOS installed in your computer, and what you need to do to upgrade your PC's BIOS.

Q&A

Q You didn't mention bugs as a reason to upgrade your BIOS. Is this another possible reason?

A Yes, it is. It does not happen that often, but sometimes manufacturers release a BIOS upgrade to repair a bug that has been discovered in a previous BIOS release. This is another reason to periodically check your manufacturer's Web site for notices of BIOS upgrades.

Q Why did manufacturers switch from BIOS on chips to flash BIOS?

A To make it easier to issue upgrades. Although it is a lot safer to embed your BIOS on chips that you cannot erase or accidentally delete, it is also considerably more expensive both for the manufacturer and for you, the user, to upgrade the BIOS. Flash BIOS is a good compromise between ease of use and safety. As you've seen in this hour, it's fairly easy to locate a flash BIOS upgrade and use it to upgrade your BIOS, and at the same time, you can't easily delete your BIOS using flash BIOS upgrades.

Q Can my BIOS be infected by a virus?

A Since BIOSes can be flashed, yes. It is most likely to occur when you are booting your PC with an infected floppy disk, so make sure you scan any suspect floppy disks before you boot your PC.

Part III

Upgrading Your Drives

Hour

HOUR 11

Replacing, Upgrading, or Adding a Hard Disk Drive

Just as we've seen memory prices nose dive over the past few years, prices on hard disk drives have also dropped. In 1984, a Seagate 30MB hard disk drive cost around $350. Now you can easily pay less money for a drive 200 times larger and considerably faster.

As an added bonus, although hard disk prices have been dropping steadily, the storage capacities on hard disk drives have been steadily inching upward. Now, it's fairly common to see new PCs advertised with hard disk storage capacities in the 12–14 *gigabyte* range.

NEW TERM A *gigabyte* is a thousand megabytes, and a megabyte is one million bytes, so a gigabyte is one billion bytes. Gigabyte is commonly abbreviated GB. To give you a real-world example of how big a gigabyte is, the text in this chapter is approximately 70K. On a 1 gigabyte hard disk drive, I could store more than 14,000 copies of this chapter.

If the PC you are currently using has less than 4GB of disk storage, you are long overdue for an upgrade. You will find that installing a hard disk drive in your PC is extremely easy.

During this hour you will learn the following:

- The differences between an IDE and a SCSI interface and hard disk drive, and how to decide which is better for your PC
- How to install a hard disk drive as either an addition or a replacement for the drive you currently have installed

Is Your Upgrade an Addition or a Replacement?

Like memory, when you upgrade your hard disk drive, in most cases you are actually adding a second disk drive to your system rather than replacing a smaller, slower hard disk with a larger, faster drive. In most PCs, accommodating a second hard disk drive is no problem. There are very few reasons why you should ever be forced to remove your existing hard disk and replace it with a new one. The following are the exceptions:

- Your PC physically does not have room (an empty drive bay) for a second hard disk drive.
- You are switching from IDE drives to SCSI drives.
- Your hard disk drive fails and has to be replaced.

IDE Versus SCSI

The first major decision you have to make in upgrading your hard disk is choosing between the two types of drives—IDE and SCSI. In most cases, the decision is made for you by the type of disk controller installed in your PC. For the last five years, most PCs have been manufactured with an IDE controller built in to the system, but in the last year or two some PC manufacturers have offered customers a choice between *IDE* and *SCSI*.

NEW TERM *IDE* stands for Integrated Drive Electronics, and *SCSI* (pronounced "scuzzy") stands for Small Computer System Interface. You might also see IDE listed as EIDE, for Enhanced Integrated Drive Electronics, which is a newer and faster enhancement on the original IDE specification.

SysChk, the systems diagnostic/configuration program you ran in Hour 3, "Examining Your PC's System Configuration," should have identified the type of *disk controller* and drive you have installed in your PC.

NEW TERM   A *disk controller* is the interface that connects your disk drives to your mother-board. The controller can either be built in to the motherboard, as are most IDE controllers in most PCs built in the last few years, or they can come in the form of an interface card that is installed into one of the slots on your motherboard.

IDE is currently the more popular and widely used of the two disk types, primarily because IDE devices are cheaper to manufacture than SCSI devices. IDE also seems to have a slight edge in disk performance. Depending on how you have your PC configured and what operating system you are planning to use, SCSI can actually give you better overall system performance. This is particularly true if you install two or more hard disk drives in your PC and use a true 32-bit operating system, such as Windows NT 2000.

Even though IDE drives are slightly faster than SCSI drives, SCSI drives do offer some significant advantages over IDE drives:

- SCSI drives put far less strain on your CPU than IDE drives. This can result in overall higher levels of system performance and reliability.

- SCSI drives perform better in 32-bit multitasking operating systems, such as Windows NT 4.0 or 2000, because SCSI controllers and drives can perform disk reading and writing tasks while other operations and programs are running.

- You can attach up to seven SCSI drives or devices to a single SCSI controller; IDE drives and devices are limited to two devices per controller.

- A slower SCSI device, such as a CD-ROM drive, does not degrade the performance of a faster device (a hard disk, for example) if both are connected to the same con-troller. On older IDE controllers, a CD-ROM drive degrades the performance of a hard disk if both are on the same controller. That is why most PCs in the past were shipped with two IDE controllers on the motherboard—one for the hard disk drives and one for your CD-ROM drive. On newer systems with EIDE (Enhanced IDE drives), each device can operate at its optimal level of performance.

- A SCSI cable can be up to 10 feet long, enabling you to install multiple external (outside of your PC) SCSI devices; IDE cable can usually be no longer than about 15 inches, which limits most IDE devices to being installed inside your PC.

Although SCSI controllers and drives can be configured to produce a higher level of per-formance, SCSI drives are still mainly used in high-end workstations and network file servers rather than standard desktop PCs. Perhaps the biggest incentive for using IDE drives is their cost. A comparable IDE drive can easily cost half the price of a SCSI drive. Also, because SCSI controllers are rarely built in to motherboards, you also need to purchase a SCSI controller (minimum of about $100) to install SCSI drives and devices.

11

Installing an IDE Drive in Your PC

As I mentioned earlier, you can install only two IDE drives or devices on a single IDE controller. Most manufacturers now build two IDE controller connectors on their motherboards so that you can install two hard disk drives on one controller and a CD-ROM drive on the second controller. IDE controller connectors are easy to spot on your motherboard. Just look for two 40-pin connectors side-by-side (see Figure 11.1).

FIGURE 11.1

IDE controller connectors on a motherboard.

IDE drives use a series of jumpers on the drives to designate whether a single drive is installed on one controller or whether multiple drives are installed on the same controller. The jumpers are installed on a 3×2 matrix of pins often found on the end of the drive near the power connector, but can also be found on the hard disk drive circuit card. When you purchase a hard disk drive, the instructions indicate where the jumper pins are located and how you are to designate the drives.

When multiple drives are installed on the same controller, one drive is designated the primary or "master," and the other drive is designated the secondary or "slave."

If two drives are installed on one controller, you need to install the jumpers on one drive as you see in Figure 11.2 to designate it as the primary or master. You need to install the jumpers on the second drive to designate it as the secondary or slave (see Figure 11.3). If a single drive is installed on a controller, no jumpers are installed.

FIGURE 11.2
Jumpers designating one drive as the primary or master.

FIGURE 11.3
Jumpers designating one drive as the secondary or slave.

11

Replacing an Existing Hard Disk Drive

The easiest way to install a hard disk drive is by replacing an existing drive with a new drive because you can use the existing drive as your model for installing the new drive. All the mounting screws and connecting cables should be the same, eliminating any guesswork on your part.

When replacing an existing drive with a new drive, one of the first consider-ations is to determine how you are going to back up or transfer the files from the old drive to the new drive. If you have some sort of backup device (for example, a tape drive or a removable media drive, such as a Zip drive), this greatly simplifies the file transfer process. If you do not have a backup device, your only option is to back up your data files onto floppy disks and reinstall your operating system and programs onto the new drive after it is installed. A number of disk image copying programs are available on the market—such as Norton Ghost, Partition Magic, and Drive Image—that can simplify this task, but these programs usually require some sort of large storage or backup device to temporarily store the disk image. If you have access to a network file server, these disk image copying programs can be a godsend.

A disk image program reads your hard disk drive and makes an exact copy of the drive contents sector-by-sector regardless of what you have stored. The program then makes an exact copy of your drive byte-for-byte and notes where on your hard disk each byte or sector is stored.

To Do: Replacing an Existing IDE Drive

To replace an existing drive with a new drive:

1. Unplug your PC and exercise all the safety precautions previously mentioned, such as grounding yourself to prevent static electric discharges.

2. Locate the existing drive in your PC. Diagram how each cable is connected to the drive and how the drive is mounted in your PC. Note all connecting screws and mounting hardware and how the drive is physically installed in your PC.

3. Disconnect the power connector from the hard disk drive.

4. Disconnect the ribbon cable from the hard disk drive. Note how the ribbon cable is attached to the drive (that is, the position and orientation of the red stripe, if there is one, on the ribbon cable).

5. Remove any screws used in mounting the hard disk drive to your PC. Some PC manufacturers place the hard disk into a mounting bracket, and some manufactur-ers mount guide rails onto the sides of the drive. Most manufacturers try to install two mounting screws on each side of the drive for a total of four mounting screws to hold the drive securely in place.

6. Check to see whether any jumpers are installed on the existing drive. Follow the guidelines mentioned earlier for correctly installing jumpers on the new drive. Use the existing drive as your model, and make sure you place the jumper (if there is one installed) on the new drive the same as the jumper is installed on the existing drive.

7. Attach the new drive to any mounting hardware or bracket, if one is used in your PC, and reinstall the drive into a drive bay or mounting position in your PC.

8. Reattach the ribbon cable and the 4-wire power cord to the drive.

> Although it is impossible to incorrectly reattach the power cord, it is possible to misalign the ribbon cable as it is reattached. Put it on, and if it doesn't work, reverse it. You have a 50/50 chance of getting it right (or getting it wrong).

When you turn on your PC for the first time, you will probably have to re-run your CMOS hardware Setup program to configure the new drive. This procedure varies from PC to PC—some newer PCs do a considerable amount to automate this process, whereas some older PCs may require you to enter hardware values for the new drive, such as the number of drive heads, tracks, and sectors. This information is supplied with the drive, so make sure to hold onto your documentation.

> If your computer does not recognize your hard disk drive or reports a storage capacity far smaller than the reported size of the drive, it is possible you have an older BIOS in your PC that does not recognize large (larger than 550MB) drives. See Hour 10, "Upgrading Your PC's BIOS," for more information on replacing your existing BIOS.

Adding a Second Hard Disk Drive

Adding a second drive is usually easier than replacing an existing drive provided you have an empty drive bay available. Again, you can use the existing drive as a template for how the second drive will be installed. When adding a second IDE drive, remember that one drive has to be designated the primary or master, and the other drive has to be designated the secondary or slave. In most cases, the existing drive is designated the master, and the drive you are adding is designated the slave. By designating the new drive as the secondary or slave, you do not need to concern yourself with backing up the files on the existing drive or installing an operating system on the new drive. The new drive (after it is formatted) will simply appear as the next drive letter after your existing drive (usually drive D:).

If you have a CD-ROM drive installed in your PC and you are adding another hard disk drive, your CD-ROM drive will be bumped down a drive letter. For example, if your CD-ROM drive is designated drive D:, after you add another hard disk drive, the new hard disk drive becomes drive D: and your CD-ROM drive becomes drive E:. Usually this is not a problem except when the software you install from a CD-ROM requires you to leave the CD-ROM in the drive while the program is running (like many games). In this scenario, your program is looking for your CD-ROM files on drive D: instead of drive E:. If this happens to you, see if there is a way to reconfigure your program to look on E: from the CD-ROM. If you can't reconfigure the software, you will have to reinstall it.

You also need to note how the ribbon cable is attached to the existing drive and attach the ribbon cable in the same position to the new drive you are adding. Note, too, that there are two connectors on the ribbon cable for attaching IDE devices. Because you are designating one drive the master and one drive the slave, it does not matter which connector you attach the new drive to (see Figure 11.4).

FIGURE 11.4

This figure shows two IDE drives and the positioning of jumpers and the ribbon cable.

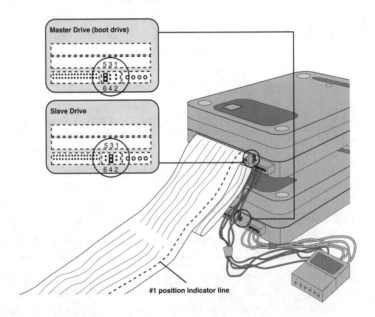

Just make sure before you begin that your PC has sufficient physical room for a second drive (that is, you have an empty drive bay), and make sure you have all the mounting hardware (for example, support frame, guide rails, and so on). Many hard disk drive kits now come with several sets of mounting hardware to cover all contingencies, but it never hurts to tell the sales representative what type of computer you have to ensure that the drive kit you purchase will work with your system. Most computer stores that sell hard disk drives also sell mounting kits (if the hard disk drive you purchase does not come with a mounting kit), and the kits usually identify most of the computers they are designed to work with.

Also, if you find yourself missing a 4-wire power cable, you can pick up a Y-connector (see Figure 11.5) at almost any computer store for around $5.

FIGURE 11.5

A Y-connector used to attach two devices to a single power connector.

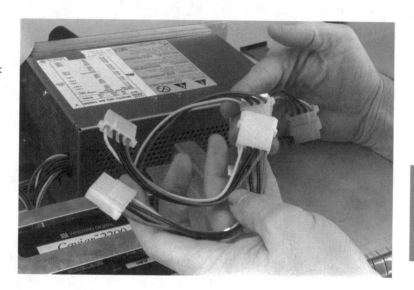

11

Installing a SCSI Drive

Installing SCSI hard disk drives and devices is quite different from installing IDE drives. When you install SCSI hard disk drives and devices in your PC, you are creating what is called a "SCSI chain." The SCSI chain consists of a SCSI controller card, a SCSI cable, one or more SCSI devices, and a SCSI *terminator* at each end of the chain. It is important to remember that the terminators are always at both ends of the SCSI chain. I mention this because the end of a SCSI chain can be any of the following:

- A SCSI controller card with a built-in terminator
- A SCSI device, such as a hard disk drive, a CD-ROM drive, a tape backup drive, a scanner, and so on, also with a built-in terminator
- A physical SCSI terminator

Most newer SCSI controller cards are designed with both an internal and external connector for attaching SCSI devices (see Figure 11.6). Because of this design, a SCSI controller card can be in the middle of your SCSI chain or at either end, depending on whether you have internal or external SCSI devices or both. Most newer SCSI controller cards can also be self-terminating if they are at the end of the SCSI chain.

NEW TERM When we say you need a *terminator* it does not mean you need the big guy with the Austrian accent from the movies by the same name. You need an electronic component that signals the end (both ends) of the SCSI chain. They come in various shapes and sizes, but usually connect to the end of your SCSI chain using the same type of connectors as your other SCSI devices.

FIGURE 11.6

A typical SCSI controller card showing both internal and external connectors.

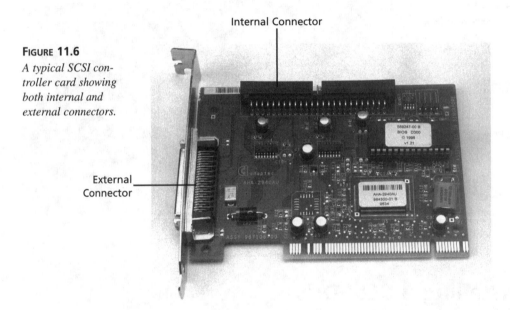

Internal Connector

External Connector

Another important difference in installing SCSI disk drives and devices is that every device on a SCSI chain has to have a unique ID number. SCSI ID numbers are simply a means of identifying one device from another on the SCSI chain. This is similar to designating one IDE drive the master and one the slave. For example, if you have three cats, you would not name them all "Max" because they would get confused when you called them. The same applies to SCSI devices. Unless they have unique ID numbers, confusion can occur when you need to access a particular drive or device.

In most instances the SCSI controller is given the SCSI ID number 7, which means you can use ID numbers 0–6 for your SCSI drives and devices. For hard disk drives, SCSI ID numbers are usually set using a series of jumpers, much the same way you used jumpers to designate IDE drives connected to the same controller. The instructions accompanying the drive explain how to install the jumpers for a specific ID number.

You do not designate a SCSI drive as master or slave as you do with IDE drives. If you plan to boot your PC from the SCSI drive, its ID number must usually be set to 0. If you have both IDE and SCSI drives in your PC you must boot your PC from the IDE drive, in which case the SCSI drive ID can be any number from 0–6.

Physically installing the SCSI drive into your PC is about the same as installing an IDE drive in regards to physical location and mounting hardware. You may have a bit more latitude and room to work because SCSI cables can be a lot longer than IDE cables.

To Do: Installing a SCSI Disk Drive

To install an internal SCSI hard disk:

1. Install the SCSI controller card in an empty slot.

2. Set the SCSI ID on the drive according to how you plan to use it (that is, will you boot from the SCSI drive, will the SCSI drive exist in the PC with an IDE drive, and so on). In most cases the ID number is set using jumpers.

3. Install the SCSI drive using the mounting hardware you have.

4. Attach the power cable to the SCSI drive.

5. Attach the SCSI cable to the drive. In every case I have seen, SCSI cables are notched or in some way designed so that the cable can only be attached to the drive in one way (see Figure 11.7).

FIGURE 11.7
*A notched SCSI con-
nector on a SCSI
cable.*

11

6. If the internal SCSI drive is the only SCSI device you are installing, make sure the SCSI cable (that is, the SCSI chain) is terminated after the drive. Make sure the

▼

▲

other end of the SCSI chain, which should be the SCSI controller, is also terminated. Many newer SCSI controllers will self-terminate if they detect that they are
at the end of the SCSI chain.

> If you install an external SCSI device such as a scanner, termination is no
> longer at the controller card but at (or after) the last external device.
> Likewise, if you install an additional internal SCSI device such as a SCSI CD-
> ROM drive after the hard disk on the SCSI chain, the termination now falls
> after the last device on the chain. Just remember, terminate *both* ends of
> the SCSI chain. Be sure to remove any other terminators so that there are
> only two on the chain.

If the SCSI drive is the only drive in your PC, you do not have to make any changes in
your CMOS settings unless you are removing an IDE drive and replacing it with a SCSI
drive. In this case, you have to turn off or disable all *IDE parameters* (settings) in your
CMOS hardware settings. You will need to run your hardware Setup (CMOS) program
and in most cases set your IDE drive settings to "unused" or "disabled."

NEW TERM *IDE parameters* are the settings you make in your hardware Setup (CMOS) program to identify the characteristics of your drive. These include the number of
read/write heads on your drive, the number of physical platters (the metal disks that actually make up your hard disk), and the number of tracks and sectors defined on each platter surface. The surface of each hard disk platter is divided into a number of concentric
rings. These rings are tracks. Each track in turn is again divided into a number of wedge-
shaped units called sectors.

Adding a Second SCSI Drive

If you ever decide to add a second SCSI drive, you need only to set the SCSI ID number
(to a number not being used) before installing the drive into an empty drive bay. For
example, if the first SCSI drive has the SCSI ID number 0, set the SCSI ID number of
the second drive to 1. The next time you start up your PC, your SCSI controller will
automatically detect the new SCSI device inserted in the SCSI chain.

Preparing Your Drives for Software

Before you can install files and software onto your new drive, you need to create one or
more disk partitions using FDISK or a similar utility and format the drive. A partition is
nothing more than a defined area on your hard disk that you use to store files.

Using FDISK to Create a Disk Partition

If you use FDISK (which is stored on your DOS disk), you simply start up your computer using your DOS disk, and then start FDISK by typing **FDISK** at the DOS prompt.

To Do: Using FDISK to Create a Partition

To create a partition using FDISK:

> You have to set one, and only one, partition to be the active partition. The active partition is on the drive you start up your computer to. If you are adding a second drive, do not accidentally reset the active partition to the second hard disk drive or your computer will not start.

1. Select option 1 to Create DOS Partition (see Figure 11.8) In most cases, you create a single partition on your entire hard disk drive.

> If you want to divide your hard disk into two or more logical drives, FDISK enables you to create more than one partition on a new hard disk drive that you install. If you decide to create multiple partitions on a single physical drive, the usual configuration is to divide the drive 50/50—make 50% of the drive into the first partition and 50% of the drive into the second partition. But you can divide the drive in any configuration you want. Remember, too, that each partition you create exists as a drive with a separate drive letter (for example, C:, D:, and so on) on your PC.

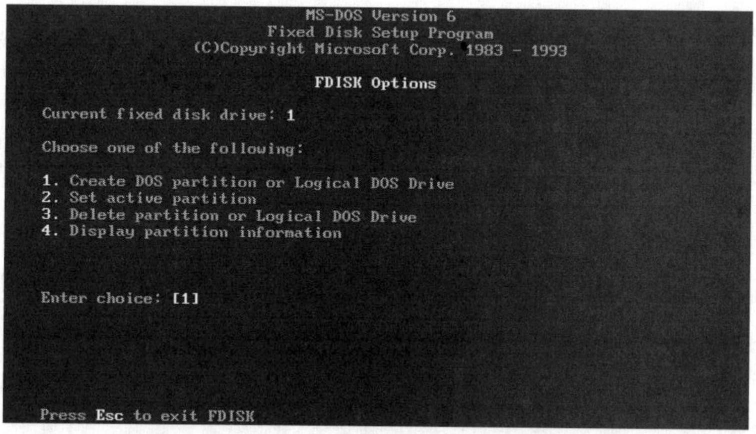

11

FIGURE 11.8

The main menu in FDISK.

```
                          MS-DOS Version 6
                       Fixed Disk Setup Program
                 (C)Copyright Microsoft Corp. 1983 - 1993

                            FDISK Options

        Current fixed disk drive: 1

        Choose one of the following:

        1. Create DOS partition or Logical DOS Drive
        2. Set active partition
        3. Delete partition or Logical DOS Drive
        4. Display partition information


        Enter choice: [1]




        Press Esc to exit FDISK
```

▼   2. Make one partition the active partition. This will be the partition (drive) you will
         start up your PC to (see Figure 11.9).

FIGURE 11.9
*FDISK showing one
partition set as the
active partition.*

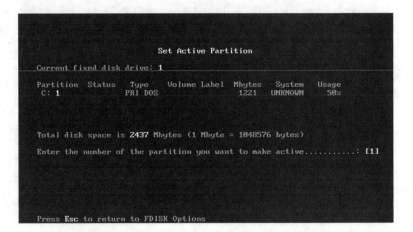

▲   3. Press ESC twice to exit FDISK and restart your PC.

Using Partition Magic to Create Your Partitions

One problem with using FDISK to create your partitions is that FDISK is typically a
DOS-based utility and limits your partition sizes to 2 GB. If you are using Windows 98
you can create large partitions (larger than 2 GB), but you will need to create them as
FAT32 partitions.

 FAT32 is a partition type used exclusively in Windows 98 for supporting larger
partitions and for more efficient file storage on large hard disk drives.

Partition Magic is a disk partition creation utility that will not only allow you to create
partitions larger than 2 GB, but will allow you to resize your partitions (make them
larger or smaller) regardless of whether you are running Windows 95/98 or Windows
NT 4.0/2000 (see Figure 11.10).

Formatting Your Drive

After you create your partition(s), you need to format your hard disk. Formatting pre-
pares your hard disk to accept and store files. Regardless of which operating system you
eventually plan to install on your PC, you can first perform a simple DOS format. Then,
if you need to change the formatting, you can safely reformat the drive.

FIGURE 11.10

Partition Magic's main interface showing one partition.

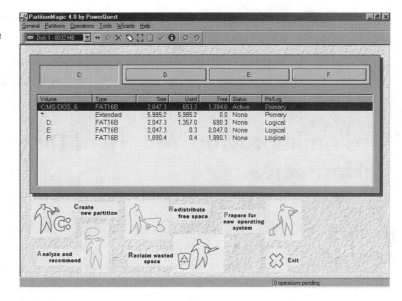

To Do: Formatting Your Hard Disk Drive

To format your hard disk:

1. Start up your PC with your DOS disk.

2. If you are formatting the hard disk as your startup drive, type

   ```
   format c: /s
   ```

   to format the drive and install DOS system files to make the drive bootable.

3. If you are formatting a drive that will not be a bootable drive, type

   ```
   format x:
   ```

   where *x*: is the drive letter of the drive your are formatting. Just make sure you format each partition you create.

> On IDE drives, make sure you don't perform what is called a "low-level" format. This is a procedure that is done at the factory and should not be performed by an end-user because you can ruin the drive if you do.

11

Installing an Operating System on Your PC

After your hard disk drive is formatted, you can decide what operating system you want to install on your PC. Follow the instructions accompanying the operating system you plan to use on whether any additional preparation is necessary before you install the operating system.

Tips on Improving Your Hard Disk Performance

After you finish installing a hard disk drive in your PC and get your operating system installed, there are still a few things you can do to keep your drive operating in peak form.

Defrag Your Hard Disk Regularly

As you use your computer, you are continually creating and deleting files even if you are not aware of it. Many software programs create temporary files that are deleted when you exit the program. When you format your hard disk, you are actually dividing it into small areas called sectors. Without going into a lot of very technical detail, every time you create a file, your operating system saves a set number of bytes into every sector. When a sector is filled, your operating system uses the next available sector to save more of the file, and so on, until all the file is saved into however many sectors it needs. The sectors do not have to be next to each other to store parts of the same file. The operating system keeps track of which sectors are storing which files. So in a relatively short period of time it's not only possible, but very likely, that your files are scattered all over your hard disk.

Although your operating system does a good job of keeping track of your files and finding all the sectors where a file is stored, locating files scattered all over your hard disk can take time and slow your PC's performance. To solve this problem and literally put your files back together, or at least move the files into adjacent sectors, you can use programs called hard disk defrag (defrag being short for defragmentation) utilities.

You should regularly defrag your hard disk to keep the performance at peak levels. Figures 11.11 and 11.12 show before and after defrag shots of hard disk drive partitions. "Regularly" can vary depending on how you use your PC, but you should make a habit of checking your drives for fragmentations at least once a week.

FIGURE 11.11

A hard disk drive before it is defragged.

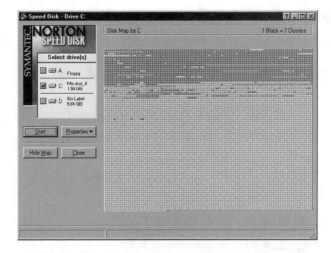

FIGURE 11.12

A hard disk drive after it is defragged.

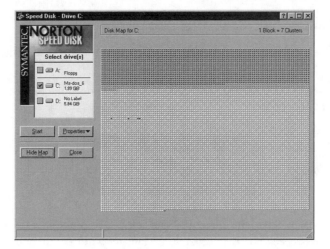

Never use a defrag utility unless it is specifically made for your operating system and its file store system. Many users who used a defrag utility designed for DOS on their PC with Windows 95 discovered after it was too late that the DOS defrag utility damaged most of the files on the PC. Also, if you are using Windows 98 and have your hard drive formatted for FAT32 (a file storage system used in Windows 98), make sure your defrag utility can work with FAT32.

Delete Unneeded Files

As I said earlier, many programs create temporary files on your hard disk and are supposed to delete these files when you exit the program. But sometimes, for various reasons, these temporary files remain on your hard disk. Unneeded files take up valuable space on your hard disk and slow its performance.

All versions of Windows include a service or a utility that you can use to locate and remove these unneeded files. Most of the time these files have the extension .TMP or .BAK.

One way to locate and remove these unneeded files is by using File Manager, which is included in every version of Windows.

To Do: Removing Unneeded Files

To remove all files with the extension .TMP:

1. Start File Manager. If you don't see an icon for File Manager, use the Windows RUN command and type **WINFILE** to start File Manager.

2. Select the drive you want to check by selecting the drive letter icon in File Manager.

3. Select the File menu and choose Search to open the Search dialog box (see Figure 11.13).

FIGURE 11.13

The File Manager Search dialog box.

4. Type ***.TMP** in the dialog box and select OK. Make sure the Search All Subdirectories check box is selected. File Manager will perform a thorough search of the drive you select and locate every file with the extension .TMP (see Figure 11.14).

5. Highlight the files with the extension .TMP and press the Delete key to delete these unneeded files.

Some temporary files in Windows are files that Windows is using. While Windows is using these files, you cannot delete them.

FIGURE 11.14

File Manager locates all files with the extension .TMP.

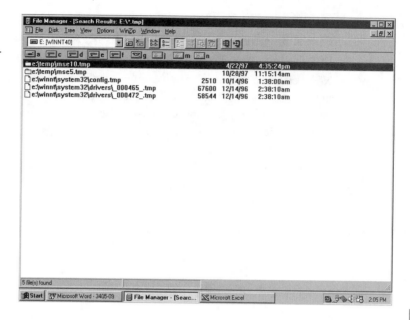

Summary

In the past hour you learned how to install a hard disk drive into your PC regardless of whether you are replacing your existing drive with a new, larger drive, or merely adding a second drive in your system. You learned the differences between IDE and SCSI hard disk, and hopefully learned enough to decide which one to purchase. You also learned a few tips on what you can do to keep your hard disk drives operating at peak levels of performance.

Q&A

Q Besides cost, are there any other reasons to use IDE drives over SCSI drives?

A Cost is still the big reason why the majority of PCs are manufactured with IDE drives. Other than that, SCSI drives seem to have the advantage in every other category. Performance-wise they are about the same, with only some minor discrepancies between different manufacturers, but remember that IDE drives place a greater strain on your CPU than do SCSI drives, something like 60% of CPU resources for IDE drives versus about 2% for SCSI drives. For users concerned about squeezing all the performance they can out of their CPUs, SCSI seems the way to go. You can also add more SCSI drives in your PC than IDE drives.

Q I bought a SCSI drive and the documentation says to use the manufacturer's FDISK program instead of the DOS FDISK. Is there a problem with using the DOS FDISK program on SCSI drives?

A No. It could be that some manufacturers simply supply their own FDISK program in the event you don't have DOS, or they have built extra functionality into their own FDISK program. In most cases you can safely use either unless the manufacturer specifically says not to use the DOS FDISK program. The DOS FDISK program will also only allow you to create partitions with a maximum size of 2048MB (2 gigabytes), which is the maximum size that DOS can address.

HOUR 12

Replacing Your Floppy Disk Drive

During this hour the focus will be on replacing rather than upgrading your floppy disk drive because floppy disk drives have not seen much in the way of advancements in the last six years or so. Perhaps the last change in floppy disk drives occurred several years ago when most manufacturers standardized on the installation of a single 3 1/2-inch floppy disk drive, removing the 5 1/4-inch drive as a standard feature. If you haven't noticed, software is no longer shipped on 5 1/4-inch disks, and they seem to have gone the way of the dinosaurs.

Although there was a brief flirtation by some manufacturers with the 2.88MB floppy disk drive, this device never really caught on and the standard is still the 1.44MB 3 1/2-inch floppy disk drive.

Whereas upgrading your floppy is not an issue, periodically these workhorses do go bad and you find yourself having to tear out the old one and replace it with another 3 1/2-inch drive. This chapter teaches you all you need to know to accomplish this minor repair.

During this hour you will learn the following:

- What changes have occurred in floppy disk drives since the days of the original 5 1/4-inch 160K models
- How to safely remove a floppy disk drive and replace it with a new unit

A Brief History of Floppy Disk Drives

Since the original IBM PC was released in 1981, floppy disk drives have evolved considerably. The first PCs were equipped with single-sided drives with a capacity of only 160K. When IBM released DOS 2.0 to support the IBM PC/XT and its hard disk drive, it also slightly upped the ante on floppy disk drives with a slight change in its disk formatting layout from eight sectors per track to nine, which also effectively increased storage capacities on both single-sided and double-sided drives. Shortly thereafter, single-sided drives began to be phased out and the standard was double-sided drives.

During the next few years floppy disk drives on PCs evolved remarkably, as shown in Table 12.1.

TABLE 12.1   Evolution of the Floppy Disk Drive

Type	Capacity	Size
Single-sided, single density (8 sectors/track, 40 tracks)	160K	5-1/4"
Single-sided, single density (9 sectors/track, 40 tracks)	180k	5-1/4"
Double-sided, single density (8 sectors/track, 40 tracks, 2 sided)	320K	5-1/4"
Double-sided, single density (9 sectors/track, 40 tracks, 2 sided)	360K	5-1/4"
Double-sided, double density (15 sectors/track, 80 tracks, 2 sided)	1.2M	5-1/4"
Double-sided, high density (9 sectors/track, 80 tracks, 2 sided)	720K	3-1/2"
Double-sided, double density (18 sectors/track, 80 tracks, 2 sided)	1.44M	3-1/2"

Replacing Not Repairing

In the past few years, many books on upgrading PCs have included chapters on repairing floppy disk drives. But floppy disk drives have been reduced to inexpensive commodity status and can be readily purchased at most weekend computer fairs for as little as $10–$15, so it makes little sense to worry about repairing what has literally become a "throw-away" computer component. There's also no concern with compatibility issues because all 3 1/2-inch floppy drives are virtually the same, nor do you have to be concerned with whether you have the correct mounting hardware because all the mounting hardware is already in place inside your PC.

> Even though floppy disk drives are not as essential to day-to-day computer operations as they once were, at roughly $10–$15 a pop, it makes good sense to keep a spare on hand as an emergency repair unit.

Diagnosing a Broken Floppy Disk Drive

Diagnosing a problem with a floppy disk drive is usually pretty simple and straightforward. In most cases you discover the problem when you attempt to use the drive, such as reading from or writing to a floppy disk. Following is a small list of symptoms that can appear when your floppy disk drive is malfunctioning. Be sure to check using multiple disks to make sure your problem is drive related and not disk related:

- Disk activity light does not come on when attempting to use the drive
- Cannot read a disk in the drive
- Cannot write to a disk in the drive
- Programs fail to recognize that a disk is in the drive
- Cannot format a disk in the drive

Keep in mind that any or all of these symptoms can also occur if the ribbon cable or power cord attached to the drive is loose or removed (see Figure 12.1).

So before you break out your toolkit and swap out the drive with your spare, make sure you check the cables. You'd be surprised how easily and frequently cables come loose. Be sure to check your cables first.

If you check the cables and they are securely in place, be sure to also check your CMOS settings. Make sure they show a 3-1/2", 1.44MB floppy disk drive as your A: drive.

12

FIGURE **12.1**

*Loose cables can
cause your floppy disk
drive to appear to be
malfunctioning.*

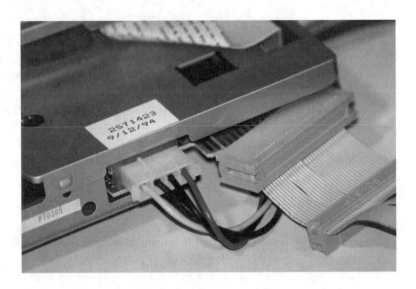

If your cables are secure and your CMOS settings are correct and your drive still is not functioning correctly, it's a safe bet your disk drive is malfunctioning and you need to replace it.

Replacing a Broken Floppy Disk Drive

Replacing a broken floppy disk drive is as easy, if not easier, than installing a hard disk drive (see Hour 11, "Replacing, Upgrading, or Adding a Hard Disk Drive").

To Do: Replacing a Floppy Disk Drive

To replace a floppy disk drive:

1. Unplug your PC and ground yourself before removing the cover.

2. Examine your PC to see how the floppy disk drive is installed in your computer's case. Note how many screws are holding the drive in place and the cables attached to the drive. You may have to remove the front bezel (face plate) to slide the drive out.

3. Identify (and label, if necessary) where and how the cables are attached to the drive before you remove the cables. If you have to remove any other cables to gain access to your floppy disk drive, make note of these also. Notice that the power connector for a 3 1/2-inch drive is smaller than the standard power connector (see Figure 12.2).

▼ **FIGURE 12.2**

Power connector for a 3-1/2" floppy disk drive.

4. Remove all screws holding the drive in place (see Figure 12.3), and carefully remove the drive from the drive bay.

FIGURE 12.3

Removing floppy disk drive mounting screws.

12

5. Insert the new drive into the drive bay.

▼ 6. Replace all hardware mounting screws.

▼ 7. Reconnect the ribbon cable to the drive, making sure you reattach the cable the same way it was attached to the original drive. You'll notice also that your ribbon cable may have two different connector types (see Figure 12.4). The other connector on the ribbon cable was previously used to connect your drive B:, which on earlier model PCs was a 5-1/4" floppy disk drive.

FIGURE 12.4

The ribbon cable attached to your floppy disk drive.

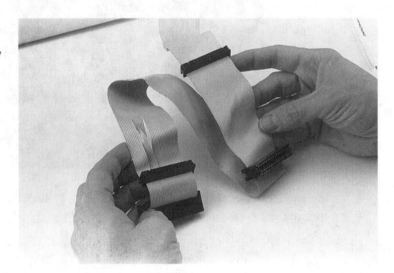

▲ 8. Reconnect the smaller power cord to the new drive.

When everything has been reattached and reconnected, turn on your PC to test your work. Notice whether the light on the drive comes on when you start up your PC. If the light comes on and stays on, it means you have the ribbon cable on backward (reverse the cable). Place a floppy disk into the new drive and perform a few routine tests on the drive. Try issuing the DIR A: command to see if you can read the contents of the disk. If there's no light, which usually indicates a setup problem, try DIR B:. If you are using Windows 95, 98, NT or 2000, you can use Explorer to test your drive instead of DIR A:. Try formatting a disk in the drive and copying a few files to the disk. If all these tests work satisfactorily, you can be fairly certain that the disk you just installed is working okay.

Alternatives to a Standard 1.44MB Floppy Disk Drive

If your floppy disk drive goes belly up, there are alternatives when selecting a replacement drive. You might want to consider one of several high capacity removable media drives (see Hour 15, "Adding a Removable Media Drive") that will also read and write standard 3-1/2", 1.44MB floppy disks. Most of these drives plug into one of your two IDE ports—the same connectors you connect your hard disk drives to. Although these high capacity drives will read, write, and boot from standard 3-1/2" disks, they will set you back a few more bucks than a standard 3-1/2" drive. If you choose to use the high capacity media they are designed for, expect to also pay a bit more than you will for formatted 3-1/2" high-density floppy disks.

Summary

In the past hour you learned about the evolution of floppy disk drives, how to diagnose some problems that can occur with them, and how to replace a malfunctioning floppy disk drive.

Q&A

Q Why did manufacturers abandon the 5 1/4-inch floppy disk drive?

A It's only speculation, but it appears there are probably several reasons. PC users have always looked for better methods of storing more data. The 3 1/2-inch 1.44MB floppy disk is smaller and more convenient than the 5 1/4-inch 1.2MB floppy disk and stores (slightly) more. The 3 1/2-inch drive is also a better storage medium than the 5 1/4-inch because it is more rigid and less susceptible to physical damage.

Q Do you think it is likely that the 3 1/2-inch floppy will be replaced by another storage medium?

A If history is any indicator, the answer is yes. Software manufacturers have for years used the medium of choice as a means for distributing software. In the last year or so, most software has been distributed on CD-ROMs, which unfortunately are read-only, making them unsuitable as a replacement for the current 3 1/2-inch floppy disk and drive. Even though there are CD-ROM drives and disks that are read/write and bootable, because of cost and the (sometimes) complexity of using the accompanying software, it does not appear that this medium will be replacing the 3 1/2-inch drive. Some manufacturers have been giving buyers the option to replace their 3 1/2-inch drive with a 100MB Zip drive (see Hour 15). The price of Zip drives has been dropping steadily and it does appear to be gaining a certain amount of acceptance, but it is probably still too soon to tell if the 100MB Zip disk and drive will replace the 3 1/2-inch floppy disk and drive. Some manufacturers have also developed high capacity drives that will read and write to standard 3-1/2", 1.44MB disks, but no PC manufacturer has standardized on this type of hardware.

12

HOUR 13

Upgrading or Adding a CD-ROM Drive

A few years ago, a CD-ROM drive was somewhat of a luxury item and something many computer users still considered an extravagance. Nowadays, a CD-ROM drive is practically standard equipment in a PC. In fact, virtually all manufacturers now include them in every PC that rolls down the assembly line.

Two factors that have helped to push the CD-ROM drive into the mainstream are its continuing drop in price and its continuing improvement in performance. A top-of-the-line 50x (50 speed) CD-ROM drive is in the $75–$100 price range.

Whether you're looking to upgrade the old CD-ROM drive you have in your PC to a more advanced model or to add a new CD-ROM drive to your system, you need to know the ins and outs of installing.

During this hour you will learn the following:

- How to select a CD-ROM drive
- Whether to choose an IDE drive or a SCSI drive
- How to install both internal and external CD-ROM drives
- How to improve or maintain your CD-ROM drive's performance

Selecting a CD-ROM Drive

Despite all the hoopla you've read and heard about *DVD* drives replacing CD-ROM drives and making them obsolete, it hasn't happened yet. Considering the rate at which manufacturers are still cranking out new models of CD-ROM drives, this switch to DVD technology doesn't appear to be happening anytime soon.

NEW TERM   *DVD* stands for *Digital Video Disk* and is a rather new digital technology very similar to CD-ROM technology. DVDs differ in that they are able to store several times the capacity of CD-ROM disks, which is approximately 650MB.

The first thing you need to understand about selecting a CD-ROM drive is its speed terminology. The first CD-ROM drives transferred data at a rate of 150KBps (kilobytes per second). This initial speed came to be known as "single-speed" and was written as "1x." As CD-ROM drives progressively got faster, their speeds were measured in comparison to the initial single-speed drives. For example, a double-speed (2x) drive transferred data at a rate of 300KBps (150KBps×2=300KBps). A quad-speed (4x) drive transferred data at a rate of 600KBps (150KBps×4=600KBps). A six-speed (6x) drive transferred data at a rate of 900KBps, and so on.

At last report (or the last time I bothered to check the computer shop ads in the Sunday newspaper), several manufacturers had released 52-speed (52x) drives, and if history is any indicator, the advancement in CD-ROM technology won't stop there.

In selecting a drive, the data transfer speed is likely to be the first factor you consider, but it should not be the only factor. How fast a CD-ROM drive can transfer data is important, but how fast your CD-ROM drive can locate data (called *seek time*) is also important.

Just like on your hard disk drive, the structure on a CD-ROM drive is composed of sectors and tracks. Seek time is defined as how fast the magnetic head (or in the case of a CD-ROM drive, the laser read head) that reads data can move from one track to another. Although CD-ROM drives cannot approach the seek time speeds of hard disk drives, around 8ms–10ms (milliseconds), a CD-ROM drive seek time of around 110ms is considered excellent.

Another factor to consider is the cache size on your CD-ROM. A cache is a holding area of memory built in to the drive to temporarily store data as it is being processed. Most drives have a cache of between 256K and 1MB; anything larger is a premium.

SCSI Versus IDE

Just as you had to decide between IDE and SCSI when you were selecting a hard disk drive in Hour 11, "Replacing, Upgrading, or Adding a Hard Disk Drive," when selecting a CD-ROM drive you also have to decide between IDE and SCSI. The same factors concerning performance and cost apply when selecting a CD-ROM type.

If you already have a SCSI controller installed in your PC, you are way ahead in terms of performance with selecting a SCSI CD-ROM drive because SCSI CD-ROM drives, like SCSI hard disk drives, do not place as much strain on your CPU. So, if you already have a SCSI controller in your PC for your SCSI hard disk(s), you will most likely want to select a SCSI CD-ROM drive. If your hard disk drive is IDE, you will most likely select an IDE CD-ROM drive for your PC.

Installing the Drive in Your PC—Internal Versus External

If you plan on installing a CD-ROM drive with an IDE interface, the decision on internal versus external has already been made for you. All IDE CD-ROM drives are internal because the IDE interface does not allow for a cable long enough to connect an external drive. Another major advantage an internal drive has over an external drive is cost. An internal drive is generally about $50–$75 cheaper than an external drive because an external CD-ROM drive requires a case and a separate power supply. The only real consideration you have for installing an internal drive is whether your PC has physical room for it. If you are out of drive bays, you have no choice but to install an external drive. Internal CD-ROM drives are all a "standard" size and will occupy what is called a "full-sized" drive bay slot (see Figure 13.1).

FIGURE 13.1
An internal CD-ROM drive in a drive bay slot.

13

To Do: Installing an Internal IDE CD-ROM Drive

Installing an internal CD-ROM drive is no more difficult than installing a hard disk drive.

> Just as you did before, when handling any delicate electrical components inside your PC make sure you properly ground yourself to protect against static electricity.

To install an internal drive:

1. Select a drive bay in your PC that you can use to install the drive. Make sure you have also removed the front panel on the case covering the empty bay if there is one. Make sure you have an unused power connector you can plug in to the drive. If you don't have an unused power connector, go to your local computer store and pick up a Y-connector. Unplug one of your power connectors from another device and attach the Y-connector.

2. On most PCs built in the last three or four years, you find two IDE interfaces, usually labeled primary and secondary (see Figure 13.2). Your hard disk drive (if you have an IDE hard disk installed in your PC) should be attached via cable to the interface labeled primary. Make sure you have a cable that will reach from the secondary interface to the bay where you are installing your new drive.

FIGURE 13.2
Primary and secondary IDE interfaces on the motherboard.

Primary IDE interface

Secondary IDE interface

▼   3. If you have to install any guide rails on the sides of your drive, install them accord-
       ing to the instructions accompanying the drive (see Figure 13.3). If drive rails are
       not included, but needed, be sure to pick up a set from your local computer store.

FIGURE 13.3

*Guide rails of various
sizes used for
installing CD-ROM
drives and other
peripheral devices.*

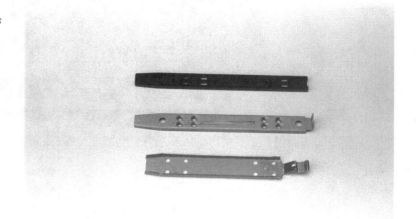

4. Insert the drive into the drive bay and attach the ribbon cable from the secondary
   (slave) IDE interface to the 40-pin IDE interface on the rear of the drive (see
   Figure 13.4).

Even though IDE interfaces can accommodate two IDE devices, do not connect the CD-ROM drive to the same interface you connect your IDE hard disk
drive to. The CD-ROM drive, which is a much slower device than a hard disk
drive, will degrade the performance of the hard disk drive.

If your PC has only one IDE interface connector, don't panic. Instead, just
make a quick trip to your local computer store and purchase an IDE interface card. It usually runs in the vicinity of $25–$30. Don't worry about it conflicting with any of your existing IRQs or memory addresses. Most
manufacturers realize it is added as a secondary interface and usually assign
it IRQs and addresses that would be the same as a secondary interface. Just
remember, when in doubt, ask the salesperson or the store's in-house technical guru.

▼

13

The rear of a typical IDE CD-ROM drive showing interface, power, and sound connections.

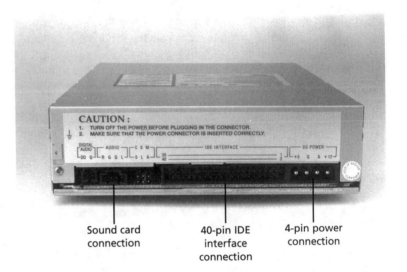

Sound card connection

40-pin IDE interface connection

4-pin power connection

5. If you also have a sound card in your PC (see Hour 20, "Upgrading or Adding a Sound System to Your PC"), you can connect the audio cable to the audio connector on the rear of the CD-ROM drive. Without the audio cable, you will not be able to play audio CDs through your sound system.

6. After you have everything connected to your drive, go ahead and adjust your drive even with the front opening of the drive bay and tighten the screws securing your drive in place.

7. Just as you did when you installed your hard disk drive, you will probably have to run your computer's hardware Setup program to complete the hardware installation. Also, you should have some type of software installation disk that you will need to run to install the appropriate driver, depending on the operating system you are running. If you are running Windows 95/98 or 2000, when you restart your PC Windows should automatically detect your newly installed CD-ROM drive and install the proper driver (a feature known as "plug and play").

▲

In addition to a hardware driver for your drive, the disk that comes with your CD-ROM drive also includes a number of utilities for your drive. One of the most enjoyable utilities is one that enables you to play music CDs on your new CD-ROM drive. If you don't have a sound card in your PC, you can simply plug a set of headphones into the connector on the front of the drive next to the volume control.

Installing an Internal SCSI Drive

Installing an internal SCSI CD-ROM drive is almost exactly the same as installing an internal IDE drive. The cable is a bit different, and just like with installing a SCSI hard disk drive, you have to set the SCSI ID on the CD-ROM drive according to the instructions that came with your drive. Remember, too, that the SCSI ID (0–6) has to be unique.

> All SCSI devices, such as hard disk drives and CD-ROM drives, leave the factory with a preset SCSI ID, which in most cases you can leave as is. Just be sure to check that the ID set on the device isn't an ID you are already using on your SCSI chain. Two devices on a SCSI chain with the same ID will not operate.

Remember to check the termination on your SCSI chain. Some SCSI CD-ROM drives come with a factory-installed terminator. If your CD-ROM drive is not placed at the end of your SCSI chain, you have to remove the factory-installed terminator or the devices on the chain after the CD-ROM drive will not operate. Check your CD-ROM documentation on how to remove the terminator. In many cases, you simply will need to remove a jumper.

Installing an External Drive (SCSI Only)

Installing an external CD-ROM drive is even easier than installing an internal drive. External CD-ROM drives are always SCSI drives and almost always ship with the appropriate cable needed to connect your drive to our SCSI card.

> Many external SCSI CD-ROM drives also ship with a SCSI interface card, which saves you the trouble and expense of having to purchase a SCSI card separately. If you find that you do have to purchase a SCSI interface card, check with the manufacturer of the drive to see if there are any types of SCSI cards recommended or if there are any types of SCSI cards that may not work with your CD-ROM drive.

13

After you have the drive, cable, and interface card, literally all you have to do is plug them together. Insert the card into an empty slot in your PC (see Figure 13.5). Next, connect one end of the cable to the connector on the end of the card (the connector protruding out of the back of your PC) and the other end of the cable to the connector on the drive (see Figure 13.6).

FIGURE 13.5

Inserting the SCSI interface card into an empty slot in your PC.

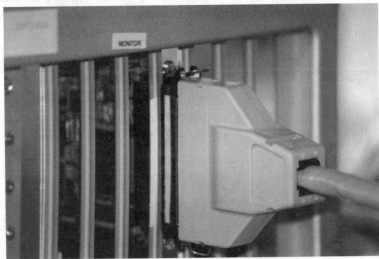

FIGURE 13.6

Plugging the SCSI cable into the interface card and into the CD-ROM drive.

With some SCSI CD-ROM drives, you receive a SCSI terminator. The terminator looks like the plug on the end of the SCSI cable without the cable attached (see Figure 13.7).

If you need to use the terminator to terminate your SCSI chain, you will see two SCSI connectors on the back of the SCSI CD-ROM drive. Plug the terminator into one connector and plug the SCSI cable into the other connector.

FIGURE **13.7**

A typical SCSI termi-nator.

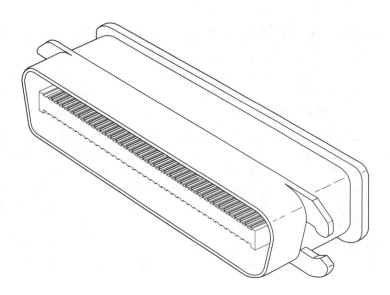

Remember that only the device at the end of the SCSI chain should be terminated. If the CD-ROM drive is not at the end of the SCSI chain, you do not
have to terminate the chain at the CD-ROM drive.

Don't panic if one or both of the SCSI connectors on the back of your CD-
ROM drive looks different than the typical 50-pin Centronics connector commonly found on many SCSI devices. Four types of SCSI connectors are used
on SCSI devices—the 50-pin Centronics connector, the 25-pin D-connector,
the 50-pin mini-SCSI connector, and the 63-pin SCSI connector.

Now, just plug-in the electrical cord supplying power to the external drive, run the Setup
program for your PC, and install the driver for the CD-ROM drive from the disk included
with your drive, and you're done. If you are running Windows 95/98 or 2000, your newly
installed CD-ROM drive should be detected when you restart your PC, and Windows will
attempt to automatically install the appropriate driver. Make sure you have your
Windows disks handy. If you are using Windows NT 4.0 or another operating system,
you will need to check your CD-ROM documentation on how to load the appropriate driver for your OS.

13

Improving Your CD-ROM Drive's Performance

Just as all versions of Windows use a disk caching utility to improve disk reading performance, likewise, you can use a disk caching utility to improve reading performance. The caching utility that comes with Windows provides some minimal caching functionality for CD-ROM drives, but is designed primarily for hard disk drives, not CD-ROM drives.

A CD-ROM cache works by using special algorithms to store frequently used data or to try to anticipate what data you might need next. Either way, it copies the data from the CD-ROM disk to either memory or your hard disk drive where the data can be accessed faster than it can from the much slower CD-ROM drive. Obviously, the cache works better if you have a lot of memory in your PC, but if you don't have much memory to spare, the cache instead uses your hard disk drive as its caching area.

Although there are several commercially available caching programs on the market that you can acquire from your local computer store, there are also shareware versions you can download off of the Internet and "try before you buy." One such program is CD-Quick, available from Circuit Systems (see Figure 13.8) at `http://ourworld.compuserve.com/homepages/circuitsys`.

FIGURE 13.8

The Web site of Circuit Systems, makers of CD-Quick.

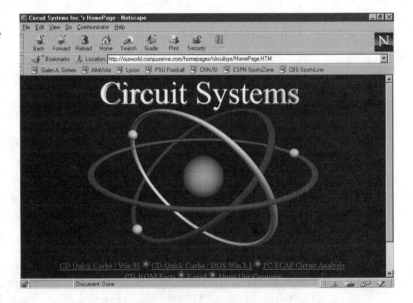

The main caution in using CD-ROM caching utilities is to steer clear of programs that attempt to copy most or all the contents of a CD-ROM disk to your hard disk drive. These programs typically do a poor job of caching and merely consume space on your hard disk drive.

What About DVD?

Undoubtedly you've heard or read a lot of the recent press that DVD has been receiving and may be wondering if you want to upgrade to a DVD drive instead of a CD-ROM drive. If you do, consider the following:

- DVD drives (at least the second-generation DVD-2 drives) are compatible with commercial CD-ROM disks and CD-R (CD-Recordable) and CD-W (CD-Writeable) disks. The first generation of DVD drives did not read CD-R and CD-W disks. Make sure you read the fine print and get a second-generation DVD-2 drive or upgrade kit.

- DVD drives are going through many of the same growing pains that early CD-ROM drives went through, namely, speed and cost. DVD drives read CD-ROM disks at 8x speeds.

- Upgrade kits for DVD drives can be a bit confusing and problematic for some users to install, especially because the upgrade kits include a "decoder" interface card that must be compatible with your existing video card. It is also possible to encounter IRQ conflicts with the installation of a new card in your PC.

- DVD upgrade kits are currently running in the neighborhood of about $300–$400. But just like the initial price of CD-ROM drives, DVD prices are expected to drop as they become more plentiful.

On the plus side, however, reports say that nothing currently on the market can match the quality of audio and video delivered by DVD. DVD was originally designed as a new distribution medium for home movies to compete with (or replace) analog VHS. The main requirement for the original DVD specification was the capability to store a typical two-hour movie on a single side of the disks. DVD disks currently store about 4.7GB of data (compared to only 650MB for CD-ROM disks) and include multiple audio tracks or vastly improved digital audio. Many DVD upgrade kits include adapters for connecting the output from your PC to your TV to enable you to watch DVD movies either on your PC monitor or on your living room TV. Acceptance among the major Hollywood studios has been quite good, and by early 1999, there were more than 1,000 titles released in the new DVD movie format. Software manufacturers have not responded quite as fast. Early 1999 saw only a handful of software titles, but vendors are promising that titles will be forthcoming.

If you do find that you want to purchase and install a DVD drive in your PC, head straight for Hour 14, "Adding a DVD Drive to Your PC."

13

Summary

In the past hour you learned about CD-ROM drives and how to select a drive as either an upgrade or a new component in your PC. You also learned about the differences between IDE and SCSI CD-ROM drives and how to install each type. You learned about DVD drives as well and some of the information to help you decide if you want to upgrade to a DVD drive.

Q&A

Q Are CD-ROM disks like phonograph records? In other words, is there something written on both sides of the disks?

A No, CD-ROM disks only contain information on one side—the side opposite the label, regardless of whether it is a software or music CD-ROM. Some DVD disks, however, will have information on both sides. The tip-off is if you see a label: If you see a label on one side of the disk, it's a safe bet there is information only on the other side.

Q Because CD-ROM drives and DVD drives both read disks using reflected light from a laser rather than a needle in a groove like a phonograph record, does this mean that CD-ROM and DVD disks are immune from scratches?

A No, not at all. Although there is no physical contact between the device and the medium, CD-ROM and DVD disks can be damaged if scratched. Scratches on CD-ROM and DVD disks can interfere with the capability of lasers to properly read the data stored on the disks. You should exercise the same level of caution with your CD-ROM and DVD disks that you did years ago with your phonograph records. Even though there are so-called "scratch repair" kits on the market, don't rely on these to bail you out for careless handling.

HOUR 14

Adding a DVD Drive to Your PC

Even though they've been around for about two years, many PC users still think of DVD drives as the newest, hottest technology, especially because so few PCs currently have them.

PC software vendors still haven't totally embraced DVD technology as rapidly as the movie industry, but you can find a few titles currently available on DVD, especially those that would still require a stack of CDs, such as the first 110 years of the National Geographic (see `http://www.nationalgeographic.com/cdrom/`). The CD edition comes on 31 CDs!

Regardless of your reasons for wanting to acquire a DVD drive, during this hour you will learn:

- What a DVD is and how it differs from CDs
- What to look for in a DVD installation kit
- How to install a DVD drive in your PC

So What Is a DVD?

DVDs look a lot like CDs, but there is a world of difference between the two media. Both are 120mm in diameter, but whereas CDs store a maximum of about 650MB of data, DVDs top out at around 4.75GB of data—about seven and a half times larger.

DVD originally stood for Digital Video Disk because the intended used for DVDs was as a new storage medium for full-length movies. But as the new storage medium began seeing usage as a repository for software and other mega-storage items, the name was officially switched to Digital Versatile Disk. Almost no one calls them by their official name, so just refer to them as DVDs.

Like CDs, DVDs store data as a series of pits etched on a reflective substrate layer of plastic, which is read by a laser. DVDs achieve their gargantuan storage capabilities by reducing the size of the data pit from 0.83 microns to 0.40 microns (a micron is $1,000^{th}$ of a millimeter) and by placing the ridges of the one concentric groove closer together— from 1.6 microns to just 0.74 microns. And with a smaller target you also need a tighter laser beam. Whereas the laser in CD-ROM drives uses a 780-nanometer wavelength, the laser beam in DVD drives uses only a 640-nanometer wavelength.

Enough with the rocket science! Just think of it as smaller data bits packed a lot closer together.

What You Will Find in Your DVD Upgrade Kit

When you purchase a CD-ROM drive you get a drive and maybe a ribbon cable to attach the drive to your IDE or SCSI port. In a DVD upgrade kit, you will find a little bit more than just your DVD drive. In addition to the DVD drive you will (should) also find what's called an *MPEG-2* decoder card.

 MPEG-2 is an international graphics standard established by the Motion Picture Entertainment Group (MPEG) for audio and video compression and playback.

The decoder card (see Figure 14.1) is attached to your existing video card to allow DVD playback through your PC's video system.

When you purchase a DVD kit, make sure you choose one that includes an MPEG-2 decoder (hardware) card and not one that uses software for MPEG-2 playback. The hardware option is far superior to software emulations. Also, make sure your decoder card supports resolutions up to 1,280×1,024.

You should also find an IDE ribbon cable in your upgrade kit. Most DVD drives for PCs are IDE (or more precisely, EIDE—Enhanced IDE). Most of the SCSI DVD drives you find are DVD-RAM drives.

FIGURE 14.1

A typical DVD decoder card like you will find in most DVD upgrade kits.

NEW TERM   *DVD-RAM* drives are writeable DVD drives and most are SCSI instead of IDE (or EIDE).

You will also find a video cable for connecting your decoder card to your existing video card, and a cable to connect to your sound card.

Installing a DVD Drive In Your PC

Installing a DVD upgrade kit is no more difficult than installing a CD-ROM drive (see Hour 13, "Upgrading or Adding a CD-ROM Drive") and a video card (see Hour 17, "Upgrading Your Video Card"). Basically what you will be doing is installing another device about the same size as a CD-ROM drive and another card similar to your video card.

To Do: Installing Your New DVD Kit

Just as before, whenever you are handling any sensitive electrical components inside your PC, make sure you have unplugged your PC power supply and grounded yourself to prevent static electric discharges.

To install your DVD upgrade kit:

1. Make sure you have an empty 5-1/4" drive bay in your PC and an empty slot on your motherboard. Make sure you have an unused power connector you can plug in to the drive. If you don't have an unused power connector, go to you local

14

▼   computer store and pick up a Y-connector. Unplug one of your power connectors
           from another device and attach the Y-connector. Make sure the empty slot matches
           the type of decoder card in your kit (ISA versus PCI).

      2. You should find two IDE interfaces, usually labeled primary and secondary, on
           your motherboard. Your hard disk drive (if you have an IDE hard disk installed in
           your PC) should be attached via cable to the interface labeled primary. Make sure
           you have a cable that will reach from the secondary interface to the bay where you
           are installing your new DVD drive. If you already have a CD-ROM drive attached
           to the secondary IDE port, you can also attach the DVD drive to this same cable.
           Just make sure the cable will reach the connectors on both the CD-ROM and DVD
           drives. The easiest way to assure an easy fit is to install one drive (CD-ROM or
           DVD) on top of the other in your drive bays (see Figure 14.2).

> If you decide to install your DVD drive in a PC that already has a CD-ROM
> drive, make sure you designate one of the devices the "master" and the
> other device the "slave." Your documentation will illustrate how you need
> to set the jumpers to make these configuration settings. You only need to
> make the master/slave distinction if you are placing two IDE devices on the
> same IDE port. If each device is connected to its own IDE port, you should
> be able to connect the device using the default setting configured by the
> manufacturer.

FIGURE 14.2
A DVD drive and CD-ROM drive installed together.

▼

▼   3. If you need to install any guide rails on the sides of your drive, install them accord-
          ing to the instructions accompanying the drive. If drive rails are not included, but
          needed, be sure to pick up a set from your local computer store.

       4. Insert the drive into the drive bay (see Figure 14.3) and attach the ribbon cable
          from the secondary IDE interface to the 40-pin IDE interface on the rear of the
          DVD drive (see Figure 14.4).

FIGURE 14.3

*Insert your DVD drive
into an empty drive
bay.*

FIGURE 14.4

*Attach the IDE ribbon
cable to the DVD
drive.*

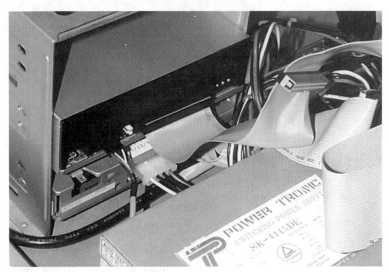

14

▼

▼

5. Connect the audio cable to the audio connector on the rear of the DVD drive and connect the other end of the cable to your sound card, following the instructions that accompanied your upgrade kit. Without the audio cable, you will not be able to hear audio when you watch DVD movies.

6. Attach the power cable to the power connector on the back of your DVD drive.

7. Insert the decoder card into the appropriate type of slot (ISA or PCI) on your motherboard (see Figure 14.5). Remove the cable from your monitor to your video card. Connect the video loop back cable in your upgrade kit from the decoder card to your video card as shown on the instructions included in your upgrade kit (see Figure 14.6). Then connect the cable from your monitor to the video connector on your decoder card. You will also need to connect an audio cable (supplied with your kit) from your existing audio card to the decoder card.

FIGURE 14.5
Insert the decoder card into an empty slot on your motherboard.

8. After you have everything connected to your DVD drive, go ahead and adjust your drive even with the front opening of the drive bay and tighten the screws, securing your drive in place.

9. You should have some type of software installation disk or CD/DVD that you will need to run to install the appropriate drivers, depending on the operating system you are running. If you are running Windows 95/98/2000, when you restart your PC, Windows should automatically detect your newly installed DVD drive and install the proper drivers (a feature known as "Plug and Play"). If you are running Windows NT, check the documentation accompanying the drive for instructions on installing the proper driver and software.

▼

▼ **FIGURE 14.6**

▼ **FIGURE 14.6**
Connect the video loop back cable from the decoder card to your existing video card.

10. Replace your PC's cover. Plug your PC in, and turn it on. If your kit comes with sample DVDs, pop one in and see how it looks. If your kit doesn't include one or more sample DVDs, it's time to make a trip to your local video rental store.

Summary

In the past hour you learned about DVD drives, what features are important to look for when selecting a new DVD upgrade kit, and how to install the upgrade kit in your PC.

Q&A

Q Since DVD drives can also play CDs, doesn't it make since to simply remove my old CD-ROM drive and just use my DVD drive for both CDs and DVDs?

A You could do that, but if you have a relatively new CD-ROM drive (one purchased in the last year or so), your DVD drive is going to be considerably slower than your CD-ROM drive. If you have a relatively new CD-ROM drive, chances are it operates at speeds around 32x–50x. Chances are your DVD drive will operate somewhere in the range of 10x–24x when playing CDs—a tad slower but it shouldn't be much of a problem.

14

HOUR 15

Adding a Removable Media Drive

Another category of devices that has seen a huge surge in popularity is read/write removable media drives. Excluding CD-R, optical disk drives, and floppy disk drives, there are basically two types of mainstream removable media drives: tape backup drives and removable disk drives (removable disk drives that mimic floppy or hard disk drives).

Even though we are including tape drives in this category, when we mention removable media drives, most users think of the types of drives that mimic the functionality of floppy or hard disk drives and give users a source of cheap (or cheaper), unlimited file storage.

During this hour you will learn the following:

- The different types of removable media drives
- About the types of tape drives available for use on PCs
- How to install an internal removable media drive
- How to install an external removable media drive

Removable Hard Disk Drives

Removable hard disk drives have become extremely popular in the past several years. The price of these drives has dropped and some models duplicate the performance of standard hard disk drives while giving the user the potential for unlimited disk storage and the ability to quickly back up data.

Two of the biggest players in the removable disk market are Iomega (see Figure 15.1) and SyQuest (see Figure 15.2).

FIGURE 15.1

Iomega, one of the largest manufacturers of removable disk drives.

The Iomega Zip Drive

Iomega (http://www.iomega.com/) and SyQuest (http://www.syquest.com/) make the most popular removable hard disk drives. Both companies produce low-end and high-end models. Iomega produces the most popular low-end model—the zip drive—in both an internal and an external model (see Figure 15.3).

Zip drive cartridges are capable of storing 100–250MB of data, and the drives are available in both internal and external models. The external models use either a SCSI or parallel port interface. The internal models use either a SCSI or IDE interface. Zip drives are typically installed as a backup device because their performance is not quite up to par with standard hard disk drives, especially the models using an IDE or parallel port interface, which are somewhat slower than the SCSI models.

FIGURE 15.2

SyQuest, another large player in the removable disk market.

15

FIGURE 15.3

An external model of the new Iomega USB Zip 250 drive.

You install the SCSI models using the same procedures as you would to install a SCSI CD-ROM drive (see Hour 13, "Upgrading or Adding a CD-ROM Drive"). The IDE model zip drive installs the same as an IDE model CD-ROM drive. To install a zip drive with a parallel port interface (available only as an external model), you merely plug the drive into your parallel port and install the software.

Some computer manufacturers have started offering zip drives as a replacement for a standard floppy disk drive. Although some users find this arrangement satisfactory, many experts think this option is still a bit premature because zip drives still have not achieved universal status and they do not read or write existing 1.44MB 3-1/2 inch disks.

The Iomega Jaz Drive

Iomega also manufactures the most popular high-end model removable hard disk drive—the Jaz drive (see Figure 15.4).

FIGURE 15.4

The Iomega Jaz drive.

The original Jaz drive used a cartridge capable of storing 1GB of data, and its performance closely rivaled that of standard hard disk drives. To achieve this kind of performance, the Jaz drive is available only with a SCSI interface. In late 1997, Iomega released a new model of its Jaz drive to counter competition from SyQuest. The SyQuest model, the SyJet, equals the performance of the Jaz drive and uses a cartridge capable of storing 1.5GB of data. Iomega's new model, the Jaz-2, which also requires a SCSI interface, uses a cartridge capable of storing an amazing 2GB of data.

Because both the Jaz models and the SyJet equal the performance of many hard disk drives, it is possible to use them in place of standard hard disk drives. You install them the same as you would any other internal or external SCSI device (see Hour 11, "Replacing, Upgrading, or Adding a Hard Disk Drive" and Hour 13).

You can also install Jaz or SyJet drives as your primary hard disk drive, an option that enables you to switch operating systems as easily as you switch disk cartridges. To start up your PC using either a Jaz or SyJet drive, you need to make sure you set the SCSI ID number to 0. And just like starting up to a standard SCSI hard disk drive, you cannot combine SCSI and IDE hard disk drives in the same PC and start up to the SCSI drive.

The SyQuest SyJet 1.5 Gigabyte Drive

The SyJet (see Figure 15.5) is SyQuest's high-end drive. It comes in SCSI (external), IDE (internal), and parallel port (external) versions. Its performance is roughly comparable to the Iomega Jaz drive in the same configuration (that is, IDE, SCSI, or parallel).

FIGURE 15.5

The SyQuest SyJet removable media drive.

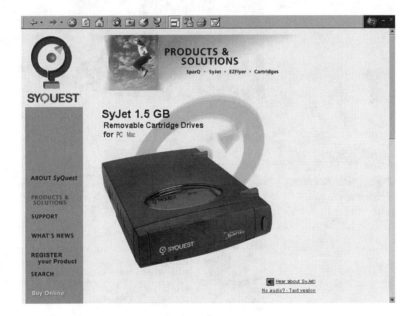

The SyQuest SparQ 1 Gigabyte Drive

The SparQ (see Figure 15.6) is SyQuest's middle-level drive. SyQuest only manufactures the SparQ in IDE and parallel port versions. The performance of the SparQ is roughly comparable to Iomega's IDE and parallel port Jaz models.

The SyQuest EZFlyer Drive

The third model in the SyQuest lineup of removable media drives is the EZFlyer (see Figure 15.7). The EZFlyer is SyQuest's low-end model targeted against the Iomega zip drive. The EZFlyer comes in four different configurations:

- SCSI (internal and external)
- IDE (internal)
- parallel port (external)

FIGURE **15.6**

The SyQuest SparQ removable media drive.

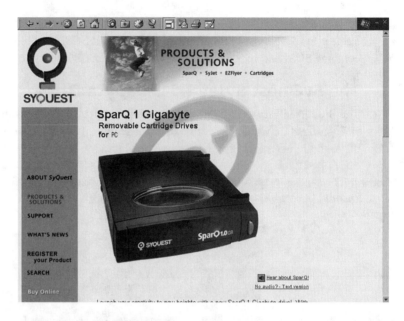

FIGURE **15.7**

The SyQuest EZFlyer removable media drive.

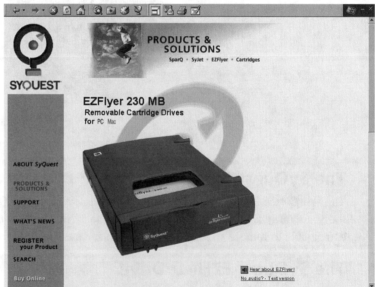

Other Removable Disk Options

Don't think for one second that if you want to add a removable disk to your PC that Iomega and SyQuest are the only games in town. They aren't, even though they do command the lion's share of this market.

Other companies attempting to carve out their piece of this niche market include Sony, Castlewood Systems, and several manufacturers of the LS-120 drive.

Sony HiFD

Sony released a removable media drive positioned as a replacement for your 1.44MB floppy disk drive. Sony calls its 200MB drive HiFD (see Figure 15.8).

FIGURE 15.8

Sony's HiFD removable disk drive—a 200MB replacement for your floppy disk drive.

Sony is attempting to carve out a portion of the low-end removable disk market with its HiFD drive (http://www.ita.sel.sony.com/jump/hifd/index.html). In addition to providing 200MB of storage on each disk, the HiFD drives are also capable of reading and writing to standard 3-1/2 inch, 1.44MB floppy disk drives. So far Sony has not made much of a dent in the zip drive market because many analysts think the HiFD drive is over-priced despite its impressive performance.

Castlewood Systems

Castlewood Systems (http://www.castlewood.com/)is a company attempting to dethrone Iomega's Jaz drives from the top of the high-end removable disk market. The company produces the ORB, a line of two 2GB removable disk drives priced considerably under Iomega's price for its Jaz and Jaz-2 disk cartridges (see Figure 15.9).

Despite its extremely aggressive pricing, the ORB is not yet making a noticeable dent in Iomega's Jaz market.

The LS-120 Drive

The LS-120 is another removable media drive you may have heard about. The LS-120 is made by several manufacturers and looks very similar to a standard 3-1/2 inch floppy disk drive. The LS-120, as the name implies, uses a disk with a capacity of 120MB in addition to being able to read and write to standard 3-1/2 inch 1.44MB floppy disks. The LS-120 is mostly sold as an internal model with an IDE interface but can also be purchased as an external model that connects to a parallel port.

FIGURE **15.9**

The Castlewood Systems' Orb removable disk drive.

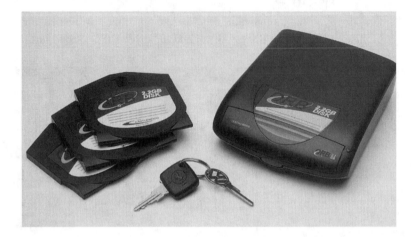

The LS-120 is a good replacement consideration for the standard 3-1/2 inch drive considering it is bootable. Some PC manufacturers, such as Gateway and Compaq, also offer it as a replacement for the standard floppy drive.

Tape Backup Drives

Tape backup drives currently come in an assortment of sizes and capacities. At one time tape backup drives were almost exclusively used to back up network file servers. Now tape backup drives are growing in popularity among individual computer users. Hard disk drives have grown in size to where it is inconceivable to think of backing them up using floppy disks, and tape drives have been following the lead set by hard disk drives and have also been dropping in price.

Choosing a tape backup drive is still largely a matter of how much you want to spend. An expensive tape backup drive won't back up any better than a cheaper model, but an expensive drive will most likely back up your hard disk faster and use fewer tapes.

Tape drives come as both internal and external models and use both IDE and SCSI interfaces, and a few tape drives come with their own proprietary interface. There are even external tape drives that plug in to the parallel port on the back of your computer the same as zip drives.

15

Some leading tape backup manufacturers include

- **OnStream**—http://www.onstream.com/
- **Sony**—http://www.ita.sel.sony.com/
- **Compaq**—http://www.compaq.com/
- **Advance Digital Information Corp.**—http://www.adic.com/
- **Aiwa**—http://www.aiwa.com/
- **APS Technology**—http://www.apstech.com/
- **Artecon, Inc.**—http://www.artecon.com/
- **Digital Equipment Corp.**—http://www.digital.com/
- **Exabyte, Inc.**—http://www.exabyte.com/
- **Hewlett-Packard**—http://www.hp.com/
- **IBM**—http://www.ibm.com/
- **MicroSolutions, Inc.**—http://www.micro-solutions.com/

One of the best sources for finding up-to-date information on PC hardware components is the hardware section of CNET's Computers.com (http://computers.cnet.com/ hardware/0-1016.html). Besides listing just about every tape drive (and removable media drive) you could possibly think of, this site also does comparison reviews and allows you to compare prices on the products listed. Where applicable, this site also lists specifications on the products listed and points you to the manufacturer for more information. If you're looking for more technical information, you should make a point of also bookmarking Tom's Hardware Guide (http://www.tomshardware.com/).

External Tape Backup Drives

The parallel port type drives are probably the easiest type of tape drive to install because all you do is plug the drive in to your parallel port and install the tape backup software. You don't have to worry about connecting cables, running your PC's Setup program, or even taking the cover off your PC. The drawback to these types of tape drives is speed— they are among the slowest tape drives on the market. Most users get around this limitation by performing their backups overnight or by dividing their backup procedure into sections that fit onto one tape.

Other external tape drives use a SCSI interface and install pretty much the same way as an external CD-ROM drive (see Hour 13). All you need to do is set the tape drive to use an available SCSI ID number and insert it into your SCSI chain. If you place the drive at the end of the chain, remember to move your terminator.

Internal Tape Backup Drives

Internal tape drives use IDE, SCSI, and proprietary interfaces. Internal drives are installed pretty much the same as internal CD-ROM drives. You must take into account the same considerations, such as an available drive bay, reach of the interface cable, and so on (see Figure 15.10).

FIGURE 15.10

An internal tape backup drive being inserted into an empty drive bay.

Tape drive
data cable

Tape drive
power cable

SCSI tape drives are typically faster and more expensive than IDE drives, so take this into consideration when deciding what type to purchase. Remember, too, that with a SCSI drive you need a SCSI interface card, if you don't already have one (see Figure 15.11).

When deciding on what type of tape drive to get, pay attention to the storage capacity of the tapes each drive uses (see Figure 15.12).

Although the general rule of thumb is that you should be able to back up each hard disk drive in your PC with one tape, all tape backup software enables you to span a backup session across multiple tapes. It's just easier and more convenient to use one tape, especially if you perform your backups overnight. Pay attention to the cost of tape cartridges. Tape cartridge prices vary considerably from manufacturer to manufacturer, and capacity is not always an indicator of cost. Make sure you also purchase a tape head cleaner for your tape drive (and be sure to use it as recommended) to make sure your tape backup unit is always performing in peak condition.

FIGURE 15.11
A SCSI interface card.

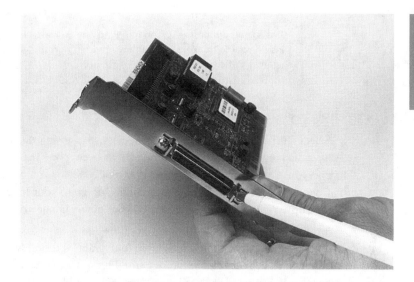

FIGURE 15.12
A typical tape backup cartridge.

Installing a Removable Media Drive

Removable media drives come in two basic designs—internal models and external models. Internal models connect to either an IDE or SCSI interface inside your PC.

To Do: Installing an Internal IDE Removable Media Drive

Installing an internal removable media drive is no more difficult than installing a hard disk drive.

> Just as you did before, when handling any delicate electrical components inside your PC make, sure you have properly grounded yourself to protect against static electricity.

To install an internal drive:

1. Select a drive bay in your PC that you can use to install the drive. Make sure you have also removed the front panel on the case covering the empty bay if there is one. Make sure you have an unused power connector you can plug in to the drive. If you don't have an unused power connector, go to your local computer store and pick up a Y-connector. Unplug one of your power connectors from another device and attach the Y-connector.

2. On most PCs built in the last three or four years, you find two IDE interfaces, usually labeled primary and secondary (see Figure 15.13). Your hard disk drive (if you have an IDE hard disk installed in your PC) should be attached via cable to the interface labeled primary. Make sure you have a cable that will reach from the secondary interface to the bay where you are installing your new drive.

FIGURE 15.13

Primary and secondary IDE interfaces on the motherboard.

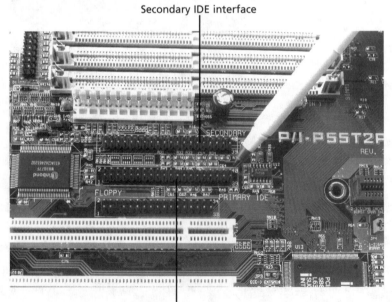

Secondary IDE interface

Primary IDE interface

▼   3. If you have to install any guide rails on the sides of your drive, install them accord-
         ing to the instructions accompanying the drive (see Figure 15.14). If drive rails are
         not included, but needed, be sure to pick up a set from your local computer store.

FIGURE 15.14

*Guide rails of various
sizes used for
installing removable
media drives and other
peripheral devices.*

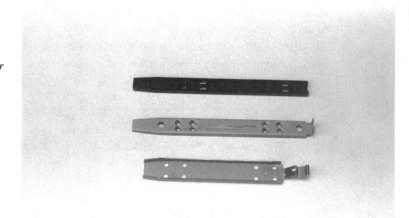

4. Insert the drive into the drive bay and attach the ribbon cable from the secondary
   (slave) IDE interface to the 40-pin IDE interface on the rear of the drive.

Even though IDE interfaces can accommodate two IDE devices, do not connect the removable media drive to the same interface you connect your IDE
hard disk drive to. The removable media drive, which is a much slower
device than a hard disk drive, will degrade the performance of the hard disk
drive.

If your PC has only one IDE interface connector, don't panic. Instead, just
make a quick trip to your local computer store and purchase an IDE interface card. It usually runs in the vicinity of $25–$30. Don't worry about it
conflicting with any of your existing IRQs or memory addresses. Most manufacturers realize it is added as a secondary interface and usually assign it
IRQs and addresses that would be the same as a secondary interface. Just
remember, when in doubt, ask the salesperson or the store's in-house technical guru.

▼

▼ 5. After you have everything connected to your drive, go ahead and adjust your drive even with the front opening of the drive bay and tighten the screws securing your drive in place.

6. Just as you did when you installed your hard disk drive, you will probably have to run some type of software installation disk to install the appropriate driver, depending on the operating system you are running. If you are running Windows 95/98/2000, when you restart your PC Windows should automatically detect your newly installed removable media drive and install the proper driver (a feature

▲ known as "Plug and Play").

In addition to a hardware driver for your drive, the disk that comes with your removable media drive also includes a number of utilities for your drive. These will vary from manufacturer to manufacturer.

Installing an Internal SCSI Removable Media Drive

Installing an internal SCSI removable media drive is almost exactly the same as installing an internal IDE drive. The cable is a bit different, and just like with installing a SCSI hard disk drive, you have to set the SCSI ID on the removable media drive according to the instructions that came with your drive. Remember, too, that the SCSI ID (0–6) has to be unique.

All SCSI devices, such as hard disk drives and removable media drives, leave the factory with a preset SCSI ID, which in most cases you can leave as is. Just be sure to check that the ID set on the device isn't an ID you are already using on your SCSI chain. Two devices on a SCSI chain with the same ID will not operate.

Remember to check the termination on your SCSI chain. Some SCSI removable media drives come with a factory-installed terminator. If your removable media drive is not placed at the end of your SCSI chain, you have to remove the factory-installed terminator or the devices on the chain after the removable media drive will not operate. Check your removable media drive documentation on how to remove the terminator. In many cases, you simply will need to remove a jumper.

Installing an External Removable Media Drive

External removable media drives offer you a few more choices depending on what configuration each manufacturer decides to offer. External models will attach to either a SCSI, parallel, or USB port on your PC.

If you select a removable media drive that connects to your USB port make sure your operating system will support a USB port. Windows 98 and 2000 will support USB. Windows 95 will only support USB ports with the proper upgrades. Windows NT does not support USB.

To install your external removable media drive simply plug it in to the appropriate connection port on your PC and then run the accompanying software to install the appropriate hardware driver. Remember, if your are installing a SCSI external removable media drive be sure to check the SCSI ID to make sure it is not already being used by another device on your SCSI chain. Make sure too that if your drive is at the end of your SCSI chain it is properly terminated. In most cases the drive will come with a terminator and your documentation will explain how to activate the terminator.

Tips for Getting the Most Out of Your Backup Drive

Whether you use a tape drive or a removable media drive as your backup unit, here are a few tips for getting the most out of your backup system:

- *(Extremely Important)* After you install your backup system, be sure to test it. Make sure you fully understand how to back up the files on your hard disk drives. Be sure to test the restore procedure as well as the backup procedure. Try restoring a few files to a temporary directory.

- If you use a backup tape drive, make sure you purchase top quality tapes. Remember: The tapes you buy are your only insurance against disaster. Just as you wouldn't want to trust a cheap, cut-rate parachute, don't trust cheap, cut-rate backup tapes.

- Don't overuse your tapes. Tapes are a much more fragile medium than hard disk drives. Tapes do wear out with extensive use. Extra tapes are a lot cheaper than the time it takes to replace unrecoverable data.

- Create a backup schedule and stick to it. This way you know which backup tape contains the data you are looking for.
- Tape backup drives require regular maintenance. Be sure to read the documentation and perform whatever routine maintenance the manufacturer prescribes, including regularly cleaning the read/write heads of your tape drive.

Summary

In the past hour you learned about many of the options available to you if you decide to add a removable media drive to your PC. You learned about both high-end and low-end drives and about the selection of interfaces each model uses.

Q&A

Q Why are all the drives that use a parallel port interface so slow?

A Because the parallel port was not designed to pass a data stream very quickly. The parallel port was designed as a standard output port to pass data bits in parallel sequence, eight bits at a time, to devices such as printers.

Q If it is so slow, then why is it used at all?

A The parallel port is used as an interface because every PC has one and every parallel port works just like every other parallel port. It is a standard interface that does not require any configuration on the part of the user, and it works on every PC as they come out of the box. Attaching drives to IDE or SCSI ports requires the user to perform some degree of configuration to make them work. The parallel port is literally Plug and Play at its easiest, but you pay a price—speed.

PART IV

Upgrading Peripheral Devices

Hour

HOUR **16**

Replacing Your Keyboard, Mouse, and Other Input Devices

After reading the title of this chapter, you may start wondering what's wrong with your keyboard and mouse. Actually, the keyboard and mouse you are now using may be fine, but over the course of this hour (well actually, maybe in a little less time) you will learn about some better alternatives for the common keyboards and mice usually shipped with PCs.

During this hour you will learn:

- About ergonomic design
- That most keyboards are not ergonomically designed
- How to select an ergonomically designed keyboard
- How to select a more comfortable mouse or other pointing device

Is Anything Wrong with My Keyboard or Mouse?

The title of this lesson might prompt you to skip it because nothing is wrong with your keyboard or mouse. Well, the idea is not that anything is wrong with the keyboard and mouse that came with your PC, but that replacement keyboards and mice can make long hours of PC use easier and much more pleasant.

Keyboards and mice have improved considerably over the past few years, in both functionality and *ergonomics*.

NEW TERM   *Ergonomics* is the study of the relationship between people and their work environments. In simpler terms, it means producing tools in the workplace, such as chairs, desks, keyboards, and so on, that conform more to the way human bodies are designed and how they function rather than making human bodies conform to workplace tools. The idea is to increase comfort and reduce the possibility of injuries or stress.

Functionally, probably nothing is wrong with your keyboard, or at least we hope nothing is mechanically or electronically wrong with it. Like thousands of other PC keyboards, however, yours may be contributing to a physical problem that hundreds of orthopedic surgeons are seeing more and more of each year. You may have encountered the terms *repetitive stress injury* and *carpal tunnel syndrome*. These are medical terms used to describe an extremely painful and sometimes disabling condition brought on by continuously repeating a physical action that places your hands, arms, or legs in an unnatural position. Whether you are aware of it or not, most of us do this every time we use our keyboard.

Although we can absolutely in no way offer a diagnosis on whether you've suffered a repetitive stress injury or whether you've actually developed carpal tunnel syndrome, we can offer you some advice that may help you avoid problems down the road. Now that we've gotten the legal stuff out of the way (which should make the lawyers and suits happy), let's move right along.

The average flat keyboard forces you to bend your wrist outward so that your fingers are in position to reach all the keys. If you're a hunt-and-peck typist, this problem may not be so bad. If you are a touch typist, however, your wrists are probably angled outward at about 30 degrees. If you extend the legs on your keyboard to lift the back of your keyboard upward, you are putting more strain on your wrists because now you are also hyper-extending them backwards another 30–40 degrees.

This unnatural bending of your wrist for long periods of time, day in and day out, eventually can place stress on the nerves in your arms, hands, and wrists. You may have noticed after using your keyboard for several hours that you experience some tingling or numbness in your wrists or fingers. This could be the start of more serious problems.

After studying this problem for several years, designers have come up with what they call the ergonomic keyboard (see Figure 16.1).

FIGURE 16.1

A typical ergonomic keyboard.

16

The basic idea behind the ergonomic keyboard is that it places your wrists and hands into a more comfortable and natural position, with your palms facing more toward each other. This position places much less stress on the nerves and ligaments in your wrists and hands.

Ergonomics, however, is not the only direction keyboard makers are going. Added functionality is another. Keyboards are no longer just keyboards. You can now purchase keyboards with additional devices such as scanners (see Figure 16.2), trackballs, or touchpads built in.

Whether you purchase a keyboard for more comfort and functionality, or if you are just looking for a keyboard with a better feel than the one you are currently using, you need to make sure that you get a keyboard with the correct type of plug for your PC. Most PCs today are manufactured with ports for the newer, smaller 6-pin PS/2-style keyboard plugs shown on the left in Figure 16.3.

This type of plug is easy to identify because it is the same size as the plug used on mice. The other type of keyboard plug is the original AT-style plug, which is noticeably larger than the PS/2 plug.

Don't panic if, when you purchase a new keyboard and attempt to plug it in to your PC, you discover that your new keyboard has the wrong size plug. Most computer stores sell keyboard plug adapters for $5–$10 that convert PS/2 to AT and vice versa (see Figure 16.4).

FIGURE 16.2
A keyboard with a built-in sheet-feed scanner.

FIGURE 16.3
A 6-pin PS/2-style keyboard plug on the left and an older AT-style keyboard plug on the right.

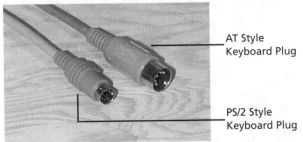

AT Style
Keyboard Plug

PS/2 Style
Keyboard Plug

FIGURE 16.4
Keyboard adapters for converting PS/2- to AT-style plugs.

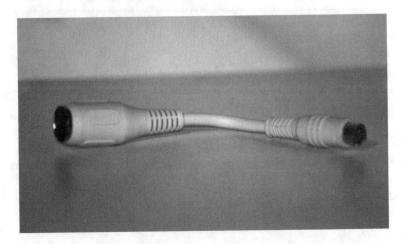

Fixing a Keyboard?

Even though some texts attempt to explain how to fix your keyboard, depending on the type of keyboard you have, you could start tearing it apart only to discover that it's about as difficult to put back together as grandpa's old pocket watch. But this doesn't mean you can't occasionally perform some routine maintenance to help keep your keyboard clean.

Keyboards are great for attracting and collecting dust. And if you're like me and occasionally catch a quick snack while working, you'll find that your keyboard is also quite good at attracting and collecting crumbs. Later in this hour, I'll give you some handy tips on how to clean your keyboard and mouse.

16

Mice and Other Pointing Devices

For many users, the mouse is purely a functional device; either it is functioning, or it isn't! Mice and other types of pointing devices today, however, offer a lot more than mere functionality. Ergonomic mice have been designed to fit your hand. Cordless mice eliminate the cord's getting in your way. Some mice have two buttons; some have three; some are left-handed; and some mice even have built-in gyroscopic mechanisms that you can wave through the air instead of dragging across a pad.

Another mouse innovation for people who surf the World Wide Web a lot is a mouse with a special scrolling wheel placed between the two buttons. The scrolling wheel enables you to scroll up and down long Web pages quickly and smoothly. A lot of applications now also support this scrolling action, including Microsoft's Office suite.

If you are a Windows 95/98 or Windows NT 4.0/2000 user, you can run a program that enables most mice to behave as if they have a scrolling wheel. Go to `http://www.pointix.com/download/index.htm` (see Figure 16.5) and download the Pointix Scroll utility.

And there's a new twist on the old standard Microsoft Mouse. It's called the *IntelliMouse* (`http://www.microsoft.com/insider/mice/default.htm`). Instead of a ball, the IntelliMouse is an optical mouse that scans your desktop 1,500 times per second and, according to Microsoft, gives you tracking precision greater than any other mouse on the market (see Figure 16.6).

If you have limited desktop space and prefer to move your hand rather than move your pointing device, you should opt for a *trackball* rather than a mouse (see Figure 16.7).

NEW TERM A *trackball*, simply stated, is a mouse turned upside down. The ball inside the pointing device is not moved across a pad, but instead your hand motions move the ball (usually a much larger ball).

FIGURE 16.5
The Pointix Web site where you can download the Pointix scroll utility.

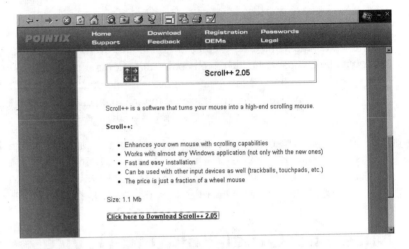

FIGURE 16.6
Microsoft's optical tracking IntelliMouse Explorer.

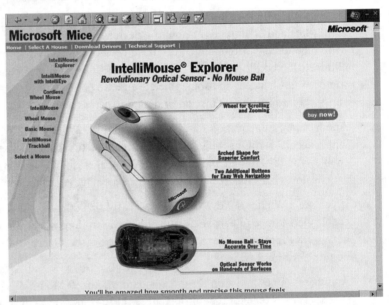

Another pointing device that can help you save desktop space is a touchpad. A touchpad is about the same size as a trackball, but instead of a large ball that you move to position your pointer, you touch a touch-sensitive pad with your finger to position your pointer. Just like a trackball, a touchpad can take a little getting used to, but it is another pointing device you may want to consider.

FIGURE 16.7

A typical trackball pointing device.

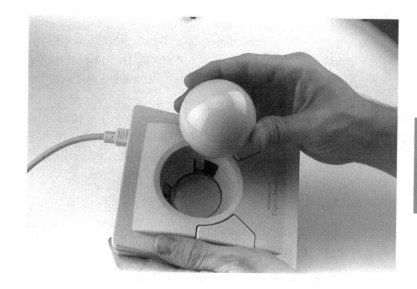

Just as you can purchase a keyboard with the wrong type of plug, mice also come out of the box with one of two types of connectors—a 6-pin Din connector and a 9-pin serial connector. To give you the option of using either type connector, most manufacturers now include a mouse plug adapter with their mice (see Figure 16.8).

FIGURE 16.8

A mouse plug adapter.

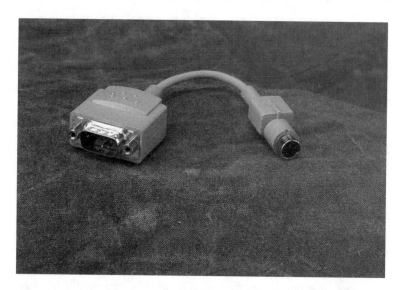

What's most important when selecting a new mouse is comfort and ease of use. In other words, the mouse or trackball should move smoothly. Many large computer stores have a selection of mice on display that you can try to see how they feel and operate. Take this opportunity to try different sizes and styles of mice to see which type you prefer.

If you're in the market for a new keyboard or mouse, one of the best sources for finding up-to-date information on PC hardware components is the hardware section of CNET's computers.com (http://computers.cnet.com/hardware/01016.html). Besides listing just about every keyboard and mouse you could possibly think of, this site also does comparison reviews and allows you to compare prices on the products listed. Where applicable, this site also lists specifications on the products listed and points you to the manufacturer for more information.

Tips on Cleaning Your Input Devices

Over time and with normal usage, your keyboard, mouse, and other input devices get dirty. The best way to tell when your devices are dirty and need to be cleaned is when they start to behave erratically, such as your mouse pointer not moving in the direction you are trying to position it, or your keyboard keys becoming hard to press.

Cleaning Your Keyboard

Over time, your keyboard accumulates dust, crumbs (if you eat and work as many computer users do), and other small bits of debris, which can cause keys to stick or make your keys slightly harder to depress. The easiest method you can employ to clean your keyboard of these small bits of debris is simply to turn it over so that the keys are facing down toward your desktop and shake your keyboard firmly. Don't shake it hard enough to jar loose your keys, but give it a few good shakes to clear out the crumbs and other small particles.

If you have the misfortune of accidentally spilling a liquid on your keyboard, such as a soda or other soft drink, you may quickly discover that the sugar or other sweetener causes your keys to become sticky. If this happens, immediately stop what you're doing. Save any work you're doing and shut down your PC. Unplug your keyboard and take it to an empty sink. Soda and other liquids can be easily removed using simple alcohol (the rubbing type, not the drinking type). Take a bottle of alcohol out of your medicine cabinet and slowly pour it into the keyboard in about the same area where the spill occurred. The alcohol does not harm the electrical contacts in your keyboard and does a fairly good job of cleaning the spilled liquid. You may need to use more than one bottle of alcohol. You can usually tell when you have completely cleaned your keyboard by simply pressing the keys to check whether they still feel sticky. Just make sure you allow sufficient time for the alcohol to dry (evaporate) before you plug your keyboard back in to your PC and begin using it again.

Don't use any cleaning products commonly used to clean your kitchen or bathroom because some can damage the plastics in your keyboard and others can leave residues, which can cause more damage. Isopropyl Alcohol is about the safest (and often cheapest) cleaning product you can use.

Although some professionals advocate opening and dismantling a keyboard, I generally don't make this recommendation because it can be extremely difficult to reassemble all the small pieces. If you find that a good cleaning with alcohol does not clean anything you might accidentally spill on your keyboard, you are probably better off pitching the keyboard and purchasing a new one.

Cleaning Your Mouse

Mice also get dirty. Usually the parts that get dirty are the rollers inside the mouse, which come in contact with the ball. Just as you did with your keyboard, reach for your bottle of alcohol. This time, instead of pouring the alcohol over the ball and rollers, you want to remove the ball and, using a cotton swab soaked with alcohol, clean the rollers of any build-up of dirt and grease, which can accumulate over time. The instructions that came with your mouse can explain how to open it and remove the ball. Usually, it is just a matter of sliding or twisting a panel holding the ball in place. Just make sure you understand how to replace the ball before you begin removing it.

Again, just as with your keyboard, don't use common household cleaning products that can damage your mouse.

Summary

In the past hour, you learned how to select a better and more comfortable keyboard and mouse and how important comfort and ergonomics can be when using them. You also learned how to overcome the problem of purchasing a mouse or keyboard with a plug that doesn't match your PC mouse and keyboard connections.

16

Q&A

Q **What can be done to prevent repetitive stress injuries such as carpal tunnel syndrome short of purchasing a new ergonomic keyboard?**

A Actually, you can do several things. First, make sure your keyboard is lying flat. If you have the legs on your keyboard extended, fold the legs back down. Second, give yourself frequent breaks when typing. Stop every 10–15 minutes for a minute or two and let your hands and wrists relax. You might also consider purchasing a keyboard and/or mouse rest pad. These are soft, gel-filled devices that provide additional support and comfort for your hands and wrists.

Q **If I develop a repetitive stress injury such as carpal tunnel syndrome, what can be done?**

A Again, you have to see your doctor for diagnosis and treatment. Some cases that have not progressed too far can be treated with some of the corrective actions mentioned in this chapter. If the injuries are severe, however, often the only treatment is surgery.

Q **Should I ever attempt to fix a broken keyboard?**

A There's nothing wrong with attempting to repair a keyboard. There is no danger involved, but chances are you will find it difficult, depending on the type of keyboard it is, to get all the pieces back together and functioning. If you have an old keyboard you are no longer using, go ahead and take it apart (or at the very least remove a few keys) and then try putting it all back together. You may find it is a lot harder than it first appears.

Hour 17

Upgrading Your Video Card

For most users, upgrading a video card is like getting your appendix taken out—you don't do it until you need to. Most users make do with whatever video card came with their PC when it was purchased.

There's actually nothing wrong with this video card philosophy. Chances are the video card installed in your PC by the manufacturer is more than adequate for 98 percent of the applications you run. So, why should anyone want to upgrade their video card? The answer is the same for any decision to upgrade a component in your PC—to get better performance!

Better performance in a video card can mean several things—higher video resolution, faster screen refreshes, better graphics, or more colors on your screen. For most users, the need for better performance in a video card is usually driven by a specific application: a high-end graphics art program, a CADD or engineering design program, or even a game using enhanced 3D graphics.

Regardless of your reasons for wanting to get better video performance out of your PC, during the next hour you will learn:

- What features are currently being touted in video cards
- What to look for in selecting a video card upgrade
- How to install a new video card in your PC

What's Currently Available in Video Cards

Nowadays, it is extremely difficult to purchase a bad video card. Video cards have been one of the fastest developing technologies in the computer industry in recent years, and surprisingly, this advancement has been driven largely by the computer gaming industry.

NEW TERM *Video cards* are also referred to as *video adapters*, *graphic adapters*, and *graphic cards*. These terms all refer to the same device—the interface card installed in your computer that controls and produces video on your monitor. Although the term mostly applies to separate interface cards installed in your PC, the term video card can also refer to video display circuitry built in to the motherboard.

For years, computer gaming software has been pushing the display envelope for faster and more complex graphics and animation. Consequently, the entire computer industry has benefited from this small but demanding segment of the industry because these same video cards also deliver improved graphic performance for the more mainstream business application uses of computers.

The big buzzword in video cards is *3D graphics*, which refers to a means of displaying or rendering onscreen graphic objects so that they appear to have 3-dimensional texture and look more realistic. Again, the gaming side of the computer industry is light years ahead of the business side in terms of its use of 3D graphics.

What to Look for in a Video Card

Currently, you need to look for two main features when selecting a video card: memory and speed. It's fairly easy to determine how much memory each video card has installed. The amount of memory installed on the card is usually printed in big, bold letters on the outside of the box. In the not too distant past, most video cards left the factory with 2, 4, or 8MB of memory installed. Nowadays it is very common to see video cards equipped with 16–32 MB of video memory. Video memory is also usually referred to as VRAM.

NEW TERM *VRAM*, short for Video RAM (Random Access Memory), is a special type of high-speed memory designed for use in video cards.

How Important Is Video RAM?

Video RAM or video memory is important because it directly controls video resolution and the number of colors you can display on your monitor. Resolution is defined as the number of pixels (short for picture elements) displayed on your screen. A pixel is the smallest video display unit that can be displayed on your screen. In standard VGA mode—what you are probably looking at on your PC right now—there are 640 pixels displayed horizontally across your screen by 480 pixels displayed vertically, for a total of 307,200 pixels (640×480=307,200).

When you increase your resolution to 800×600 (800 by 600), the number of pixels increases to 480,000 (800×600=480,000). The number of pixels displayed on your screen, however, is only half the story. Each pixel is made up of a color. In 16-color mode, the lowest number of colors for VGA, each pixel can be 1 of 16 possible colors. You need four bits of memory to support 16-color mode, and if you do the math, you'll see that you need 153,600 bytes of memory to support 16-color mode:

640×480=307,200

307,000×4=1,228,800(bits)

To convert bits to bytes, divide by 8:

1,228,800(bits)/8=153,600(bytes)

Unfortunately, 16-color mode does not produce very brilliant colors. A better color mode is 256 colors. To produce 256-color mode, however, you need to jump from four to eight bits per pixel or 307,200 bytes of memory. Your display is getting better but it is still not great. An improvement would be to increase your color or color depth to 65,536 colors. To jump to a color depth of 65,536 colors, however, you need 16 bits of memory for each pixel, for a total of 614,400 bytes of memory.

No video card manufacturer produces video cards with 614,400 bytes of memory. Instead, they round this number up to a more convenient 1MB of memory. So, to display VGA resolution at 65,536 (64KB) colors, you need 1MB of memory on your video card. If you increase your resolution to 1,024×768 at 64KB (65,536) colors, you now need 2MB of memory on your video card, and if you increase your resolution to 1,280×1,024 or the number of colors displayed to 16.8MB (16,777,216), then you need 4MB of memory on your video card. Table 17.1 lists video memory requirements at various resolutions and color depths.

17

TABLE 17.1 Video Memory Requirements

Resolution	Color Depth	Colors	Video RAM	Memory Required (bytes)
640×480	4-bit	16	256KB	153,600
640×480	8-bit	256	512KB	307,200
640×480	16-bit	65,536	1MB	614,400
640×480	24-bit	16,777,216	1MB	921,600
800×600	4-bit	16	256KB	240,000
800×600	8-bit	256	512KB	480,000
800×600	16-bit	65,536	1MB	960,000
800×600	24-bit	16,777,216	2MB	1,440,000
1024×768	4-bit	16	512KB	393,216
1024×768	8-bit	256	1MB	786,432
1024×768	16-bit	65,536	2MB	1,572,864
1024×768	24-bit	16,777,216	4MB	2,359,296
1280×1024	4-bit	16	1MB	655,360
1280×1024	8-bit	256	2MB	1,310,720
1280×1024	16-bit	65,536	4MB	2,621,440
1280×1024	24-bit	16,777,216	4MB	3,932,160

If all you're working on are spreadsheets and text documents, you're not going to see much difference between 16 colors and 65,536 colors displayed on your screen. If you are a graphic artist, however, the increase in color depth to 24-bit color (16.8MB colors) is essential.

To Do: Demonstrating Video Resolution and Color Depth

To demonstrate video resolution and color depth using your existing video card, follow these steps:

1. Use SysChk or SiSoft Sandra (see Hour 3, "Examining Your PC's System Configuration") to determine how much video memory you have installed on your existing video card (see Figure 17.1).

2. If your current video mode is not VGA (640×480 resolution) and 16 colors (color depth), change to this particular resolution and color depth. If you are running Windows 3.1x, double-click the Windows Setup icon, select Video, and choose the

▼   driver for 16 Color VGA mode. If you are running Windows 95/98/NT/2000, right-
      click your desktop to open the display shortcut menu, select Properties, and then
      select Settings to open the Display Properties dialog box (see Figure 17.2). Make
      the appropriate change to Color Palette and Desktop Area.

FIGURE 17.1

SiSoft Sandra display-
ing video information.

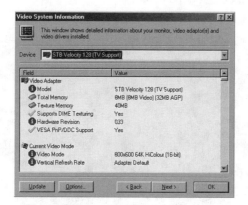

FIGURE 17.2

The Display Properties
dialog box in
Windows 98.

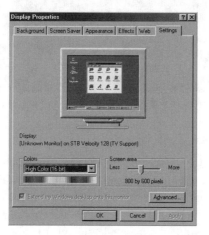

17

3. If you have Internet access, start your Web browser and proceed to the following
    Web page:

    `http://www.felixnet.com/wolfpark/wolftrip.htm`

    Select the second group of pictures and click the first picture to display it full-sized
    (see Figure 17.3). This picture has fairly vivid colors and good resolution when
▼   viewed at something better than 16-color VGA mode.

▼   4. Repeat step 2, staying in VGA mode (640×480 resolution), but select a better color
depth (such as 256 colors or 65,536 colors). Go back and view the test picture
again and note the change in appearance. Take a few minutes to try various screen
resolutions and color depths to see which combination produces the best results
using your video card and monitor.

FIGURE 17.3

*Test picture for various
video modes and color
depths.*

▲

Video Speed

Video speed is often referred to as *refresh rate*, the speed at which the video card can
redraw or refresh your display screen at certain resolutions. Most experts agree that your
video card should have a minimum refresh rate of 72 Hz at every resolution to avoid
flicker, which can cause eye strain and fatigue. While the type of memory installed on
your video card can definitely affect refresh rate, the other factor controlling refresh rate
is the speed of the Digital Analog Converter (DAC). You should look for a video card
with a DAC speed of at least 175 MHz.

Ultimately, speed is important for a video card because a faster card is able to redraw or
refresh your display screen and produce smoother animation when you are displaying
moving objects on your screen. Again, this is a feature more important to graphic artist
programs, Web designer applications, CAD engineering software, and video games than
to a word processing program. But video speed is also important if you are working in

any type of business graphic program or if you are viewing graphics or animation on the Internet. The bottom line is that any application benefits from a higher quality video card (especially Windows) and eventually you are faced with using some sort of graphical application.

Video card speed is a little harder to determine. Often it takes sophisticated testing programs to determine the relative speed of a particular video card. Most users lack the testing software and resources to test numerous video cards, so we must rely on the various computer industry journals to test and publish their results. These testing reviews can often be valuable sources of information that you as a consumer and computer user should regularly check before making any computer purchase.

A few magazines you might want to browse for product reviews on video cards are *PC Magazine, PC World, Windows Magazine, Windows Sources*, and *Windows NT Magazine*.

17

So, what does all this mean when deciding whether you need a new video card? If you are an ardent game player and you are trying to keep pace with the latest gaming technology, you most likely want the fastest video card you can get with at least 16–32 MB of memory and one that can display ultra-fast 3D graphics.

If you are using any type of sophisticated graphics or animation software, you also want to consider upgrading to a video card that fits the same bill. However, an even less demanding reason technologically for upgrading your video card is purchasing a larger monitor. Although VGA mode (640×480 resolution) is perfectly acceptable on a 14" or 15" monitor, if you are looking at a 17", 19", or even a 21" monitor, you want to crank up the resolution to a higher level in order to take advantage of your larger display. For monitors 17" and above, it is fairly common to use a resolution of 1024×768 or higher. In addition, if you look back at the preceding section, you see that higher video resolution and higher color depth require a video card with more memory. Once again, you can refer back to Hour 3 and use SysChk to determine the specifics of your existing video card.

Although SysChk indicates the basics of your video card, if you are interested in expertly testing your video card and tuning your monitor, you should look into a professional testing utility such as DisplayMate from Sonera Technologies, located at `http://www.displaymate.com` (see Figure 17.4).

Figure **17.4**
*Sonera Technologies,
the developer of
DisplayMate.*

Installing a Video Card

There is very little setup involved when installing a new video card.

Regardless of which version of Windows (3.1/95/98/NT/2000) you are using, before you remove your existing video card and install a new one, do this: Set your video mode to VGA and your colors to 16. This ensures that Windows, with the standard VGA driver installed, will work with your new video card.

To Do: Installing Your New Video Card

To install a new video card, follow these steps:

1. If you are running Windows 95/98/NT/2000, right-click your desktop to open the display shortcut menu. Select Properties and Settings to open the Display Properties dialog box.

2. Select the Change Display Type button to open the Change Display Type dialog box (see Figure 17.5).

3. Select the Adapter Type Change button, and then select the Show All Devices radio button.

4. Select Standard Display Adapter (VGA).

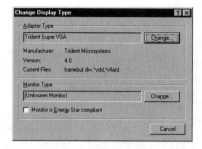

▼ **FIGURE 17.5**

*The Change Display
Type dialog box in
Windows 98.*

If you install a new video card that requires a video driver that is incompatible
with the driver required by your previous video card, it is possible your PC will
not start Windows 95/98/NT/2000. To prevent this from happening, you can
install the generic VGA video driver, which should work with just about every
video card on the market.

17

5. Turn off and unplug your PC. Ground yourself and then remove the cover.

6. Unplug the cable from your monitor, which is connected to your current video
   card.

7. Remove your current video card and insert the new video card into the same slot
   on your motherboard (see Figure 17.6). If you are removing a card from an ISA
   bus slot and the new card requires a PCI bus slot, be sure to insert the new card
   into the proper slot. If you are removing a card from a PCI slot and the new card
   requires an AGP slot, be sure to insert the new card into the proper slot.

AGP, short for Accelerated Graphics Port, refers to a special graphics slot
designed by Intel, which began appearing about 1-1/2 to 2 years ago in PCs
with Pentium II motherboards. Read the next section for more details on AGP.

Some motherboards have built-in video cards, which you need to disable
before adding an upgraded video card. To disable a built-in video card, you
need to consult the documentation that came with your PC. In many instances,
you can disable a built-in video card by running the hardware Setup program
used to configure your PC. To disable some built-in video cards, however, the
manufacturer might have included a special video configuration utility.

▼

▼ FIGURE 17.6
*Inserting a new video
card into your PC.*

8. Replace your PC's cover, and attach the video cable to your new card. Plug your
   PC in and turn it on.

9. Install the video driver for your new card following the instructions accompanying
   the new card. If you are running Windows 95, 98, or 2000, there is a good chance
   the operating system will detect the new card and begin the driver installation for
   you. Just follow the prompts to install the new video driver.

▲

What About AGP?

If you regularly read the computer trade journals, another hot term you may have seen
lately is *AGP*, which stands for *Accelerated Graphics Port*. Strictly speaking, it is not an
upgrade item. You cannot add AGP to your existing computer.

> **NEW TERM** A *chipset* is nothing more than a specialized processor or group of processors
> designed for a specific task.

In addition to the 440LX chipset, you also need to be running either the Windows 95
OEM Service Release 2.1, Windows 98, or Windows 2000 because these are the only
operating systems that fully support AGP. You also need a video card that is AGP compliant and software written to utilize AGP's advanced capabilities.

So what does all this AGP hardware and software buy you? Amazing graphics texture
and silky smooth animation, but surprisingly no additional display speed. In tests con-
ducted on similar computer systems using an AGP video card and a PCI video card, the

AGP card was not significantly faster, and in some tests, the AGP turned in the same speed as the PCI or lower.

Another drawback to AGP is that Intel set a rather relaxed standard. The only real qualification for AGP is that the AGP card fit into the proprietary AGP slot. In early models released by several manufacturers, some cards did not fully implement the full texturing features for enhanced 3D graphics. There are even different implementations of display speed on the so-called compliant video cards. Some cards operate at 66 MHz and provide 264 megabytes per second of display video data, whereas other cards are able to effectively double these numbers. Reportedly, some manufacturers are working on cards that quadruple these figures.

Finally, little software is written to take full advantage of AGP. The largest category, as you might guess, is games. Even the best AGP video cards do nothing to improve existing graphics software.

17

Summary

In the past hour you learned about video cards, what features are important to look for when selecting a new video card, and how to install a video card in your PC. You have also learned about the newest video specification AGP, what it will do, and what it will mean for you in terms of improving graphics software.

When you are in the market for a new video card, one of the best sources for finding up-to-date information on PC hardware components is the hardware section of CNET's computers.com (`http://computers.cnet.com/hardware/0-1016.html`). Besides listing just about every video card you could possibly think of, this site also does comparison reviews and allows you to compare prices on the products listed. Where applicable, this site also lists specifications on the products listed and points you to the manufacturer for more information. If you're looking for more technical information, you should also make a point of bookmarking Tom's Hardware Guide (`http://www.tomshardware.com/`).

Q&A

Q Are there video resolutions higher than 1280×1024? If so, what are they used for?

A The highest advertised video resolution I have ever seen is 1800×1440. Resolutions this high are typically used in CAD/CAE (Computer Aided Design/Computer Aided Engineering) and usually require 21" or larger monitors.

Q **Is it possible to install two video cards in a PC, attach two monitors, and view information on each monitor?**

A Yes, but to do so requires either special software or an operating system (Windows 95/98/2000, Linux) to support this type of operation. Also, unless your software is designed for multiple views, you will see the same display on both monitors.

Q **What is the Color Palette under display settings for? How many colors should I set my PC to display?**

A The Color Palette, as you might have guessed, is used to set the maximum number of colors displayed for your video card. The maximum number of colors you can display is determined by the amount of video memory on your video card and the resolution you have set. You should definitely set your color palette to display more than 256 colors to avoid what looks like a "washed-out" display. Any setting higher than 65,536 (64K) is merely a matter of preference unless you are playing games that require a higher color palette or you are editing high-resolution photos or similar graphics.

Hour **18**

Upgrading Your Video Monitor

During the last hour, you learned about upgrading your video card and the benefits you can gain from a new video card. If you are still using the same old 14- or 15-inch monitor, however, you're cheating yourself out of the very benefits you sought in upgrading your old video card with a new one. The main reason most users upgrade their video cards is to gain higher resolution, which enables them to see more on their screen. But resolutions of 1024×768 and 1280×1024 are nearly unreadable on 14- and 15-inch monitors unless you have a passion for squinting.

In the past, the biggest deterrent for most users interested in purchasing larger monitors was cost. As recently as 2–3 years ago, most 21-inch and larger monitors hovered in the $2000–$2500 range. Nowadays, these same monitors are advertised with prices in the $600–$1000 range, in part because of competition from the newly released 19-inch monitors in the $400–$600 price range. For the average PC user, selecting an upgrade among this glut of lower priced, larger monitors can be confusing.

This hour will help you wade through this morass and hopefully, you will learn enough about selecting a new monitor to choose one that meets your needs and your budget. In this hour, you will learn:

- What all the benefits are in obtaining a larger monitor
- What monitor features such as dot pitch, refresh rate, and viewable area are and how important they are in selecting a larger monitor
- What other features are important to look for in selecting a new monitor
- Some tips and advice in setting up your new monitor

Why You Should Purchase a Larger Monitor

In the last hour, you learned about upgrading your video card and that to fully appreciate many video card upgrades, you need to consider upgrading your monitor as well, especially if you're still using a 14- or 15-inch monitor.

Plain and simple, the reason you want a new, larger monitor is that it enables you to see more of what is displayed on your screen. For example, if you are currently using a 15-inch monitor, upgrading to a 17-inch monitor may not seem like a big deal, but a 17-inch monitor gives you about 30 percent more onscreen viewing area. Upgrading from a 15-inch monitor to a 21-inch monitor gives you more than 50 percent more onscreen viewing area because you are able to comfortably set your display to a higher resolution. Table 18.1 shows the recommended resolution for 15-, 17-, 19-, and 21-inch monitors. Keep in mind that these are just recommendations, not chiseled-in-stone guidelines.

TABLE 18.1 Optimal and Acceptable Display Resolutions

15-inch	17-inch	19-inch	21-inch
640×480	640×480	640×480	640×480
800×600	800×600	800×600	800×600
1024×768	**1024×768**	**1024×768**	1024×768
	1280×1024	**1280×1024**	**1280x1024**
		1600×1200	**1600×1200**
			1800×1440

Optimal, *Useable,* Not advisable

To give you an idea how resolution can affect how much you can view onscreen, take a look at Figures 18.1, 18.2, and 18.3. These three figures display the same information onscreen, but as you can see, as the resolution increases, so too does the amount of information visible onscreen.

FIGURE 18.1

Resolution set at 640×480.

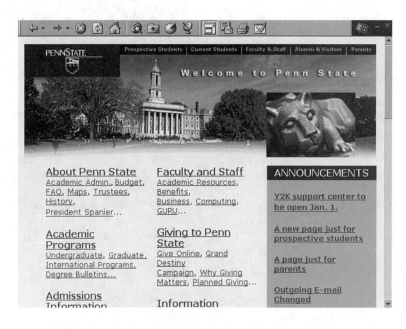

FIGURE 18.2

Resolution set at 800×600.

18

FIGURE 18.3
*Resolution set at
1024×768.*

Larger monitor prices have also been dropping in the past year. A good 17-inch monitor can be purchased now in the range of $300–$600. A good 21-inch monitor can be purchased now for between $700 and $1000.

Purchasing a larger monitor has a downside. Larger monitors are just that—larger monitors! They take up more room on your desktop, and more importantly, larger monitors weigh a lot more. Some 21-inch models can tip the scales at upward of 75–80 pounds.

Another reason to upgrade to a newer monitor is that monitor technology has improved in the last few years. Monitors are not just bigger, but they are also better. Monitors now produce clearer, sharper images with less distortion and flicker on the screen, which means if you regularly spend hours in front of your PC, you are less likely to suffer eye strain (or at least less eye strain than before). Newer monitors also generally are equipped with better controls (such as horizontal and vertical controls, contrast, brightness, and so on), which enable you to do a better job of fine-tuning your monitor to your own personal preferences.

Selecting Your New Monitor

Before you head out and plop down your hard-earned cash for a new monitor, there are a few guidelines you need to know about selecting a monitor:

- *Be careful of dot pitch claims.* A short time ago the big buzzword for monitors was dot pitch. A computer monitor's screen is composed of thousands of very small dots called pixels (short for picture elements), which when set to the correct color, create the appearance of images. Dot pitch is the measurement between these dots. Unfortunately, not every manufacturer measures dot pitch the same way, so using dot pitch to compare one monitor to another quickly becomes a comparison of apples and oranges.

  Another problem with using dot pitch to compare monitors is that it only works on monitors using the dot-trio shadow-mask picture tube. In the dot-trio shadow-mask picture tube, a thin sheet of perforated metal coated with light sensitive phosphor is what creates the actual dots. On monitors using this type of picture tube, you want to measure the shortest distance between the perforated dots. Some manufacturers measure the distance from the center of one dot to the center of an adjacent dot, but not every manufacturer uses the dot-trio shadow-mask picture tube in their monitors.

  Some manufacturers use what is called the aperture-grille picture tube. The aperture-grille type picture tube uses an array of stretched wires coated with phosphor instead of a sheet of perforated dots.

  A third method is called slot-mask, which combines portions of shadow-mask and aperture-grille technologies.

- *Look for a high refresh rate.* Another important factor to consider in selecting a new monitor is the monitor's refresh rate. The refresh rate is the speed at which the monitor can refresh or redraw the onscreen display. You want a monitor with a fast refresh rate because this tends to reduce onscreen flicker. Refresh rates are not determined by the type of picture tube that the manufacturer uses, so refresh rate turns out to be a more legitimate gauge for comparing monitors. Refresh rates do vary according the resolution used on the monitor. You want to elect a monitor with a refresh rate of at least 72 Hz (which means the screen is refreshed about 72 times a second) for the highest resolution you intend to use.

- *How much control you have over your monitor.* As strange as this may sound, many experts also suggest that you check to see the number of controls available on the monitor. A monitor with a lot of controls enables you greater latitude in fine-tuning your monitor.

18

> While we're on the subject of controls, if you can select a monitor with all the controls on the front rather than on the back, adjusting your monitor will be a lot easier.

- *Check the actual size of the viewing area.* Keep in mind one additional fact when selecting a larger monitor. The advertised size of the monitor is not the size of the display screen. Table 18.2 shows you approximately what you can expect for your display size (measured diagonally) when you purchase a certain size monitor. Keep in mind that, just like with your television set, the measurement is made diagonally.

- *Is it a flat screen monitor.* Having a flat screen as opposed to the slightly rounded screen will display images with less distortion. But be prepared to pay a little extra for a flat screen.

TABLE 18.2   Monitor Display Sizes

Monitor Size in Inches	Approximate Viewing Area
14	12.5
15	13.5
17	15.5–16
19	17.5–18
20	18.5–19
21	19.5–20

You really don't need a degree in electrical engineering to be able to compare monitors and select the best one for your needs. If you really want to get down to a low-level technical comparison between monitors, a number of good software programs are available that you can use to test monitor performance. Two of the best are the WinBench series from ZD Labs (www.zdnet.com) and a program mentioned in the last hour, DisplayMate by Sonera Technologies (www.displaymate.com).

For many users, however, the best way to choose one monitor over another is by performing a few simple tests in a local computer store.

When you're in the market for a new monitor, one of the best sources for finding up-to-date information on PC hardware components is the hardware section of CNET's computers.com (http://computers.cnet.com/hardware/0-1016.html). Besides listing just about every monitor you could possibly think of, this site also does comparison reviews and allows you to compare prices on the products listed. Where applicable, this site also lists specifications on the products listed and points you to the manufacturer for more information. If you're looking for more technical information, you should also make a point of bookmarking Tom's Hardware Guide (`http://www.tomshardware.com/`).

To Do: Performing a Simple Set of Tests on a New Monitor

The following are a few simple tests you can perform on any monitor you are contemplating purchasing:

1. Start Windows (any version) and check for uniform focus. Place a few icons around the screen—in the center and in the corners—and see if all the icons seem to have the same clarity and brightness. Look at the vertical and horizontal lines. Are they straight, or are any lines bowed? Are all the colors crisp and clear without any slight tints on any of the images?

2. Use a graphics program to draw a circle on the screen. Is the circle a circle or is it an oval? If you see an oval, this monitor causes some degree of distortion when using graphics-intensive programs.

3. Load any word processing program. Type a sentence on the screen and set the font to an eight-point or smaller serif type font such as Times Roman. Are the characters crisp, clean, and legible, or are they fuzzy?

4. Turn the brightness up and down while examining the corners of the screen. Does anything change? Do any images swell or bloom?

5. Repeat the previous steps at different resolutions.

Don't immediately dismiss the monitor if it comes up short on any of these simple subjective tests. The monitor could just be connected to a lesser quality video card. See whether you can get the sales representative to plug the monitor into a computer with a better card. Better yet, check to see what type of return policy the computer store has (such as 30 days with no restocking fee) in case the monitor does not perform well with your graphics card. Keep in mind that seemingly identical monitors can produce differing results. Another method for choosing one monitor over another is to regularly check product reviews by several of the popular trade magazines. One recurring feature present in most computer magazines is product reviews and comparisons on computer hardware and software. Most have gone through the trouble of setting up extensive testing laboratories specifically designed to put a product through its paces.

Some computer magazine publishers have even set up online testing programs you use to test your monitor. *PC Magazine* has an online testing section specifically for monitors located at `http://www.zdnet.com/pcmag/features/monitors/test/_test.htm` (see Figure 18.4), and *Windows Magazine* has an online version of its WinTune 98 program located at `http://www.winmag.com/wintune98` (see Figure 18.5).

The PC Magazine test was created with the help of Sonera Technologies and is a subset of their complete online testing utility. If you want to try the full test, go to http://www.displaymate.com/.

FIGURE 18.4
PC Magazine's *online monitor testing page.*

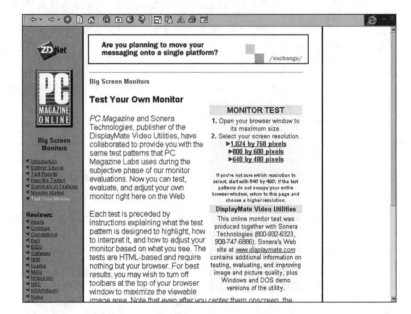

FIGURE 18.5
Windows Magazine's *online WinTune 98 testing page.*

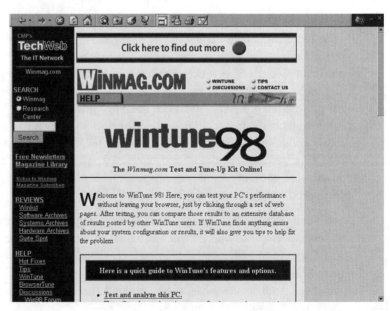

Setting Up Your New Monitor

As mentioned earlier in this chapter, a larger monitor takes up more room on your desktop, so make sure you have the available desktop real estate before you unbox your new monitor.

To Do: Setting Up Your New Monitor

▼ To Do

To set up your new monitor, follow these steps:

1. Turn off and unplug your old monitor. Turn off the power to your computer. Then disconnect your old monitor from your PC and remove it from your desktop.

2. Unbox your new monitor and carefully examine it for any signs of transit damage. Examine the video cable and connector, which plugs into your PC.

3. Place your new monitor on your desktop. Do not place it on top of your PC. If a separate base accompanies your monitor, follow the instructions for assembling and placing your monitor on the base.

> Larger monitors tend to be very heavy, too heavy, in fact, to place on top of your PC as many users are accustomed to doing with 14- and 15-inch monitors. Most PC cases cannot adequately support monitors weighing upwards of 50–60 pounds and could bow or crack and damage your PC.

18

4. Adjust the height of the monitor so that the approximate center of the screen is at eye level.

5. Plug your monitor's video cable into your PC and connect the monitor's power cable.

6. Turn on your monitor and your PC.

> There is still a lot of controversy over whether you should turn on your monitor or your PC first, or whether you should plug them both into a combination surge protector/power strip and turn them both on together. I have heard so-called experts recommend each method. Personally, I previously owned a PC where the instructions stated to turn the monitor on first, so I always turn my monitor on first and then turn on my PC.

▼

▼   7. Your new monitor should come with a disk containing drivers for Windows 95/98,
         NT 4.0, and 2000. These drivers enable your Windows operating system to prop-
         erly adjust certain settings to those required by your monitor. Windows 3.1 does
▲   not make these adjustments. If you are using Windows 95/98/NT 4.0/2000, follow
         the instructions that come with your monitor for installing these drivers.

> If you are running Windows 95/98/2000 and your monitor is Plug and Play,
> these versions of Windows will attempt to make these adjustments for you.
> Just follow the onscreen prompts.

NEW TERM   *Plug and Play* is a combination hardware and software feature that enables an
                operating system such as Windows 95/98/2000 to identify and configure hard-
ware you add to your PC. In order to work, the hardware item has to have special chips
built in that identify the hardware item. Also, the operating system, such as Windows
95/98/2000, has to be Plug and Play–enabled in order to be able to read those chips and
use the information contained within to configure the hardware.

After your monitor is installed correctly and set up, be sure to adjust the resolution to the
optimum setting, as recommended in Table 18.1. If you are installing a 17-inch monitor,
adjust the resolution to at least 1024×768. If you have a 19-inch monitor, set your resolution at 1024×768 or 1280×1024. If you have a 21-inch monitor, adjust the resolution to
either 1280×1024 or 1600×1200. Keep in mind these are merely suggestions for what
many experts consider the optimum settings for certain size monitors. Your own preferences may dictate a higher or lower resolution. The best judge is what feels comfortable
to you.

LCD Monitors

Another type of monitor you need to be aware of when deciding to purchase one is the
LCD monitor (see Figure 18.6).

LCD stands for liquid crystal display, and is the type of monitor you see on laptop computers. You can also purchase freestanding LCD monitors that you can attach to your
desktop PC. LCD monitors have low glare screens and consume considerably less power
than their CRT cousins (5 watts versus about 100 watts). LCD monitors excel when it
comes to color quality and are actually better than many standard monitors.

LCD monitors are still limited in size—you still don't see many larger than 15 inches
and they still cost considerably more than CRT displays. A 15-inch LCD monitor will set

you back anywhere from $800–$1000. But LCD monitors have one indisputable advantage over CRT displays—size. LCD monitors can easily be 1/10th the depth of CRT displays and weigh on average between 5 and 10 pounds.

FIGURE **18.6**

A typical LCD monitor from IBM, one of the leading manufacturers of LCD monitors.

If you've got more money than desktop real estate, then by all means go for an LCD monitor.

Summary

In the past hour you learned about selecting a new, larger monitor. You learned some of the factors you need to consider when selecting a new monitor and a few methods to test monitors before you make a purchase. Finally, you learned some tips for setting up your monitor for optimal use.

Q&A

Q What about monitors larger than 21 inches? I don't see them mentioned very much.

A There are monitors larger than 21 inches, but they mainly fall into two categories that have prevented them from being widely used. The first category is monitors larger and more costly than the current batch of 21-inch monitors. These are extremely high-resolution monitors that can adequately display 1600×1200 resolution. They are also extremely costly, usually in the range of $2500–$4000. The second category is large home-use monitors usually in the size of 28–32 inches. To keep the cost down for the home market, these monitors are usually limited in the resolution they support. Most only display a maximum of 800×600.

Q Should I consider buying an LCD monitor?

A Just like most other PC components, the price of LCD monitors has been steadily heading south and most likely this trend will continue. Price, which was once the biggest obstacle for most users is not the first factor to consider. Comparably sized (screen size, that is) LCD and CRT monitors will still have a noticeable gap in price, but not nearly so much as a year ago. The primary reason most users cite for purchasing an LCD monitor is the smaller footprint. If deskspace is a major consideration, by all means go for an LCD. They are fairly comparable in displaying text and images.

HOUR 19

Upgrading or Adding a Modem or Other Communications Device

Like larger monitors, another item formerly considered an extravagance but has long since been seen as standard equipment is the modem. Originally brought to prominence by online services such as CompuServe and AOL, the modem became indispensable with the rise in popularity of the Internet.

Modem technology used to be one of the fastest developing computer technologies and, consequently, one that seemed to demand a continuing cycle of upgrades. But with the development of 56K modems, this technology seems to have reached its technological limit over standard telephone lines.

If you're considering upgrading your modem, this hour should prove valuable to you in deciding whether to get a 56K modem or one of the other newer communications technologies.

During the this hour you will learn:

- How modems work
- Whether you want to upgrade your existing modem to one of the new 56K modems
- Whether you want to try one of the alternative digital communications technologies such as ISDN, ADSL, or cable modems

Understanding Modems

Modem is short for modulate/demodulate, which is what a modem does to send and receive data from one computer to another. Your computer stores data in digital form. But standard telephone lines transmit information as sound, which is an analog signal. The modem in your computer system converts the digital information in your computer to an analog (sound) signal and transmits the analog signal over telephone lines to another computer. The modem there converts the analog signal that your computer transmitted back into a digital form.

NEW TERM   *Analog* and *digital* are terms used quite freely and they have taken on several popular meanings. In the context of computer communications, analog refers to communicating by means of converting the signal in your computer to a measurable frequency and modulation, which happens to be sound waves. Digital refers to communicating by means of transmitting your message using a representation of the binary symbols 0 and 1 just as they are created in your PC.

Most standard modems today transmit data in the range of 28,800–56,000bps (bits per second). Don't be surprised (or disappointed) if you purchase a modem advertised to operate in this range but only get a maximum transmission speed of between 26,400bps and 50,000bps. Modem transmissions at higher speeds are largely governed by the quality of your telephone lines. Telephone lines for the most part are simply unshielded, twisted copper wire and are extremely vulnerable to interference from a variety of sources. Interference reduces the audio quality of the call you are making to your mother (whether you notice it or not), and reduces the transmission speed of your modem as well.

 Don't confuse the terms bps (bits per second) and baud rate. The confusion arose years ago when modems only transmitted at 300bps. The baud rate is the rate at which a signal between two devices changes in one second. Originally, that rate for 300bps modems was 300 times per second, which also equals 300 baud, so the terms were used interchangeably. Bits per second is the actual transmission speed of the data between modems. As modem speeds (bps) improved, it was not necessary (or in some cases possible) for the signaling change rate to keep pace. Now most modems transmit several bits per baud. If all this sounds complicated, just remember that the transmission speed of modems is described in terms of bits per second, not baud. A 28.8 modem is transmitting 28,800 bits per second, not 28,800 baud.

Selecting a Modem

Modems are available in both internal and external models. An internal modem is installed inside your PC (see Figure 19.1) and requires a slot on your motherboard. An external modem (see Figure 19.2) plugs in to one of your serial ports (via a serial cable).

FIGURE 19.1

An internal modem.

19

One question that many beginning modem users continue to ask is "What type of modem do I need to access AOL (America Online)?" The answer is simple—virtually any type of modem enables you to access AOL. AOL is designed to accommodate a wide range of PC systems and modem types, and you should be able to find a communications line ranging in speeds from 9600bps up to ISDN speeds of 128,000bps. If you are having trouble with your modem, give AOL technical support a call. That's part of what you're paying for each month.

FIGURE **19.2**

An external modem.

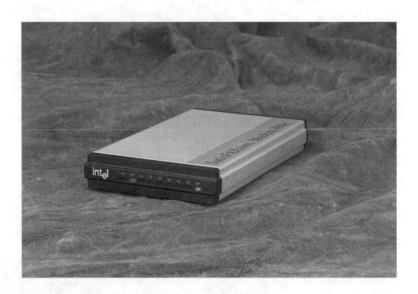

Functionally, you do not see any differences between an internal and an external modem; both operate exactly the same. When deciding which type to purchase, consider that an internal modem generally costs less than an external modem because it lacks a case and a power supply, but it takes up a slot in your PC. Both require an interrupt (IRQ) signal from your PC (the internal modem requires its own interrupt, whereas the external modem uses the interrupt signal assigned to the serial port the modem is connected to).

Again, in deciding on a brand, you might want to refer to product reviews by the popular trade magazines. Though all brands that adhere to the various international specifications for modems operate, theoretically, at the same speed, there are some differences in how certain modems handle error correction. As I mentioned earlier, modems use standard telephone lines that are subject to interference from various sources. When a transmitted signal encounters interference, the modem attempts to resend the portion of the signal that encountered the interference. Different manufacturers use different methods for detecting and correcting interference, and these methods can result in some variance in actual transmission speeds.

When you're in the market for a new modem, one of the best sources for finding up-to-date information on PC hardware components is the hardware section of CNET's com-puters.com (`http://computers.cnet.com/hardware/0-1016.html`). Besides listing just about every modem you could possibly think of, this site also does comparison reviews and allows you to compare prices on the products listed. Where applicable, this site also lists specifications on the products listed and points you to the manufacturer for more information. If you're looking for more technical information, you should also make a point of bookmarking Tom's Hardware Guide (`http://www.tomshardware.com/`).

And finally, if you select an internal modem be sure to check whether the modem needs to be inserted into an ISA or a PCI slot (see Hour 8, "Replacing Your Main System Board," for information on the differences between ISA and PCI slots). Internal modems used to all be designed for ISA slots, but in the last year or so many manufacturers have started switching to internal modems that are inserted into PCI slots. This is mainly because many motherboard manufacturers have started to reduce the number of ISA slots installed on motherboards on their way to total elimination of ISA slots and boards.

Installing Your Modem

The only difference in installing an internal modem and installing an external modem is what you do with the hardware. The software you need to install with your modem—the modem hardware driver and the communications software you plan to use with your modem—is exactly the same.

Installing an Internal Modem

Installing an internal modem is fairly simple because all you have to do is insert the modem into one of your available motherboard slots and then configure your PC or operating system to recognize the modem.

If you are running Windows 95/98/2000 on your PC, make sure any internal modem you purchase is designated Plug and Play (PnP). Plug and Play is a feature Windows 95/98/2000 uses, which enables the operating system to automatically detect and configure your modem to work with your PC. Plug and Play is not available in Windows 3.1 or Windows NT 4.0.

19

To Do: Installing an Internal Modem

To install an internal modem, do the following:

▼ To Do

1. Read the documentation that accompanies your modem thoroughly before you begin to install the modem. Check the documentation for your modem to determine whether there is a certain communications port (COM1, COM2, and so on) that your modem prefers to use. Check also to see if there are any switches or jumpers you need to set for the communications port you will be using. If you have jumpers on your modem, they are used to set your modem to use one of your two main serial ports, COM1 or COM2. If you are running Windows 95/98/2000 and your modem is Plug and Play, you can skip this step. If you have to set your modem by setting a jumper, make sure you are not setting your modem to use a serial port

▼ that is being used by another device, such as a serial mouse. This will create a device conflict and neither device will function properly. You can check this using SysChk (see Hour 3, "Examining Your PC's System Configuration," for information about using SysChk).

> **NEW TERM** *Communications ports* are connection points your computer uses for communicating with some peripheral devices. Most computers have two basic types of communications ports: serial and parallel. The major difference between the two types of ports is in how they communicate. A parallel port transmits data eight bits at a time. A serial port communicates data one bit at a time. Your computer typically uses parallel ports to communicate with printers. Serial ports are used primarily for communicating with modems (and other serial devices) and are often referred to as COM (short for communications) ports. Your computer is designed to operate with two main serial ports, COM1 and COM2, but can be configured to have more.

2. Turn off your PC, unplug the cord from the wall or power supply, ground yourself to prevent static electric discharges, remove the cover, and insert your modem into an empty slot (see Figure 19.3).

FIGURE 19.3

Inserting an internal modem in your PC.

3. Follow the instructions for installing any additional software that came with your modem. Make sure you follow the instructions specifically for the operating system you are running (DOS/Windows 3.1, Windows 95/98/2000, Windows NT 4.0, and so on).
▼

▼
▲
 4. Make a note of which communications port you use in installing your modem. You
    need this information when you install the communications software you intend to
    use with your modem.

Installing an External Modem

External modems are even easier to install than internal modems.

To Do: Installing an External Modem

To install an external modem, follow these steps:

1. Turn off your PC.

2. Plug one end of your serial cable into an unused serial port on the back of your PC
   and one end into the serial connector on your modem.

3. Turn on your modem and then your PC.

4. Follow the instructions for installing any additional software driver that came with
   your modem for the operating system you are running (for example,
   DOS/Windows 3.1, Windows 95/98/2000, or Windows NT 4.0).

5. Make note of the communications port used by your modem when you install the
   modem driver. You need this information when you install the communications
   software you intend to use with your modem.

What About Those 56K Modems?

In the last few years, 56KB (56,000bps) modems have been getting a lot of press coverage, and you are probably wondering if you should upgrade your current modem to one
of the newer 56KB modems. It depends on how fast you are communicating now. If you
use your existing modem to communicate over the Internet, you are probably eager to get
any additional boost in speed; however, upgrading from a 33.6KB to a 56KB modem
may not buy you as much of an increase in speed as you are expecting.

56KB modems communicate over the same phone lines as the modem you are currently
using, which means that if you are experiencing any degree of interference with your
existing modem, the interference problem only gets worse because a 56KB modem is
more sensitive and susceptible to any transmission line interference. For example, if you
are currently using a 33.6KB modem but you almost always connect at 28.8KB or
slower, you will most likely connect at speeds far slower than 56KB with a 56KB
modem. Another fact you need to be aware of is that in all product testing reviews I have
read by the major trade journals, I have never read one where a 56KB modem was tested
and achieved transmission speeds of 56KB. Most of the test reports stated transmission
speeds of around 36–44KB, and this was only in one direction.

19

If you read the small print on the boxes of all 56KB modems, you see that 56KB transmission speeds are (theoretically) attainable only when downloading information from a host computer. When uploading, or transmitting data to a host computer, the transmission speed is only (theoretically) 33.6KB.

Another problem you may encounter is that you may accidentally purchase a 56KB modem that is not following the international standard for 56KB modems. Originally, there were two competing technologies and no real standard for 56KB modems. In early 1998, however, a standard was finally worked out (v.90 is the designation of the 56K modem standard). Just make sure you don't accidentally purchase an older modem that was manufactured before the standard was created. Make sure the modem you purchase says that it meets the 56KB (v.90) standard. Also, if you have a 56KB modem, you can only communicate at 56KB speeds (theoretically) with another computer that also has a 56KB modem. If you are planning to purchase a 56KB modem in order to connect to the Internet at higher speeds, make sure your Internet service provider also has communications lines configured at 56KB.

Alternatives to Standard Modems

One of the problems mentioned earlier with modems is that they transmit an analog signal (sound) over standard phone lines and are subject to interference, which results in a degradation of signal and transmission speed. Alternatives to modems and analog signals do exist. For example, you can get fully digital communications lines, which are not subject to interference and signal degradation. If you decide you want to investigate digital communications lines you should start by checking with your local Baby Bell or your cable TV provider to see if they are providing digital service.

ISDN

A technology that has been around for a lot longer than 56KB modems, but continues to receive far less press coverage, is *ISDN*.

NEW TERM   *ISDN* stands for *Integrated Services Digital Network* and is a way of getting reliable communications speeds above 33.6KB using digital telephone lines, instead of the analog lines used for typical phone communication and standard modems. For connecting to the Internet at speeds of either 64KB or 128KB in both directions with the host computer, ISDN gets you the most bang for your buck right now because it is now almost universally available in the U.S.

On the plus side, ISDN works over digital telephone lines instead of your standard analog, voice-grade lines, which means they are not susceptible to interference like analog lines. Being digital means that, on an ISDN line, you will always get speeds of 64KB (or 128KB), in both directions!

On the minus side, however, ISDN has a lot that has kept it from being widely embraced. For starters, you need to have a special ISDN communications line installed. The actual line is the same copper wire the phone company uses for standard telephone lines, but it is connected differently at your end and at the phone company switching office. Prices for ISDN have been steadily coming down over the past few years, but prices still vary around the country and can be expensive for installation and monthly service. You can expect to pay anywhere in the range of about $50–$250 for installation of your line. Monthly charges also vary considerably. Some Baby Bells charge you a flat monthly rate; some offer you a tiered system of varying flat rate for a certain maximum number of hours; and some simply charge you by the minute for actual usage. ISDN is now mostly available from the Baby Bells because most other ISPs that provide digital service are opting for DSL or cable modems.

You also need a special ISDN interface, either an internal card or an external device, to access your ISDN line.

ISDN interface cards and devices are often incorrectly called ISDN modems, but they are not true modems because they do not convert a signal from digital to analog (or vice versa) as modems do.

19

ISDN interface cards and devices have also been dropping in price and currently range between $100 and $300. If you have an empty slot, it is best to get the internal interface card. The internal ISDN devices are cheaper because the external devices need a case or power supply, and internal ISDN devices attain a slightly faster speed than the external devices. The external ISDN device plugs into a serial port (the same as an external modem), but standard serial ports can only achieve speeds of 115KB, which means your ISDN device can only achieve speeds of 115KB rather than 128KB.

ISDN has been extremely popular in small offices because at speeds of 128KB, ISDN connections make it possible to provide Internet connections to multiple users simultaneously. For small offices, ISDN devices are combined with devices used to form small networks.

ADSL

ADSL is another digital service that has been getting a lot of press in the last year or so. ADSL stands for Asymmetrical Digital Subscriber Line and is a digital technology providing up to 7.1Mbps of transmission speed from the host computer to your computer and 64Kbps of speed from your computer to the host. Like ISDN, ADSL is a digital signal that is not subject to line noise or interference, which means you always have a transmission signal operating at 7.1Mbps (downstream) and 64Kbps (upstream).

Throughout most of this country, ADSL is still in the trial stage and thus not widely available. My phone service provider, Bell Atlantic, is still providing spotty ADSL coverage in its service area, but at least it is here.

ADSL works over your existing phone lines but requires some additional hardware. The first device you need is called the ADSL Terminal Unit-Remote (ATU-R). You also need an Ethernet network interface card installed in your PC to connect to the ATU-R. There is also a distance limitation to connecting ADSL to your home. You must live within about 12,000 feet (about 2 miles) of your local telephone switching office (the distance limitation for ISDN is about 3 miles).

On the plus side, besides the tremendous increase in transmission speeds, ADSL is always on. Your computer never needs to dial, which also means you should never encounter a busy signal. This dedicated access also means that communications over the Internet are more secure than they are over a service such as a cable modem, which is a shared system, the same as your cable TV service. ADSL is also split at your home, which enables you to use your regular phone when your computer is connected to the Internet.

Because ADSL is being driven largely by the local Baby Bells and because they are also learning (hopefully) from the mistakes they made with ISDN, ADSL looks, for now, like it stands a good chance of becoming the next communications medium of choice.

Cable Modems

Cable modems are an attempt by the cable TV industry to cash in on the phenomenal popularity of the Internet. The cable modem system is a shared system operating at a reported 10Mbps. If you work on a networked computer at work that is connected to the Internet, you are already familiar with the downside of a shared system. Regardless of how fast the transmission is, you are sharing it with other users, which means your communications begin to slow down as more people simultaneously log in to the system.

Another downside to widespread usage of cable modem systems is that they are designed to work over existing cable TV systems. The trouble is that those systems are designed as one-way systems—the signal is only supposed to be transmitted to your home, not back to the cable office. Converting these one-way systems to bi-directional is reportedly a monumental expense, and many cable operators are still deciding whether it will be worth it. This is the main reason, apparently, why the spread of cable modems is progressing so slowly.

Summary

In the past hour you learned how modems work, some information you need to make a selection on an upgrade modem, and whether you want to upgrade to a 56KB modem. You also learned about some of the digital communications alternatives to analog modems, such as ISDN, ADSL, and cable modems.

Q&A

Q How can 56KB modems be sold as 56KB modems if they cannot achieve 56Kbps transmission speeds?

A As the technology was being developed the design engineers did achieve speeds of 56Kbps, but these were under laboratory conditions—that is, pristine copper wires, absolutely no line interference, and so on. Unfortunately, the real world does not work that way, and in the real world, we have interference, line noise, and 30–40-year-old copper wires still being used by the phone companies. In other words, they developed the technology under conditions that don't exist in the real world.

Q Which is better, ADSL or cable modems?

A Both have their pluses and minuses. Cable modems are generally cheaper and don't have the distance limitations of ADSL. ADSL, on the other hand, offers you a connection line that isn't being shared by your neighbors and is generally more secure. If you have the choice and the cost of ADSL won't break your budget, you may be happier with ADSL.

19

Hour **20**

Upgrading or Adding a Sound System to Your PC

Computers aren't just for crunching numbers and composing text. In the last few years, large high-resolution monitors, CD-ROM and DVD drives, and digital sound systems have literally brought a multimedia explosion to PCs. Even the once conservative and staid Internet is now buzzing with dazzling animation, graphics, and thundering digital audio.

Although most of the emphasis in multimedia has been placed on animation and dazzling graphics, sound and digital audio have been steadily making inroads into the multimedia paradigm. Back in Hour 17, "Upgrading Your Video Card," you learned that the gaming industry is largely responsible for many of the advancements seen in video cards because of the demands placed on the hardware by advanced 3D graphics. Well, the computer gaming industry has also been partly responsible for the advancements in multimedia audio. Just as games have placed demands on PC video systems, they have also placed demands on your PC's audio system. Another reason some have added audio to their PCs is the proliferation of MP3 files.

But enough about what led to the advancements in PC audio; we're here to discuss what you need to do to get the best, or at least better, audio from your system.

During this hour you will learn:

- How to select a sound card for your computer
- How to select a speaker system to accompany your sound card
- How to install your sound system in your PC
- How to connect and use your home stereo as your computer's sound system

Your PC's Current Sound System

Most PCs sold today still go mainly to large corporations for general business use. Although they are potentially capable of producing a multimedia frenzy of vivid graphics, dazzling animation, and thundering sound, the vast majority of these computers are sadly lacking many of the key multimedia ingredients, especially a decent sound system.

Most PCs sold today have (ugh!) a sound system no better than what was originally placed into the original IBM PCs sold back in 1981. Look inside your PC and you'll likely see a pitiful 5.5 cm speaker, which is barely capable of producing a few odd beeps and chirps. In addition, most PCs also lack any type of hardware or circuitry enabling them to process high-quality digital audio. Don't be too quick, however, to criticize the continuing pitiful state of PC sound. The vast majority of software created for the PC in the past 18 years has made few demands on a PC's sound system.

 Two buzzwords you've probably heard in the same breath with multimedia are MMX and DirectX. MMX stands for Multi Media eXtensions, and is the term coined by Intel to describe the multimedia functions included in some of its Pentium-class processors. The MMX instructions are designed to enable faster processing of sound and graphics, and thus produce a richer multimedia experience. DirectX is a series of technologies licensed by Microsoft and incorporated in Windows 95/98/NT/ and 2000 that allow for a more robust display of graphics, 3D animation, and sound. Although designed primarily for games, we are starting to see some of these technologies incorporated into Web designs and presentation business applications.

If you did not purchase a multimedia-equipped PC, don't despair. You do not have to settle for the pipsqueak audibles now emanating from your PC. By the end of this lesson, you will have all the information you need to turn your PC into a big, mean sound machine that will do justice to Carnegie Hall.

Selecting a Sound Card for Your PC

Sound card usage basically falls into one of two categories—using your sound card to listen to prerecorded audio in the form of games and CDs and using your sound card with additional equipment for creating computer-generated audio or music. The vast majority of users fall into the first category, which is the one we concentrate on in this hour.

If the most you plan to do with your audio is listen to music and sound that someone else has recorded, such as audio tracks on games and educational CD-ROMs or the occasional Duke Ellington music CD, you need to understand that most of the audio computer world is "SoundBlaster-compatible" (see Figure 20.1).

FIGURE 20.1

SoundBlaster is the number one selling sound card for PCs.

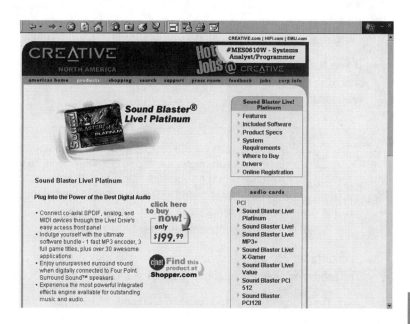

You don't really need a sound card that is SoundBlaster-compatible to listen to music CDs. In fact, you don't even need a sound card of any type in your PC to listen to music CDs. Virtually all CD-ROM players today include a headphone jack into which you can plug a set of headphones and listen contentedly for hours. If you want to hear booming bass drums, however, you likely want to channel your audio through a sound card and out to a good set of speakers, and for this, any sound will card suffice.

20

SoundBlaster sound cards currently have the lion's share of the computer audio market, a dominance that largely grew out of its early adoption by the computer gaming industry as its (so-called) standard and the SoundBlaster's early compatibility with the AdLib (a pre-SoundBlaster model) sound card.

Some of the earliest 8-bit SoundBlaster sound cards weren't really good for much except games, which really wasn't a problem for most computer users because games comprised better than 90 percent of all software with any type of sound or audio track. Today, however, SoundBlaster 64-bit sound cards are considered by some to be near the top of the line for both games and serious music composition using *MIDI* devices and electronic synthesizers.

New Term　*MIDI (Musical Instrument Digital Interface)* is an interface and a file format that enables you to connect a musical instrument to a computer and store musical instrument data. This data can then be enhanced, edited, and played back.

If you purchase a SoundBlaster sound card, or any model compatible sound card, you should not have any trouble playing any type of computer audio file or software that you encounter.

> Just remember the old computer maxim: "Compatibility is in the eyes of the beholder." Although some sound cards may claim to be SoundBlaster-compatible, there is no absolute guarantee. If you want to ensure 100% SoundBlaster compatibility, make sure you purchase a genuine SoundBlaster sound card.

SoundBlaster compatibility, however, is not the only prerequisite for a good sound card. The following are a couple other features you might want to look for in a sound card:

- If you're interested in creating MIDI audio files, make sure that your sound card has several megabytes of onboard memory and can be expanded.

- For improved sound quality in many of the newer games, make sure that your card provides support for the Microsoft Windows API DirectX including DirectSound.

When you're in the market for a sound card, one of the best sources for finding up-to-date information on PC hardware components is the hardware section of CNET's computers.com (`http://computers.cnet.com/hardware/0-1016.html`). Besides listing just about every sound card you could possibly think of, this site also does comparison reviews and allows you to compare prices on the products listed. Where applicable, this site also lists specifications on the products listed and points you to the manufacturer for more information. If you're looking for more technical information, you should also make a point of bookmarking Tom's Hardware Guide (`http://www.tomshardware.com/`).

Selecting Speakers

Selecting speakers is largely a matter of what your budget can afford. In general, the old saying that "you get what you pay for" applies to speakers. Your selection of speakers is not limited to companies that only produce speakers for the computer industry. The demand for higher quality audio has tempted several of the traditional stereo speaker makers to produce models specifically for computers. Companies such as

- Sony (`http://www.ita.sel.sony.com/products/av/`)
- Cambridge SoundWorks (`http://www.cambridgesoundworks.com/`)
- Aura Systems (`http://www.aurasystems.com/`)
- Bose (`http://www.bose.com/`)

These companies are now producing top quality speakers for computers along with companies such as

- Altec Lansing (`http://www.altecmm.com/`)
- Labtec (`http://www.labtec.com/`)
- Benwin (`http://www.benwin.com/noflashsplash2.html`)

Just make certain you purchase amplified speakers designed for use with computers, because these speakers are shielded to prevent the magnetic coils in the speakers from causing distortion or damaging your monitor if you choose to place the speakers next to your monitor.

Most computer stores that sell speakers usually have some sort of display enabling you to compare one model against another. Before you purchase, try to decide what type of audio you will be listening to. Will you mostly be playing games with your PC, or will you mostly use your sound card and speakers to listen to relaxing music CDs while you work? Having an idea of the type of audio for which your speakers will be used can help you decide how much you want to spend on speakers.

20

Although speakers have traditionally been sold in pairs, one on each stereo channel, the configuration that seems to be growing in popularity now is a pair of speakers with a third speaker operating as a subwoofer, which produces deeper, richer bass tones.

A good set of PC speakers can usually be purchased for between $100 and $200, but if you're interested in top-quality audio for your PC's sound system, high-end speakers can set you back between $500 and $700.

Some manufacturers are also making speakers that plug in to your USB port. If you are using an operating system that supports USB, such as Windows 98 or 2000, consider this another factor in your selection of speakers.

Installing a Sound Card and Speakers

Very little setup is involved to install a sound card in your PC. The sound card comes preconfigured with default settings, which work well in most PCs. If your sound card does not work after you complete the installation, there is a chance that one of the settings is conflicting with another device in your PC that is already using that setting. The most common problem is your sound card default settings using the same interrupt request (IRQ) that another device in your PC is already using. If this is the case, simply follow the instructions that accompany your sound card for changing the interrupt request used by the sound card. Usually, changing an interrupt on a sound card is accomplished by running a Setup program for the sound card. (See Hour 3, "Examining Your PC's System Configuration," for more information on your IRQ settings.) Check also to see whether your sound card needs to use a specific interrupt.

To Do: Installing Your Sound Card

To install a sound card in your PC, take the following steps:

1. Read all the installation instructions that came with your sound card. In addition to instructions for installation, you often see cautions or warnings about potential problems that other users may have encountered. Make sure you also familiarize yourself with the various connectors on your sound card. Look for microphone connectors, line-out connectors for speakers, line-in connectors for auxiliary sound devices such as CD players, and joystick or MIDI connectors (see Figure 20.2).

2. Turn off and unplug your PC. Ground yourself and then remove the cover.

3. Locate a vacant slot on your motherboard where you can install the sound card.

4. Insert the sound card into the slot (see Figure 20.3).

5. If you have a CD-ROM drive installed in your PC, attach the audio cable from the audio connector on the sound card to the audio connector on the back of the CD-ROM drive (see Figure 20.4). You may have to remove your CD-ROM drive to access the audio connector. If you don't have an audio cable (see Figure 20.5), you can pick up one from your local computer store for under $10. Make sure you

▼   write down the model of the CD-ROM drive you have installed and the type of
         sound card you just installed.

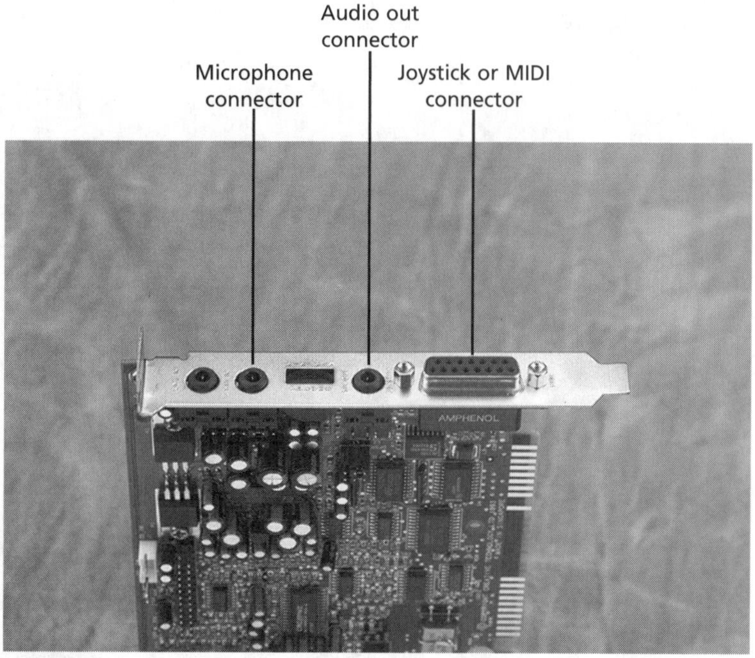

FIGURE 20.2

The connectors typically found on most sound cards.

Microphone connector

Audio out connector

Joystick or MIDI connector

FIGURE 20.3

Inserting your sound card into an available slot on your motherboard.

20

▼

▼

FIGURE 20.4

The rear connectors on a CD-ROM drive showing the audio connector for your sound card.

40-pin IDE interface

4-pin power connector

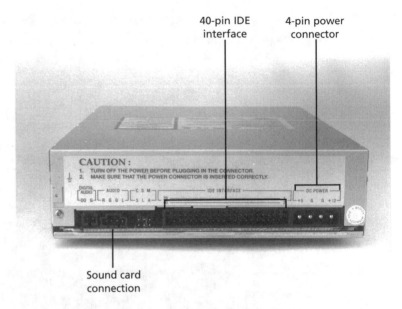

Sound card connection

FIGURE 20.5

A variety of audio cables used for connecting a CD-ROM drive to a sound card.

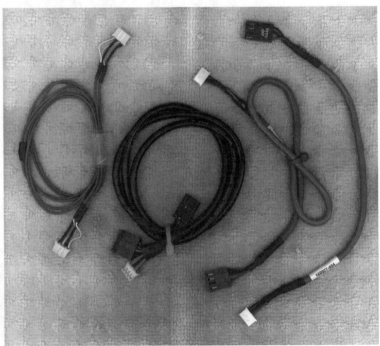

▼

▼   6. Replace your PC's cover and turn on your PC.

7. Depending on which operating system you are using on your PC, you have to run the appropriate software to configure your operating system to recognize your new sound card and to load the audio drivers. If you are running Windows 95/98/2000 and your new sound card is designed as Plug and Play, Windows 95/98/2000 should automatically recognize your sound card and begin the configuration process for you. If this happens, just follow the onscreen prompts to complete the

▲   configuration. Make sure you have your Windows 95/98/2000 disks or CD and the drivers' disks accompanying your sound card.

When you complete the configuration process, the configuration software should include a procedure to test your newly installed sound card. Make sure that your speakers are plugged into the correct connector (labeled "audio out" or "speakers" on the back of your sound card) and that they are turned on. If the audio test fails, review the instructions for your sound card, and make sure you followed each step correctly. If you still haven't found the cause of the problem, rerun the PC checklist program from the SysChk in Hour 3 to check your interrupt settings to make sure your sound card is not in conflict with another device in your PC. After you have uncovered and resolved the problem, retest your sound card and enjoy the new dimension you've just added to your PC.

If you have a CD-ROM drive installed in your PC and you connected the audio cable from your CD-ROM drive to your sound card, you might want to also try playing an audio CD in your drive. Check the software that accompanied your sound card to see whether it includes a CD player program. If it does not, you can use the Windows media player to play audio CDs.

Connecting Your Sound Card to Your Stereo

If you have your PC set up in the same room where you have your home stereo set up, it is possible to use your sound card with your stereo system. All you need is a cable connecting your sound card to your stereo amplifier or receiver. One end of the cable plugs into the same output connector on your sound card you would normally use for your speakers and the other end plugs into an auxiliary input jack on your stereo amplifier or receiver.

The cable you need to purchase is carried by most good electronics stores and can be purchased for between $5 and $10. (Figure 20.6 shows the type of cable you need to purchase.) It has two RCA-type plugs on one end, which connect into the left and right input connectors on your stereo, and the cable has what is called a miniature stereo plug on the other end, which plugs into your sound card.

20

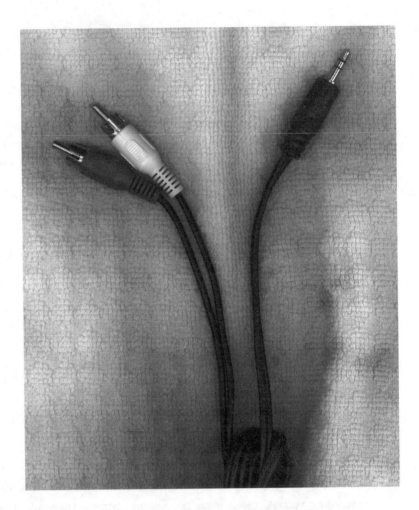

To Do: Connecting Your Sound Card to Your Home Stereo

Connecting your sound card to your home stereo is simply a matter of connecting a cable. To connect the two, do the following:

1. Purchase the cable described earlier in this section. Try to purchase a cable that is long enough to reach from your sound card to your stereo but that does not have too much slack. The cables usually come in lengths of 3, 6, 10, and 20 feet. If the distance from your sound card to your stereo is 7 feet, don't purchase a cable 20 feet in length because audio signals diminish as cable lengths increase.

2. Plug the miniature stereo plug into your sound card. Plug the cable into the connector used for speakers.

▼   3. Make sure your stereo is turned off. Plug the two RCA-type plugs into a spare auxiliary input connector on your stereo. It does not matter which plug you plug into the left jack or the right jack.

   4. Make sure the volume control is turned down on your stereo. Turn your stereo on again, and using your stereo controls, select the auxiliary input source to which you connected your sound card.

   5. Generate some type of audio on your PC (for example, start a game or play a music CD in your CD-ROM drive) and adjust the volume on your stereo to your
▲   liking.

Precautions When Using Your Stereo

You need to be aware of only two precautions when using your stereo with your PC sound card:

- Be careful when adjusting the volume levels; it is very easy to blast the room you're in if you are not careful.

- Make sure your speakers are not placed close to your PC monitor because stereo speakers typically are not shielded to prevent magnetic interference, which is generated by the speakers and can potentially damage your monitor.

If you exercise these two cautions, you can safely play your sound card through your home stereo.

Summary

In this hour, you learned how to select and install a sound card into your PC. You also learned about selecting and installing speakers to accompany your sound card and how to use your home stereo with your sound card in place of speakers.

Q&A

20

Q I was listening to a MIDI file the other day and it sounded okay but did not sound like real musical instruments. Why?

A Unlike waveform (WAV) files, MIDI files are digital representations of sound events, not actual recordings of sound. MIDI sound events are played back through a MIDI synthesizer, so what you are hearing is an electronic synthesized version of the music, not a digital recording of the music. This is another reason why MIDI files of entire songs are so much smaller than waveform files of the same musical score.

Q What about listening to MP3 files? How will they sound?

A Even though there is a slight degradation in quality because of the way the files are compressed, many users cannot tell the difference between MP3 audio and audio CDs. MP3 files sound virtually identical to the original source and do not have that "electronic synthesized" quality of MIDI files.

HOUR **21**

Selecting and Installing a Printer

One of the basic peripherals for a PC still remains a difficult installation task for many users. Desktop printers have been around as long as PCs and still connect to PCs pretty much the same as they did back in 1981.

As you will soon see, connecting your printer, or even a second printer, to your PC is not rocket science, and neither is connecting a second printer to your PC, so you can choose to print to either device.

In this hour you will learn:

- Some tips and advice on selecting a printer
- How to install a printer to work on your PC whether you are using Windows 3.1, Windows 95/98, NT, or 2000
- How to install a second printer to work with your PC
- How to set up your PC to select between two printers

Understanding the Types of Printers

All printers fall into one of two broad categories: impact or nonimpact printers. *Impact* printers employ some type of mechanical process to form characters or images by physically striking (or impacting) paper or some other printable medium. Some examples of impact printers are

- Dot-matrix printers
- Daisy-wheel printers

Nonimpact printers use a nonphysical (or nonimpact) process to transfer characters or an image to paper. Some examples of nonimpact printers are

- Laser printers
- Inkjet printers
- Thermal printers

A few years ago, dot-matrix printers reigned supreme due primarily to their speed and the fact that they were relatively inexpensive. Some of the better quality dot-matrix printers could also produce a relatively high-quality text, what was then called near letter-quality text.

Today, however, dot-matrix printers have declined significantly in popularity and have practically gone the way of the dodo now that laser and inkjet printers have dropped dramatically in price and have made true typeset-quality and color text affordable to the masses.

How to Select a Printer

For many users, price is ultimately the deciding factor in choosing between a laser and an inkjet printer. Laser printers (see Figure 21.1) are still slightly more expensive to purchase but cheaper to operate than their inkjet counterparts. By cheaper I mean that the average per-page cost is lower. Keep in mind also that, among laser printers, the average cost per page can vary significantly due to the differences in laser printer toner cartridge prices.

Inkjet printers (see Figure 21.2) are less expensive but still command a higher per-page cost to operate. Laser printers still average about one-half cent per page, whereas inkjet printers can range anywhere from about 2–10 cents per page depending on whether you are printing in monochrome or in color. It doesn't sound like much initially, until you begin to multiply these costs by several hundred or several thousand pages.

FIGURE 21.1

A typical desktop laser printer.

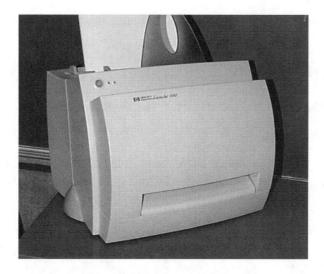

FIGURE 21.2

A typical desktop inkjet printer.

Price, however, should be only one of several factors you use in deciding what type of printer is best for your needs. In addition to price, other factors you should consider before purchasing a printer are

- Print speed
- Print quality
- Color versus monochrome
- Availability of printer drivers

21

- Demand you plan to place on your printer—that is, the number of pages you think you will print each month
- The versatility of the printer. Some manufacturers combine printers, scanners, copiers, and fax machines in one complete package.

Comparing Various Printer Models

One of best places to begin looking when you want to start comparing printer features is the Computers.com site run by CNET at `http://computers.cnet.com/hardware/0-1016.html`. CNET maintains a fairly up-to-date listing of available printer models and will periodically review printers for you and make suggestions in various categories (see Figure 21.3).

FIGURE 21.3

CNET comparison categories for its reviewed printers.

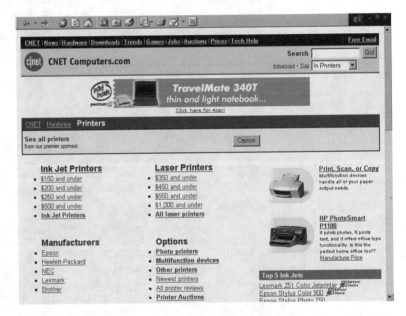

You might also consider going directly to some of the major printer manufacturers' sites for more detailed information once you have narrowed down your choices. Here are a few sites to consider:

- **Hewlett Packard**—`http://www.pandi.hp.com/pandi-db/home_page.show`
- **Epson**—`http://www.epson.com/printer/`
- **Brother**—`http://www.brother.com/us-printer/pdinfo-us.html`
- **Lexmark**—`http://www.lexmark.com/`
- **Kyocera**—`http://www.kyocera.com/KEI/printers/index.htm`

- **Tektronics**—http://www.tek.com/Color_Printers/
- **Okidata**—http://www.oki.com/english/Home.html

Print Speed

Laser printers still lead the race over the inkjet printers when it comes to churning out a large number of pages per minute, but the inkjet is rapidly closing the speed gap. Most personal laser printers print in the 6–8 ppm (pages per minute) range, whereas many inkjet printers can print monochrome text (one color text, usually black) in the 4–6 ppm range.

Print Quality

Print quality is measured in resolution, similar to video resolution. You remember from Hour 17, "Upgrading Your Video Card," that video resolution is measured by pixels (picture elements) on the entire screen measured horizontally and vertically (for example, 640×480 or 800×600). Printer resolution is also measured horizontally and vertically, but instead of the entire screen or page, the resolution is measured within a one-inch (1×1 inch) square. Instead of pixels, printer resolution is measured in dots per inch (abbreviated dpi). For example, most laser printers now print at a resolution of 600×600 (or 1200×1200) dpi.

> The dots-per-inch resolution of a printer should be described using both the horizontal and vertical measurements (600×600 dpi), but often, if the measurements are the same, the description is shortened. For example, a resolution of 300×300 dpi is shortened to simply 300 dpi. Therefore, when you see the common resolution of 600 dpi, you know that the resolution is in fact 600×600 dpi.

Although most laser printers seem to have standardized on a resolution of 600×600 dpi, in contrast, inkjet printers run the gamut from about 600×300 dpi to 720×1440 dpi. When printing text, laser printers seem to still have a slight edge over inkjet printers. However, when printing graphic images, many inkjet printers can produce much higher quality printouts than laser printers.

If you use dpi as one of your determining factors in choosing a printer, consider these suggestions:

- When printing text such as letters or manuscripts, 300 dpi is adequate. Most users are not able to distinguish between text printed at 300 dpi and text printed at 600 dpi.

21

- When printing graphics, however, higher resolution almost always means higher quality output. Most users are able to distinguish between a graphic image printed at 300 dpi and the same image printed at 600 dpi.

Color Versus Monochrome

In deciding between color versus monochrome, the decision is usually much simpler to make. If you need to print in color, you purchase an inkjet. If you are satisfied with printing only in black and white, get a laser printer.

> Color laser printers are available, but unfortunately, they are still in the $2,000–$3,000 and up price range. Most users who require color still opt for inkjet printers, which can produce output at nearly the quality of color laser printers, and at a fraction of the cost.

Keep in mind that with an inkjet printer you can also choose to print in just black and white. Many inkjet printer users produce draft copies of their output in black and white and print the final output in color.

Availability of Printer Drivers

Most printer manufacturers are targeting Windows 95 and 98 users. If you are running Windows 95 or 98, you should not have a problem getting nearly any laser or inkjet printer on the market to work with your PC. Many manufacturers are also still producing drivers for use with Windows 3.1, and a significant number are also producing drivers for Windows NT/2000. What this means is that the operating system you use should not present a problem for you with the majority of mainstream printers. If for some reason, however, you need to purchase a highly specialized printer for a specific type of print job, be sure to check first on the availability of printer drivers.

Installing Your Printer to Work with Your PC

Printers are among the easiest peripherals to install, especially if you are running Windows 95, 98, or 2000, because either of these versions of Windows will practically install the printer for you. Most printers today are designed to connect to your PC via the parallel port, so basically all you need to connect your PC and printer is a standard *Centronics parallel cable*.

A *Centronics parallel cable* is a simple communications cable with a 36-pin Centronics connector on one end and a 25-pin female connector on the other.

You can purchase a Centronics parallel cable in most computer stores in lengths ranging from 6 to 15 feet. And don't believe that myth about parallel cables having to be less than 10 feet in length. If you need a 15-foot cable, go ahead and purchase one. Many stores now carry printer cables in lengths of 25 feet and longer.

Connecting the Hardware

Connecting your printer is basically a two step process. The first step is connecting the hardware, and the second step is installing the correct printer driver.

To Do: Connecting a Printer to Your PC

The following is what you need to do to connect a printer to your PC:

1. Unpack and set up your printer according to the manufacturer's instructions. Be sure to carefully remove all the packing materials and restraints.

2. Plug the 36-pin Centronics connector of your parallel cable into the parallel port on your printer (see Figure 21.4).

FIGURE 21.4
The Centronics parallel port on a printer.

3. Plug the other end of your printer cable (the end with the 25-pin female connector) into the parallel port on the back of your PC. If you're not sure which port is the parallel port, refer to Hour 2, "Understanding the Components in Your PC."

4. Turn on your PC and your printer.

21

Installing Your Printer Driver

The second part of installing your printer, the installation of the printer *driver*, varies depending on which operating system you are using—Windows 3.1, Windows 95/98, or Windows NT/2000.

 NEW TERM Before you can use your printer, you need to install the appropriate printer *driver*. A printer driver is simply a small program that enables your PC to communicate with your printer.

If you are running Windows 3.1, follow the instructions accompanying your printer to install your printer driver. In most cases, you simply need to insert your printer driver disk, run the installation program, and follow the instructions and prompts on the screen. Make sure you have your Windows 3.1 installation disks handy.

If you are running Windows 95, 98, NT, or 2000, the installation of your printer driver begins as soon as you restart the operating system, provided your printer is designed as a Plug and Play peripheral. Just about all printers made in the last 2–3 years are Plug and Play. Simply follow the onscreen prompts and insert the printer driver disk when instructed.

To Do: Installing a Printer Driver Under Windows 95/98/2000

Windows 95,98, and 2000 begin installing your printer driver as soon as they are restarted, but if they don't, follow these steps to start the driver installation:

1. Select Start to open the Start menu.
2. Select Settings and then Printers to open the Windows 95/98/2000 Printer Control section (see Figure 21.5).

FIGURE 21.5
The Printer Control section under Windows 98.

3. Double-click Add Printer to start the Add Printer Wizard (see Figure 21.6) and follow the prompts to install your printer driver.

FIGURE 21.6

The Windows 98 Add Printer Wizard used for installing printer drivers.

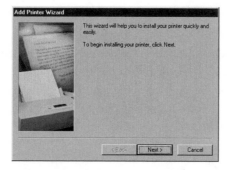

Installing a Printer Driver Under Windows NT

Installing a printer driver under Windows NT is very similar to installing the printer driver under Windows 95/98. But, unlike Windows 95, 98, or 2000, Windows NT does not automatically recognize Plug and Play peripherals, so you need to perform the same steps to manually start the NT Add Printer Wizard (see Figure 21.7) from the Start menu. Also, because of Windows NT's added security features, you need an account on the local PC that has administrative access rights in order to install the printer driver.

FIGURE 21.7

Installing a printer under Windows NT.

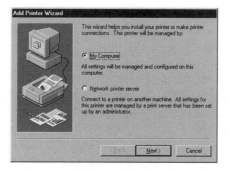

Installing a Second Printer to Work with Your PC

So far, we have discussed how to install only one printer to your PC. Now, what if you have one PC but need to connect two printers? It's not uncommon for many users to have both a laser and an inkjet printer. The remaining section of this chapter explains how you can connect both to your PC.

You can connect two printers to your PC in the following three ways:

- You can set up the second printer next to the first printer and switch the printer cable from one printer to the other.

21

- You can purchase and install a second parallel port in your PC and connect the second printer to this second port using a second printer cable.
- You can purchase a hardware device called an A/B switch and use it to switch the communication signal from one printer to the other.
- If your second printer and your PC both have USB ports and you are using Windows 98 or 2000, you can connect one printer to the parallel port and one printer to the USB port.

Years ago you could connect one printer to the parallel port and the other printer to your serial port. This option is not usually possible nowadays because very few printers are now equipped with a serial interface.

Method One: Switching the Cable

To connect two printers to one PC, switching the printer cable is the easiest but not necessarily the most convenient way to connect your two printers. You need to install printer drivers for both printers, and when you want to switch from one printer to the other, you simply unplug the cable from the back of one printer and plug the cable into the parallel port of the other printer. You don't have to turn the printers on and off and you don't even have to reboot your PC.

Regardless of which of the three possible solutions you choose, remember that you need to select the appropriate driver in Windows for the printer you are attempting to use. In most Windows applications, you can select a different printer driver from the Print dialog box.

Method Two: Installing a Second Parallel Port

Installing a second parallel port in your PC for a second printer is perhaps the most convenient of the three solutions. A second parallel port can be purchased on an interface card from most computer stores for $35 or less and installed in less than 10 minutes.

The interface you purchase for your second parallel port might contain one or two serial ports as well. To prevent any possible conflicts with your existing serial ports, simply follow the instructions with the card to disable the two serial ports.

If you purchase a second parallel port, you need to check a few settings on the interface card before you install it in your PC. First, make sure that the parallel port on the interface card is set to function as LPT2 and not set to function as LPT1. The parallel port in your PC is set to function as LPT1 by default. If both ports are set to LPT1, the two ports create a conflict and you are unable to print to either port. In most cases, this is not a problem because add-on second parallel port cards are almost always set to LPT2 at the factory. Most manufacturers seem to understand that you are adding an additional parallel port; however, make sure you check the settings before you install the card.

You also need to check the memory address and the interrupt request (IRQ) that the parallel port on the interface card is set to use to make sure they are not in conflict with the memory address and interrupt used by the parallel port (LPT1) in your PC. Use the SysChk program you used in Hour 3, "Examining Your PC's System Configuration," to check the memory address and interrupt in use by the parallel port in your PC. The interrupt most likely is 7 because this is usually the default interrupt used for LPT1. The memory address looks something like 3BC or 2BC. Just make sure that you check which settings your existing parallel port uses.

To Do: Installing a Second Parallel Port

To install a second parallel port in your PC, follow these steps:

1. Turn off and unplug your PC, ground yourself, and then remove the PC cover.
2. Insert the interface card in an empty slot in your PC.
3. Replace the cover and turn on your PC.
4. Run your PC's hardware Setup program and install or enable LPT2. If you have to include the interrupt and memory address in the setup, enter the settings the same as they are on the card.

You now can connect the second printer just the same as you connected the first printer earlier in this lesson. When you install the driver for the second printer, remember to designate the output port as LPT2, the second parallel port in your PC.

Method Three: Installing an A/B Switch

An A/B switch is like a fork in the road—it enables you to travel in one of two directions. In this case, the A/B switch is a device that enables the signal from your PC to travel to one of two connected printers.

Essentially, the A/B switch is a device or electrical connector box with one cable attached to your PC and two cables attached to each of your two printers. The device is called an A/B switch because a switch enables you to select printer A or printer B.

▼ To Do

21

The A/B switch is just a hardware device—meaning that you have no setup program to run. To install, just plug one cable from your PC into the input port on the switch. You then connect the remaining two cables from each output port to each of your printers. Now when you want to print to the printer connected to the first output port, you move the selector on the switchbox to the A position. When you want to print to the printer connected to the second output port, you move the selector on the switchbox to the B position. The biggest problem in using an A/B switch is making sure that you get the input and output cables installed correctly. But most A/B switches usually ship with more than enough documentation to walk you through the connections. An estimate of the price of an A/B switch is anywhere from about $35 to $75. You can purchase an A/B switch from most computer or office supply stores and from many electronics stores.

> Some laser printer manufacturers warn against using an A/B switch because of a possibility of damage to the printer with the sudden loss of signal (when you switch from one printer to the other). Check to make sure your printer will safely work with an A/B switch before attempting to use one.

Summary

In this hour, you learned how to select and install a printer with your PC. You learned what criteria to use to judge printers and what steps you need to follow to connect your printer and install the appropriate printer driver. You have also learned various methods of connecting two printers to your PC.

Q&A

Q Why aren't serial ports still used on printers?

A Years ago most printers came as serial communications devices. But every manufacturer implemented the serial communications port a little differently according to the needs and design of its own printers. Consequently, every serial printer required a different cable. When the original IBM PC was released back in 1981, it came equipped with a Centronics parallel port designed to work with the printer released along with it. When other manufacturers started cloning the IBM PC, they likewise cloned the Centronics parallel port to insure that their clones would also work with the IBM printer. As other vendors started manufacturing PC-compatible printers, they copied the same specifications for the Centronics parallel port to insure compatibility with the IBM PC. The Centronics parallel port very quickly became the standard for printers, and gradually, all manufacturers phased out the use of the nonstandard serial port. The serial port did ensure that printers could be connected to other types of computers and terminals, but because the non-PC printer market has mostly dried up, most printer manufacturers are now content to carve out their portion of the ever expanding PC printer market. You may have noticed also that many manufacturers are including USB interfaces to their printers as well.

Q Are there any maintenance tips I should know about for my printer?

A Just like PCs, printers do tend to attract their share of dust. Periodically—about every six months or so—open the cover and blow out as much dust as you can. It's also a good idea to have laser printers serviced about once a year. The only other maintenance advice is to use quality paper, toner, and ink cartridges.

21

HOUR 22

Selecting and Installing a Scanner or Digital Camera

In the past few years, many PC users have had the opportunity to dabble with digital imagery largely because of the availability of better quality and less expensive digital scanners and digital cameras. Scanners have never been less expensive, more available, or easier to set up and use. And digital cameras are slowly approaching the quality of film cameras while inching toward the price range considered affordable by most PC users.

In this hour you will learn:

- About the types of scanners available for the PC industry
- How to select a scanner
- How to install and set up your scanner
- How to select a digital camera

Types of Scanners

For basic home use, you can choose from three different types of scanners—flatbed, hand-held, and sheetfeed. Handheld scanners were designed basically for computer users with very limited funds to devote to a scanning device. A handheld scanner is a small device about the size of large TV remote control unit. You scan with it by slowly (and manually) sliding the scanner over the picture you are scanning. No one recommends purchasing a handheld scanner because the images they produce are almost always distorted—it is nearly impossible to move the scanner over the object you are scanning at a constant speed.

Because sheetfeed scanners were developed as a less expensive alternative to flatbed scanners, and because prices for flatbed scanners have been dropping steadily, it's likely that handheld scanners will all but disappear very shortly. If you see one for sale, even at an unbelievably low price, don't waste your money.

Although there are three types of scanners you can still purchase for home use, my recommendation for a home scanner limits your selection to just two types—flatbed and sheetfeed models.

Sheetfeed Scanners

Sheetfeed scanners are the less expensive of the two types recommended and have virtually replaced handheld scanners as the low-end model.

Besides being less expensive than flatbed scanners, one major advantage sheetfeed scanners have is that they occupy much less desktop space. The typical flatbed scanner takes up a desktop area approximately 14×20 inches, whereas the typical sheetfeed scanner only takes up an area approximately 12×4 inches (see Figure 22.1).

FIGURE 22.1

A typical sheetfeed scanner.

Although sheetfeed scanners are capable of scanning pictures and converting them to digital images the same as their flatbed cousins, most users who purchase sheetfeed scanners use them for *Optical Character Recognition* (OCR).

NEW TERM *Optical Character Recognition* (OCR) is a means of using your scanner and special software to scan a page of text, such as a newspaper or magazine article, and convert what is being scanned into a text file. Some OCR programs can also convert the scanned document into several popular word-processing formats, such as Microsoft Word and Corel WordPerfect. Keep in mind that several good OCR programs are on the market, and even the best is not 100 percent perfect.

Sheetfeed scanners can scan pictures and photos and convert them to digital images, but most sheetfeed scanners have a lower optical resolution than their flatbed counterparts. Most sheetfeed scanners have a maximum optical resolution of 300×600 dpi (dots per inch).

Just like printers that measure their output in dots per inch (see Hour 21, "Selecting and Installing a Printer"), scanners also measure their input in terms of dots per inch.

Flatbed Scanners

Of the two types of scanners recommended here, flatbed models (see Figure 22.2) are the more versatile because they allow you to scan single sheets or photos. You can also place larger, bulkier objects like books and magazines on the flatbed for scanning. On many models of flatbed scanners, you can also attach optional sheet feeders for scanning multipage documents.

Flatbed scanners also tend to have a slightly higher optical scanning resolution. Most home-use flatbed scanners have an optical resolution of 600×600 dpi.

Scanner manufacturers often present flatbed scanner resolution in two sets of numbers. They list the maximum optical resolution and they list a higher resolution value called the interpolated resolution. *Interpolation* is a means of guessing certain color values during the scanning process. Interpolation values can in some cases be fairly accurate. Nevertheless, you should never rely on the interpolated resolution as the maximum resolution your scanner is capable of achieving. Always use the optical resolution when comparing resolutions between scanner models.

Figure 22.2

A typical flatbed scanner.

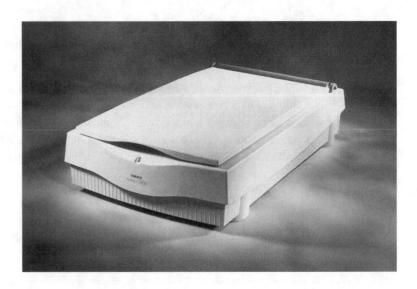

Selecting a Scanner

Now that you know about the types of scanners available, you're ready for a few helpful hints on how to select a scanner.

First, decide what you want to do with your scanner. If you just plan to scan a few documents and occasionally scan a few family photos, you can probably get by with a sheet-feed scanner. If you need a scanner for doing a lot of document OCR scanning, however, you probably will do better with a flatbed scanner with an optional sheet feeder to save you the time and effort of lifting the flatbed cover and replacing documents.

If you need to scan pictures, photos, or artwork for direct transfer to a Web site, a sheet-feed scanner is probably satisfactory. Web artwork does not need to be of very high resolution. Presently 72 dpi is good enough.

However, if you need to scan pictures, photos, or artwork and you plan to use some type of digital editing software on the scanned image—such as PhotoShop, CorelDRAW, or Paint Shop Pro—you probably need the slightly higher optical resolution offered by a flatbed scanner.

Keep in mind how much scanning you plan to do. If you will be doing a lot of scanning, you probably will want to purchase a scanner with a SCSI interface because a SCSI interface is faster than a parallel (or proprietary) interface (see Hour 11, "Replacing, Upgrading, or Adding a Hard Disk Drive," for more information on SCSI interfaces).

Originally, if you wanted a scanner attached to your PC, your choices of interfaces began and ended with SCSI. But now with scanners achieving the status of commodity items, many manufacturers have not only made scanners less expensive, but also a lot easier to connect and use. Many scanners also come with a parallel port interface. Some newer scanners can also be purchased with a USB interface.

Of the available interfaces for scanners, in most cases a SCSI interface will deliver the fastest performance, and the parallel port interface is the slowest. USB scanners will fall somewhere in between.

Although this may begin to sound like a broken record, before you purchase any peripheral, check several of the major PC journals for product reviews. It's not difficult to find a product review on scanners every other month or so, especially with the abundance of lower-priced scanners coming onto the market in recent months.

As with most of the other PC peripherals covered in this book, when reviewing scanners or digital cameras, one of the best places to begin for product information and product comparisons is CNET's Computers.Com Web site at `http://computers.cnet.com/hardware/0-1016.html`. Some other sites worth considering for more detailed information include

- **Umax**—`http://www.umax.com/`
- **Hewlett-Packard**—`http://www.pandi.hp.com/pandi-db/home_page.show`
- **Agfa**—`http://www.agfa.com/`
- **Canon**—`http://www.usa.canon.com/`
- **Epson**—`http://www.epson.com/cam_scan/`

Installing Your Scanner

Two to three years ago it was next to impossible to purchase a scanner that did not use a SCSI interface. Now you can purchase scanners that connect to your PC using either SCSI, parallel, serial, USB, or proprietary interfaces. Serial interfaces have all but disappeared on scanners, so for all intents and purposes, you only have to choose between SCSI, parallel, USB, and proprietary interfaces.

A few scanner manufacturers still use a proprietary interface and supply their scanners with a proprietary interface card. Most experts, myself included, recommend against purchasing any device utilizing a proprietary interface because they usually offer no significant advantage over other available interfaces, and they take up space in your PC (by using one of your motherboard slots) that cannot by used by other devices.

To Do: Installing a Scanner to Your PC

Because scanners are external devices, you connect them to your PC much the same as you would connect a printer, external CD-ROM drive, or an external tape backup drive. To install your scanner, follow these steps:

1. Unpack and set up your scanner, following the instructions supplied by the manufacturer. Make sure you allow sufficient space on your desktop. Be sure to "unlock" the scanner arm in your scanner. The instructions will explain how to unlock the arm, which is shipped in a locked position to protect it from possible damage. The arm must be unlocked before you can use your scanner.

2. If you need to install an interface card (SCSI or proprietary) for your scanner, turn off and unplug your PC, ground yourself, remove the cover, locate an empty slot, and install the interface card into the empty slot.

Some scanner manufacturers include a SCSI interface card with their scanners, eliminating the need to purchase a separate SCSI card if you don't already have one. Sometimes, however, these supplied SCSI cards are designed to work only with the scanner they are shipped with and will not function with other SCSI devices. In effect, you are getting a proprietary interface card.

3. Connect your scanner to your PC using the cable shipped with your scanner. Follow the manufacturer's instructions. If you install the scanner into an existing SCSI chain (see Hour 11), make sure you maintain the integrity of the chain by ensuring that it is still terminated at both ends.

Virtually every scanner manufacturer supplies a cable with their scanners. If, however, you discover your scanner does not include a cable you can usually purchase one at your local computer store. Parallel cables are usually in the $10–$15 range and SCSI cables are in the $30–$50 range.

▼

▼   4. Insert the driver disk supplied with your scanner and follow the instructions to install the scanner software and hardware driver for your particular operating system. The scanner software consists of the hardware driver needed to allow your PC to communicate with your scanner and usually also several utility programs supplied by the manufacturer.

> Bundled software is also supplied by virtually every scanner manufacturer. Some of the items they supply, besides the basic scanning software, often include an OCR program, a copy utility, and a fax utility. The copy utility can be extremely useful because it allows you to use your scanner like a photocopier, which automatically sends the output to your printer. The fax utility is similar to the copy utility, but instead of sending the output to your printer, it enables you to send faxes of items scanned, provided you have a fax modem.

5. Start your scanning software so that you can test your scanner by scanning a document or a picture. If you get an error message or the scanner fails to scan, go back and check all your cable connections, and check to make sure that the hardware driver is properly installed and configured and that your scanner is
▲   turned on.

Digital Cameras

If you are interested in producing digital images for Web site composition or digital editing, a digital camera can save you a few steps and a lot of time over using a traditional film camera. You don't have to worry about getting your film developed and then scanning the photographs.

A digital camera is just what the name suggests—a photographic camera that produces digital images. A digital camera (see Figure 22.3) does not use film. Instead, it contains memory or some type of storage medium where images you take are stored until you download them to your PC.

A digital camera is highly convenient, especially when you consider that your images are almost immediately available for use and you don't have to stop to have your film developed. Nevertheless, digital cameras do have their drawbacks:

- Digital cameras are still expensive. A good digital camera costs between $700 and $1,000. Lesser quality digital cameras can be purchased for around $300–$500.

- Digital cameras still cannot produce images at the same quality of standard film cameras. Even a moderately priced 35mm film camera can produce photos superior to digital cameras. Film can produce images with a much higher resolution than the best digital cameras, even digital cameras costing several thousand dollars.

FIGURE 22.3

A typical digital camera.

With all these negatives, you might wonder why anyone would ever bother using a digital camera. The primary reason is simple—convenience. The primary uses of digital cameras are in areas where the lower resolution produced by digital cameras is not a problem, namely Web-based graphics. Because Web-based graphics do not need to be any greater than 72 dpi, the convenience and lower resolutions offered by digital cameras make producing Web-based graphics a cinch.

Many users also purchase digital cameras because it is a lot easier to send photos as email attachments to friends and relatives.

Selecting a Digital Camera

Digital cameras can range in price from a few hundred dollars to several thousand dollars. But don't get the impression that you can't get a usable digital camera without taking out a second mortgage. There are several dozen very good digital cameras priced in the $300–$800 range (what most photographers would call "point-and-shoot" models), and several manufacturers are hard at work making more.

Just like every other product mentioned in this book, you need to check the popular PC journals for product reviews to get an idea how the various models of digital cameras in

22

your price range compare. Just like scanners, the quality of digital cameras can vary considerably for models in the same price range. And just like scanners, since this is a hot market, manufacturers are constantly coming out with new and improved models, so it pays to check often.

You should begin your selection process by comparing current models at CNET's Computers.Com at `http://computers.cnet.com/hardware/0-1016.html`. You might also want to look at the sites of some of the top manufacturers, such as

- **Kodak**—`http://www.kodak.com/US/en/nav/digital.shtml`
- **Canon**—`http://www.canon.com/`
- **Epson**—`http://www.epson.com/cam_scan/`
- **Fuji**—`http://www.fujifilm.com/`
- **Olympus**—`http://www.olympusamerica.com/p.asp?s=12&p=16`
- **Nikon**—`http://www.nikonusa.com/products/products.cfm?department=imaging`
- **Sony**—`http://www.sel.sony.com/SEL/consumer/dimaging/`

You also need to be aware of what add-on products are available for various digital cameras. Some cameras allow you to add additional memory to boost the number of photos you can take before you have to download images to your PC. Some cameras come equipped with the same type of peripheral slots found on laptop computers and allow you to use the same memory and hard disk peripherals available for laptop computers. There are also digital cameras that allow you to use floppy disks the same as you would use film in a traditional camera. When you take the maximum number of photos that will fit on a disk, you simply remove the disk, insert another, and continue shooting.

Most digital cameras come with a cable and software to allow you to connect to your PC and download the photos stored in your camera. The number of photos you can take with a digital camera will vary considerably depending on the amount of memory or storage in the camera and the resolution of the photos you take.

If you are thinking of purchasing a digital camera, here are a few features to consider:

- At what resolutions can you take pictures? The minimum now for most entry-level digital cameras is 640×480. Many manufacturers are offering lower-cost models that take photos at resolutions of 1024×768 and 1152×864.
- Does the camera include a built-in flash? You need a flash of some type if you plan to take photos indoors. Does the camera have any type of flash mode? Backlight reduction? Red-eye reduction? Effective range?

- How much memory or storage capacity does the camera have? Is it expandable? This determines how many pictures it can store at one time.

- Is the lens fixed focus, or can you zoom? What is the equivalent sized 35mm lens? Is it auto-focus or manual focus? Does it have a macro mode for taking close-up shots?

- What types of batteries does the camera use and (approximately) how long will they last (or how many photos can you take)?

- How long is the setup time between taking photos?

- Can you print directly from the camera? Does the manufacturer offer a companion printer?

- What is the color depth? 24-bit? 30-bit? More?

- Does the camera save images in the standard JPG format, or does it use a proprietary image format? If it uses a proprietary format, does it include a utility for converting to a standard format?

- Some cameras also allow you to include a few seconds of audio to help you catalog your photos. Do the cameras you are reviewing have this feature?

Although these aren't the only features that you need to be concerned with in selecting a digital camera, this list will at least give you a start in making your selection.

Summary

In the past hour, you learned about scanners and digital cameras, what features you need to be concerned about when selecting either a scanner or a digital camera, and how to install a scanner to work with your PC.

Q&A

Q I read that digital cameras last year outsold 35mm cameras. Doesn't that suggest that the quality of digital and film cameras is about the same?

A Not really. What this suggests to me is that many people are willing to pay for convenience. For the same money, digital cameras still have a long way to go to match the quality of film cameras, especially considering the broad range of film types available. To get the maximum benefit out of a good film camera, however, you need to learn a little about photography: f-stops, film speeds, macro and telephoto lenses, composition techniques with lighting, and so on. Most people just don't want to be bothered.

22

Go on the Web and find sales figures for companies like Polaroid and Kodak and compare them to sales figures for companies like Nikon and Leica. Most people who take pictures are still using point-and-shoot type cameras and don't want to be bothered with having to make settings on their camera before taking a picture. The majority of digital cameras sold are still in the point-and-shoot category.

Add to this the fact that digital cameras eliminate another headache for users—having to purchase and then take the film to a camera store or some type of processing facility before the user can see the pictures taken. Many digital cameras have not only a viewfinder for lining up the picture you want to take, but also a means of displaying the picture immediately after taking it. The increased sales of digital cameras in the last few years clearly points out that many consumers are more than willing to pay more for convenience even when it means sacrificing some quality.

Q **Manufacturers keep making more and more devices that plug into a parallel port. I know it is mainly for convenience, but are there any potential problems if you keep plugging devices into your parallel port?**

A I have yet to hear of any problems except for running out of available space in back of your PC as you keep plugging more and more devices into your parallel port. Most parallel port devices have what is called a "pass-through" connector. You plug the device into the parallel port and the connector in turn has another 25-pin connector on it you can plug your printer cable into so that you can continue to use both devices. If you were to purchase a printer, an external removable disk drive, a tape drive, and a scanner, you could conceivably plug all the devices into your parallel port simultaneously and they would all be useable. The downside is that this stack of pass-through connectors would probably extend 6–8 inches out of the back of your PC. If this is a problem, one solution is to buy an A/B/C/D switch box (an A/B switch box has two connectors, and an A/B/C/D switch box has four connectors), the same type used to connect multiple printers to your PC. The USB port has done a lot to relieve all of this parallel port congestion.

PART V

Additional Upgrading Issues

Hour

HOUR 23

Upgrading to a New Operating System

The past 22 hours have dealt exclusively with upgrading the hardware in your PC. But the latest and greatest hardware will not live up to its full potential if you are still using an antiquated operating system that is more than seven years old.

Strange as it might sound, between 20 and 30 percent of all PC users are still using the DOS/Windows 3.1 combination. In the PC world, this is tantamount to purchasing a Lamborghini Countach and never taking it out of first gear.

Now we're going to talk about upgrading your operating system. During this hour you will learn:

- About the limitations of Windows 3.1
- Why you should upgrade your operating system
- How to decide between Windows 98, Windows 2000, or another operating system, such as Linux

Limitations of DOS/Windows 3.1

If you are still using DOS, you are using an operating system that has been around in some form since 1981. Without going through the history or evolution of DOS, its biggest limitations include the following:

- DOS was written essentially for the 80286 processor, which means DOS cannot address more than 16MB of memory for program execution.

- DOS lacks any type of system or file security.

- DOS uses the 8.3 filename convention (the filename can be 1–8 characters and the file extension can be 1–3 characters).

- DOS uses the FAT16 formatting structure for formatting hard disks, which means that DOS cannot create hard disk partitions larger than 2GB (2048MB).

- DOS is a single-tasking operating system, which means you can run only one program at a time.

- DOS is text only and does not include a GUI (Graphical User Interface).

Windows 3.1 is an operating environment—not an operating system—which resides on top of DOS and still maintains most of DOS's limitations. Windows 3.1 was written to work on an 80386 processor.

But perhaps the biggest reason to upgrade from Windows 3.1 is that software is no longer being developed for it!

Now you're probably thinking that you're using Windows 3.1 and you surf the Net and use the latest versions of Netscape and Internet Explorer, so what do I mean that software isn't being developed for Windows 3.1? The versions of Netscape and Internet Explorer you're using were originally developed for Windows 95 and NT. The Windows 3.1 versions you're using are scaled-back versions created for people like you who have not upgraded yet. They are not functionally equivalent to the Windows 95 and NT versions (and are also about 3–4 versions behind what your Windows 95/98/NT/2000 brothers and sisters are using).

Speaking of the Internet, let's use it to further illustrate the point about Windows 3.1. One of the premier World Wide Web animation tools is a program called Flash by Macromedia. Go to the Macromedia Web site (http://www.macromedia.com) and see whether you can download a version of the Flash player for Windows 3.1.

Go to a few other sites and see how many programs, plug-ins, and utilities are only available for Windows 95/98/NT/2000, or are available in a scaled-down version for Windows 3.1:

- http://www.realaudio.com

- http://www.tucows.com

- http://www.download.com

- http://www.shareware.com

Still need more convincing? Here is the *coup de grace*. In late 1997, Microsoft announced it was no longer selling Windows 3.1. This announcement officially makes Windows 3.1 obsolete.

23

> In case you're wondering about IBM's OS/2 operating system, it is actually just a little better than Windows 3.1. I used to be an ardent OS/2 user and supporter, but OS/2 lacks the capability to run 32-bit Windows applications, which means that whatever applies to Windows 3.1 also applies to OS/2 in regards to software and availability (except of course for native OS/2 applications). You don't have to take my word for it. Go to your local software store and see how much software you can find for OS/2. Netscape only released a version for OS/2 in 1997.

Why You Should Upgrade

Now that I've told you why you should stop using Windows 3.1, I need to spend a few minutes telling you why you should upgrade to either Windows 98 or 2000. If you are considering an upgrade from Windows 3.1 to Windows 98 or Windows 2000, first you can set aside your number one fear—all of your existing software *will* run under Windows 98 or 2000. You will not have to junk all of your current programs and buy new software. (Actually, if you are still using software designed for Windows 3.1, you should strongly consider upgrading your software, too.)

The main reason you should upgrade from Windows 3.1 to Windows 98 or 2000 is that your existing programs will actually perform better. One major advantage Windows 98 and 2000 have over Windows 3.1 is how much better they are at managing the memory in your PC. The illustration in Figure 23.1 shows how Windows 2000 manages your PC's memory and CPU usage.

Crash Protection

If you are an active Windows 3.1 user, undoubtedly you've experienced the dreaded GPF—General Protection Fault. A GPF occurs when Windows 3.1 allows two programs to use the same area of memory. GPFs do not exist in Windows 98 or 2000 because of how well both manage memory usage.

FIGURE 23.1

Windows 2000 managing a PC's memory and CPU usage.

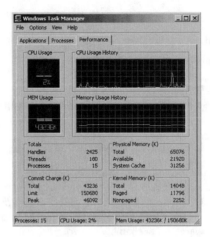

This is not to say that Windows 98 and Windows 2000 will never crash because of errant programs. If you are looking for crash protection, however, Windows 2000 has the best. Windows 2000 will not let a problem with one program affect the performance of another program. If a program crashes under 2000, only that program is affected and 2000 allows you to "gracefully" shut down the bothersome program (and then restart it if you like) without affecting the rest of your work. How many of you Windows 3.1 users have lost hours of unsaved work because another program you had open crashed and brought down the entire system?

Internet Access and Built-in Networking Capabilities

Both Windows 98 and 2000 come with all of the tools you need to access the Internet (see Figure 23.2).

You don't need to acquire extra programs or utilities to access the Internet. Of course, you can purchase or download other programs, but Windows 98 and 2000 enable you to access the Internet right out of the box (provided you have an Internet connection).

Both OSes also come equipped with all the tools you need for network setup (see Figure 23.3).

Multitasking OS

Perhaps the best reason to upgrade to either Windows 98 or 2000 is that you will be upgrading to a true multitasking operating system.

FIGURE 23.2

The Internet Setup Wizard in Windows 98.

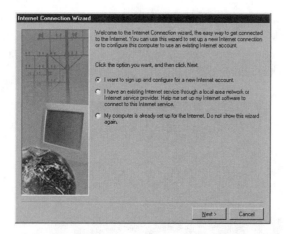

FIGURE 23.3

The Control Panel Networking setup in Windows 98.

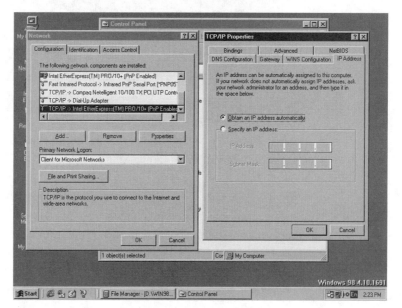

NEW TERM *Multitasking* means that several programs or tasks are capable of running simultaneously. In Windows 98 and 2000, the operating system controls the amount of CPU time allotted to each running procedure or application.

Windows 98's Plug-and-Play Capabilities

Windows 98 (the OS that followed Windows 95) is also designed as a Plug-and-Play operating system (the same as 95). That means that whenever you add, change, or remove a hardware component in your PC (provided the hardware component is Plug and Play), Windows 98 detects the change and immediately begins helping you modify your hardware setup. If it is needed, Windows 98 also helps you install the appropriate hardware driver (see Figure 23.4).

FIGURE 23.4

The Windows 98 Add New Hardware (Plug and Play) Setup Wizard.

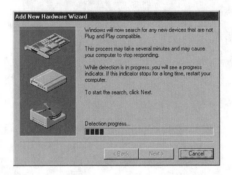

Microsoft has also included Plug-and-Play capabilities in Windows 2000.

To reiterate, here are some of the pluses and minuses of Windows 3.1 versus Windows 98/2000:

- Windows 3.1 is single-tasking; Windows 98/2000 are multitasking.

- Windows 3.1 has very limited memory management capabilities; Windows 98/2000 have extensive memory management capabilities.

- Windows 3.1 has no file or system security; Windows 98 has minimal system security; Windows 2000 has extensive file and system security.

- Windows 3.1 will run your existing (16-bit) applications; Windows 98/2000 will run your existing (16-bit) applications (and prevent them from crashing into each other) and the more advanced 32-bit applications.

- Windows 3.1 is not designed to efficiently handle large disk drives; Windows 98/2000 are both designed to manage large drives and large partitions.

- Windows 3.1 does not include applications or utilities for accessing the Internet; Windows 95/2000 both include utilities and applications for accessing the Internet.

Windows 98 or Windows 2000?

So, which operating system should you upgrade to? Windows 98 or Windows 2000? Well it depends on what you need a new operating system for, what you intend to do with your new operating system, what your level of computer experience is, and how much horsepower you have in your PC. Right now Microsoft is marketing Windows 98 as the operating system that should suffice most home users and Windows 2000 as the operating system for the corporate workplace. Windows 2000 does require a PC with a bit more horsepower, but in return for that extra bit of juice, Windows 2000 gives you better memory management, better crash protection, and better security (see Figure 23.5) than Windows 98. Windows 2000 is also a bit more complex and a bit harder to learn and use than Windows 98.

23

FIGURE 23.5

The Windows 2000 User (security) Manager.

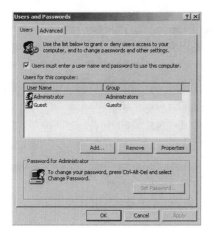

If you are planning to upgrade your home computer, odds are you'll be better off upgrading to Windows 98 because typically the needs and demands (especially in the areas of file and system security) of home users are not as pressing as those of the user in the corporate environment. Windows 98 also does a much better job of supporting games than 2000 because of the way it allocates memory resources.

Upgrading to Windows 98

Microsoft did provide an upgrade path for upgrading from Windows 3.1 to Windows 98. Although installing Windows 98 on top of an existing installation of Windows 3.1 is possible, my advice is *don't!* The installation of Windows 98 will not be done cleanly because many Windows 3.1 files will be left on your hard disk during the installation, and these files can potentially interact with similar Windows 98 files and be a potential source of problems. Similarly, if you are upgrading from Windows 95 to 98, I would not place the upgrade (Windows 98) on top of the existing operating system (Windows 95).

For best results, back up all your existing data files, delete Windows 3.1 entirely from your hard disk drive (delete the C:\WINDOWS directory), and then install Windows 98.

Afterwards, re-install all your existing software applications. This procedure will take a bit longer than installing Windows 98 on top of Windows 3.1, but you will be better off in the long run.

> If you decide to start with a really clean slate and reformat your hard disk, make sure you back up your files first.

Make sure also that you have upgraded the memory in your PC. The minimum amount of memory you should have for Windows 98 is 32MB, but you will find that Windows 98 performs best for most home users when your PC has 64MB of RAM, or more.

If you are considering instead just upgrading to Windows 95 because you feel you can likely get it for a good price (which you probably can), let me just offer the following as a few reasons why you should consider Windows 98 over Windows 95:

- *Windows 98 has better memory management.* Your programs will require less memory under 98 and actually run faster because of the improved memory management and lower memory requirements.

- *Windows 98 has FAT32.* Remember the earlier discussion on how files are stored on your hard disk and how DOS and Windows 95 use what is called FAT16, which wastes space on your hard disk. Windows 98 uses FAT32, which greatly reduces the amount of actual storage space used on your hard disk. FAT32 also works with the improved memory management to improve overall performance.

- *Windows 98 has better diagnostic and repair utilities.* Windows 98 ships with an abundant supply of diagnostic and repair utilities such as a drive defragmenter, a clean-up utility for locating and removing files you no longer need, an improved systems configuration utility, and a utility to constantly check the status of critical systems files.

- *Windows 98 has better Internet Utilities.* Windows 98 ships with Microsoft Internet Explorer 5.0 and the Active Desktop, which is a means of viewing your PC and its files through your browser and automatically getting updates and notifications over the Internet.

Upgrading to Windows 2000

Upgrading from Windows 3.1 to Windows 2000 is as easy as upgrading to Windows 98. Even though you can upgrade from Windows 3.1 (or 95/98) to Windows 2000, again, my best recommendation is that you back up everything, remove your old operating system, and install Windows 2000 as a clean install. Regardless of what you have heard or read elsewhere, it is never a good idea to install one operating system on top of another. It's also recommended that you don't attempt to run Windows 2000 unless you have at least a Pentium 266 MHz processor in your PC. Windows 2000 will run with a lesser processor, but you will not be as happy with the performance.

Although Windows 2000 will perform on PCs with as little as 16MB of RAM, most users will find that performance is rather sluggish. Windows 2000 performs better with at least 32MB of RAM; if you can install 64MB, you will enjoy excellent performance.

23

Upgrading to Linux

There is an alternative to Windows. Many users have successfully switched to the Linux operating system and have never looked back. Linux is a *UNIX* operating system clone and is not compatible with Windows or Windows-based software. But in the past few years many software manufacturers (except Microsoft, of course) have produced Linux versions of their applications and games. There are easily more than a thousand software titles and utilities available for Linux, so finding software to run should not be a major concern.

NEW TERM   *UNIX* is an operating system that actually pre-dates Windows. It is mainly used on larger, more powerful workstations and more often used in engineering and scientific settings.

In the U.S., two major vendors currently have the lion's share of the Linux market—Red Hat, at http://www.redhat.com (see Figure 23.6) and Caldera—http://www.calderasystems.com (see Figure 23.7).

Even though both companies (and many others) will sell you a copy of Linux, Linux is not actually owned by either company. Linux follows the Open Source model, which means that the program and its source code are available to anyone who wants them and who wants to download them from any of several hundred Internet sites. This means that if you are a skilled and talented computer programmer, you can not only obtain a copy of Linux but also make changes to it to your heart's content. What Red Hat and Caldera are selling you are versions of Linux that are much easier to install than to download off the Internet. Both companies also include additional applications and utilities that make Linux easier to get up and running, including Internet apps and utilities such as Netscape Navigator.

Linux will run on a lot less hardware than either Windows 98 or 2000. If you have an old 486 lying around that you have (hopefully!) discarded, you can add new life to it by installing Linux on it. Although Linux, like most other operating systems, will run better on Pentium-based PCs, it will run satisfactorily on an older 486.

FIGURE **23.6**

The homepage of Red Hat, one of the major Linux distributors in the USA.

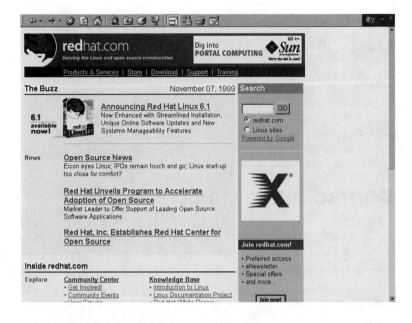

FIGURE **23.7**

Caldera, another major Linux distributor in the USA.

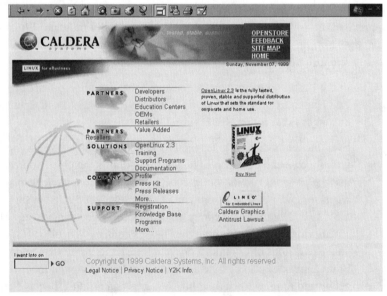

Both companies also include utilities to install Linux on your everyday PC provided you have enough free disk space, and include utilities to allow you to dual-boot to both Linux and whatever version of Windows you are running. A typical installation of Linux requires around 500MB of disk space. If you don't have this much free disk space, that's another reason to go back and re-read Hour 11, "Replacing, Upgrading, or Adding a Hard Disk Drive."

The installation procedures are different for each vendor, but a beginner or novice can install either and have Linux up and running in about an hour (see Figure 23.8).

23

FIGURE 23.8

Caldera's version of the Linux operating system.

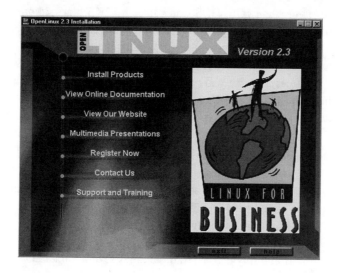

Even though you may have heard that Linux is a lot harder to use than Windows, it's actually not. It's just different, so expect a learning curve. To make that learning curve a little less steep, both companies include one or more GUIs (Graphical User Interfaces) to help shield you from an unfamiliar OS.

Summary

In the past hour, you learned about upgrading your operating system and why you should upgrade if you are still using the DOS/Windows 3.1 combination. You also learned about some of the features in Windows 98 and Windows 2000, which should help you decide which of these two operating systems you should select. You also learned about Linux, an alternative to Windows.

Q&A

Q **I've also heard that both Windows 98 and 2000 offer advantages in how they store files on your hard disk. Can you explain these?**

A Windows 98 enables you to use a file's formatting and storage system called FAT32; Windows 2000 uses NTFS. Both of these formatting and file storage systems are better at storing files than the system offered in DOS and will potentially save you significant storage space. Here's the problem with DOS: DOS uses a system called FAT16, and without going into a lot of technical detail, on hard disk drives larger than 1GB, DOS stores files in 32KB blocks. For example, if you have a file that is 50KB, DOS will take two of its 32KB storage blocks to store the 50KB file. If you do the math, you will see that there is 14KB of wasted space. If you have a file that is only 1KB in size, DOS will still store it using a 32KB block of space, meaning that you now have 31KB of wasted space. In this example of storing two files, one 50KB and one 1KB in size, you've used 96KB of disk space and wasted 45KB. In case you're wondering, DOS will not allow you to store the 1KB file in the 14KB of unused space left over from the 50KB file.

Both Windows 98 and 2000 use 2KB storage blocks instead of the 32KB blocks used by DOS. This means that to store the 50KB file in the previous example, you would need twenty-five 2KB blocks with no wasted space, and to store the 1KB file you would need one 2KB block with only 1KB of wasted space. So instead of using 96KB to store the two files and wasting 45KB of disk space, you would only use 52KB of disk space and waste only 1KB. This may not sound like much until you start multiplying this example times several hundred or several thousand (for the number of files you typically have on your hard disk) and you can start to see how much space you're wasting under DOS' FAT16 system.

Q **What are the disadvantages to upgrading to Windows 98 and 2000?**

A Well, obviously there is a learning curve. The interfaces for Windows 98 and 2000 are somewhat different than Windows 3.1. This is probably the biggest disadvantage, but like anything else on your PC, you start out learning the basics and then advance to the more difficult areas. In the long run, you will see that the advantages far outweigh the disadvantages.

Q **Does this also apply to Linux?**

A Yes, even more so. Some versions of Linux offer you more than one GUI interface. There numerous other "differences" despite the similarities. As with any new OS, take it slow and learn as you go.

HOUR 24

How to Purchase PC Components on the Internet

In the past 23 hours, you learned a considerable amount about how to upgrade the various components in your PC. You also should have picked up a few tips about how to select the upgrade items. In this hour, you will learn how to go about purchasing those items over the Internet.

During this hour you will learn:

- The pros and cons of purchasing online
- How to locate companies and components
- What you need to know about Internet security to safely purchase PC components (or anything else) over the Internet

Purchasing Over the Internet

All the PC components mentioned throughout this book can very readily be purchased directly over the Internet and delivered right to your front door. Although many computer users are starting to purchase items via mail order, not so many are purchasing over the Internet despite the fact that most of the companies selling mail order are also selling over the Internet. As expected, you have to make a few tradeoffs when purchasing over the Internet.

On the plus side

- No sales reps will bother you by trying to sell you additional items you don't want or need.
- Most companies place their entire inventory on their Web site, but place only a fraction of it in magazines and catalogs. This allows you to locate the exact model of whatever item you are looking to purchase.
- You have instant access to current pricing and inventory status. The key phrase here is "inventory status." If you are ready to purchase, you can instantly see who is ready to ship you the item you need.
- It's very easy to do comparison shopping (pricing) online and many, if not most, items can be purchased cheaper online as compared to purchasing in-store.

However, purchasing over the Internet also has a down side:

- You must know exactly what you want to purchase, which usually means manufacturer and model.
- You must purchase using a credit card. Because you are in effect purchasing from a computer system and not a person, you cannot pay with a check, a money order, or a company purchase order.
- You have to trust Internet security. This still seems to be the biggest turnoff for most potential online customers, but as you will see later in this hour, it shouldn't be.

Locating Companies

Locating computer companies and computer supply companies who do business over the Internet is relatively easy. Look in any computer magazine and you will see ads for dozens of companies—most will include a Web address of where you can find their online storefront.

You can also locate computer companies on the Internet by using the Internet. One of the best places to start looking is at Yahoo! (http://www.yahoo.com/). On the Yahoo! home page you will see a link for Shopping. Click on this link to enter the Yahoo! Shopping section (see Figure 24.1).

FIGURE 24.1

The Yahoo! online Shopping section.

There are several other links you can try on this page. In this example, you'll see how to go shopping for a new DVD player. Select the Electronics link, and then select the Video link. Finally, select the DVD Players link to open another online shopping guide (see Figure 24.2).

To compare various DVD players, select one or more of the manufacturers links. For example, if you select the Sony link you'll see the items listed in Figure 24.3.

Select one of the models listed and you will not only see more info on that particular model, but also prices where that model is offered by various online merchants (see Figure 24.4).

If you're in the market for something other than a new DVD player, here are a few other online shopping sites you might want to visit:

- **Computer Discount Warehouse**—http://www.cdw.com/
- **PC Connection** —http://www.pcconnection.com/
- **Internet Shopping Network**—http://www.isn.com/

- **Micro Center**—http://www.microcenter.com/

- **PC Mall** —http://www.pcmall.com/

- **Micro Warehouse**—http://www.microwarehouse.com/

- **Computability**—http://www.computability.com/

- **The PC Zone**—http://www.pczone.com/

- **Insight** —http://www.insight.com/

- **Buy.Com** —http://www.buy.com/

After you locate a few companies you think you might want to do business with, you need to look at a few things before you place your first order:

- *How does the company ship the order and what do they charge?* Some companies advertise what appear to be lower than competitive prices, then turn around and charge you exorbitant shipping and handling charges to make their profit. Find out what carriers the company ships with and find out if they ship overnight delivery, 2nd day delivery, or 3–5 day ground delivery. For most computer components, shipping charges should be minimal considering that most computer components are rather small and lightweight. The exception, however, is computer monitors. If you opt for a 17-inch or larger monitor, bear in mind that the shipping weights can be 60 lbs. and up; and you will often see shipping charges in the neighborhood of $60–$80 (see Figure 24.5). When comparison shopping on monitors, keep this shipping charge in mind and weigh it against possibly paying a state sales tax.

FIGURE 24.2

DVD players on the Yahoo! Shopping site.

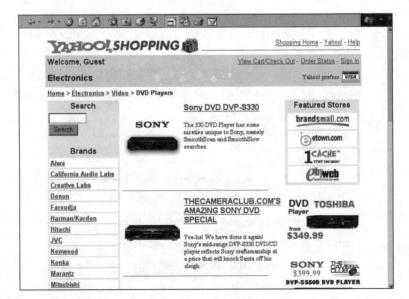

Figure 24.3

Sony DVD players that you can purchase online through the Yahoo! Shopping site.

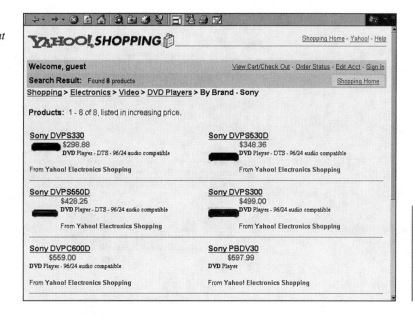

Figure 24.4

Various online merchants offering Sony DVD players for sale on the Internet.

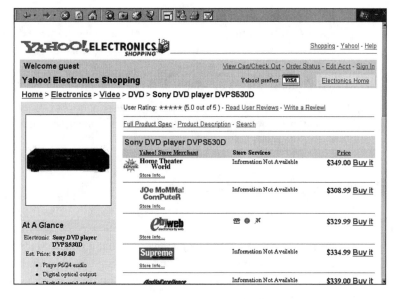

24

- *What are the company's return policies?* If you order the wrong part or if the item you order does not work with your computer can you return it? Some companies will charge a 5–15 percent restocking fee for returned items.

FIGURE 24.5

An example of ship-ping charges on a monitor.

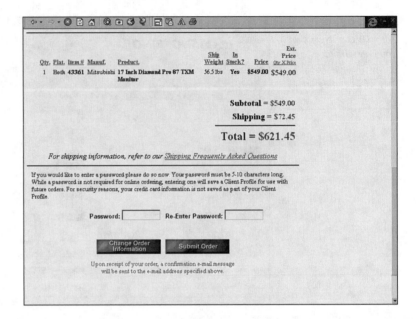

- *Will you be charged sales tax for the item?* In most cases, you will not be charged sales tax for your state (assuming your state has a sales tax) for the items you purchase unless the company has a physical presence in your state. If your state does have a sales tax and you are not charged sales tax, in many states you are required (by your state) to pay what is often called a merchandise tax.

- *Do any of the companies offer lowest price guarantees?* Some companies will guarantee theirs is the lowest price and will meet or beat a competitor's price. It never hurts to ask.

Internet Security

For online purchases, does the company use a secure Web site? A secure Web site is a means of conducting your transaction by establishing an encrypted connection between your computer and the Web site computer so that no one can tap into the communication session and see information you want to keep private, such as your credit card number. If the company is not using a secure site, make your transaction over the telephone using the company's 800 number.

The question of Internet security is probably the single most important factor still limiting online commerce. The main problem is not that the Internet commercial transactions are not secure. The main problem is that the Internet commercial transactions are not *perceived* as being secure.

Every time someone asks me if I'm worried about making purchases over the Internet and giving out my credit card number, I turn around and ask them if they have ever eaten out in a restaurant. I ask them if they worried when they gave the waiter their credit card and watched him disappear into a back room. I then point out to them that I am probably safer giving my credit card number out over a secure Internet connection than they are giving their credit card to a waiter they've never seen or met.

You can very easily identify when you have a secure connection by two visible signs in your Web browser. The first sign is the address of the Web page you are viewing. A normal or unsecured Web page address begins `http://`, but a secure Web page address usually begins `https://`.

The second sign is some symbol or indicator from your Web browser that the Web site is secure. In Netscape, you will see a closed lock (see Figure 24.6).

24

FIGURE 24.6

In Netscape you see a lock like this, which indicates a connection with a secure Web site.

Netscape's
Secure site
indicator

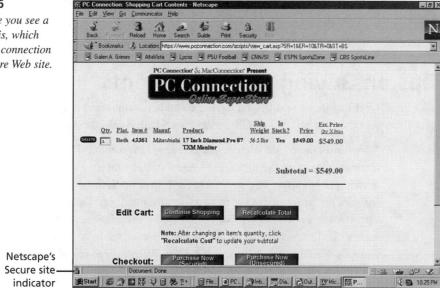

In Internet Explorer, a secure Web site is illustrated by a lock displayed on the status bar at the bottom of the screen (see Figure 24.7).

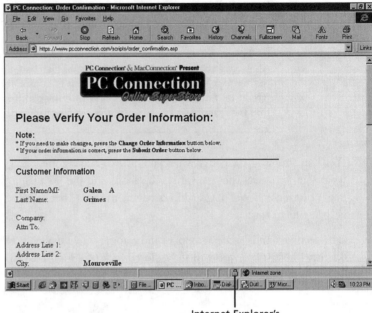

FIGURE 24.7

In Internet Explorer you see this indicator informing you that you have established a connection with a secure Web site.

Internet Explorer's
Secure site indicator

Tips on Buying PC Components

Finally, let me offer a few tips on buying computer components whether you purchase them over the Internet, call an 800 number, or simply walk into a computer store.

- *Do your research first.* Before you buy any item for your PC, read a few product reviews comparing the item from several manufacturers. For example, if you are thinking about upgrading your CD-ROM drive, look through some recent issues of some of the major computer industry journals and see what features are considered important and see what type of comparison testing has been done. Some product reviews include either an "Editor's Choice" selection or a "Best Buy" recommendation. CNET has a hardware comparison Web site you can also check at http://www.computers.com.

- *Get recent information.* Product reviews are an excellent means of getting information on products you want to purchase, but not if the information is two years old. Computer products change rapidly. Don't bother with reviews that are more than six to eight months old. If you can't find a recent review, wait a few weeks and there will be another one.

- *Make friends with the "computer guru" in your company.* Every company usually has one person who seems to know just about everything there is to know about computers. Seek out this person and become friends. Often, much of the information you need is available simply for the asking.

- *Check Usenet (Internet Newsgroups) for comments from other users.* Usenet has a category for just about everything, including computer hardware. Check out comments from other users on specific brands and models. Look for comments on customer relations with company (manufacturer and dealer), whether the product performed as advertised, and any information on problems with the product.

Online Auctions

Another source for checking out discounted computer parts and peripherals is online computer auctions. Many of these sites are selling merchandise from dealers or manufacturers who are disposing of excess or older inventories. Some are also selling used merchandise, which by law they must identify as used equipment.

Here are a few online auction sites where you can shop for computer equipment:

- **DealDeal.Com**—`http://www.dealdeal.com/`
- **OnSale**—`http://www.onsale.com/atauction/computers/computers.htm`
- **CNET Auctions**—`http://auctions.cnet.com/`
- **Ezbid**—`http://www.ezbid.com/`
- **Ebay**—`http://www.ebay.com/`

On some auction sites you are buying from the site and on some sites you are buying from a third-party seller. Check the rules of the site before you bid. Be sure to check all merchandise at the manufacturer's site before you bid to know exactly what you are bidding on, how old it is, and approximately how much it is worth.

Is it safe to buy from online auctions? The vast majority of the time, it is. But when in doubt, use one of the many escrow services available for auction buyers.

Summary

In the past hour, you learned about purchasing upgrade components for your PC over the Internet. You learned about some of the security precautions you need to be aware of in order to maintain a secure connection with the company you are purchasing from. And finally, you learned a few tips on purchasing computer products whether you buy them online or in a computer store.

Q&A

Q What should I usually pay for shipping?

A That's a hard question to answer because most online computer stores set their own shipping policies. Some charge by weight, with a minimum charge for very small items like SIMMs. Some charge by distance and weight, and some charge you a flat rate for all items under a certain weight limit. Keep in mind that shipping charges vary according to when you want to receive your purchase. Overnight delivery is the most expensive, and what is called surface transit typically is the least expensive. Shop around though. Some retailers (or e-tailers as some are now called) will discount products then jack up their shipping charges to make up for the discount.

Q Are there any other shopping concerns I should have?

A If the price on an item looks too good to be true, make sure you are not purchasing a refurbished item when you think you are purchasing a new item. It is not uncommon for manufacturers to offer refurbished items, but they must be identified as such. Also, if you do purchase a refurbished item, check to make sure what type of warranty is supplied with the item, if any, and whether you can return the item if it does not meet your needs. Check also to see if the dealer charges you a re-stocking fee for returned items.

PART VI
Appendixes

Appendix

Appendix A

Glossary

The following is a list of terms used throughout this text.

16-bit and 32-bit   Technical terms you will hear whenever the discussion turns to operating systems and/or programming, among other things. Quite simply, they refer to how computer instructions and data are processed by your computer, either in 16-bit units or in 32-bit units. Because a 32-bit unit is twice as large as a 16-bit unit, the assumption is that 32-bit programs and operating systems are twice as fast as their 16-bit counterparts. Twice as fast may be stretching it a bit, but the basic underlying assumption is generally true. 32-bit programs and operating systems are faster than 16-bit programs and operating systems.

ADSL   Asynchronous Digital Subscriber Line. A digital communications line for connecting to the Internet. Speeds can vary, but are usually between 720 Kbps and 7.1 Mbps for downloading. It's called asynchronous because upload speeds are considerably slower.

analog   *See* **digital and analog**.

BIOS   The acronym for Basic Input Output System. It is a set of instructions built in to your computer to control how information and data flow in and out of your computer.

Bit   A plus or minus electrical charge (more commonly understood as 1 or 0). Eight bits equal one *byte*.

boot, warm and cold   The terms describe two methods of rebooting or restarting your PC. As the names imply, a *warm boot* is a reboot with the power on and a *cold boot* is a reboot with the power off. The difference between the two booting methods is more than just the presence of electrical power. A cold boot is a more thorough, or complete, boot up process because it also releases any data that might still be in several system caches or memory holding areas. A cold boot runs a more thorough POST—the Power On Self Test. A warm boot is less stressful on your electrical components.

Bps   Bits per second. Usually used to describe a digital communications speed.

Bus   The bus in your PC is the connecting electronic pipeline among your processor, memory, and the PC's peripherals, such as drives and interface cards.

Bus speed   Refers to how fast data and instructions are able to move among the CPU, memory, and your PC's peripherals. Part of bus speed is controlled by how wide the bus is and the speed of the bus. Bus width refers to how many bits of data can be passed at one time—8 bits, 16 bits, or 32 bits of data. Obviously, a bus that can pass data 32 bits at a time can operate faster than a bus that can pass data only 8 bits at a time. To put this analogy into a more real-world scenario, think of a water pipe that is 1 inch in diameter versus a water pipe that is 4 inches in diameter. The 4-inch pipe allows more water to pass every second than does the 1-inch pipe.

Centronics parallel cable   A simple communications cable with a 36-pin Centronics connector on one end and a 25-pin female connector on the other. You can purchase a Centronics parallel cable in most computer stores in lengths ranging from 6 to 15 feet. And don't believe that myth about parallel cables having to be less than 10 feet in length. If you need a 15-foot cable, go ahead and purchase one. Many stores now carry printer cables in lengths of 25 feet and longer.

Clock speed   A measurement of how fast (its maximum speed) a particular CPU is set to operate. The speed is the measurement in megahertz (MHz) of an oscillating timing crystal used to control how fast the CPU can perform internal operations. Maximum implies that there is also a minimum speed, which is no longer the case. It was true with some early 286 and 386 processors for which you could adjust the speed (why anyone would ever want to use anything but the maximum speed is beyond me), but since the 486, the stated clock speed is the speed at which the CPU should be operating, according to the manufacturer.

digital and analog   These are terms used quite freely and have taken on several popular meanings. In the context of computer communications, *analog* refers to communicating by means of converting the signal in your computer to a measurable frequency and modulation, which happens to be sound waves. *Digital* refers to communicating by means of transmitting your message using a representation of the binary symbols 0 and 1 just as they are created in your PC.

DIMMs   Dual Inline Memory Modules. Memory modules used in newer Pentium II and Pentium III PCs. Sizes usually range between 32 and 256MB.

Disk controller   The interface that connects your disk drives to your motherboard. The controller can either be built in to the motherboard, as are most IDE controllers in most PCs built in the last few years, or they can come in the form of an interface card that is installed into one of the slots on your motherboard.

dpi   dots per inch.

DVD   Digital Video Disk. A rather new digital technology very similar to CD-ROM technology. DVDs differ in that they are able to store several times the capacity of CD-ROM disks, which is approximately 650MB.

Ergonomics   The study of the relationship between people and their work environments. In simpler terms, it means producing tools in the workplace, such as chairs, desks, keyboards, and so on, that conform more to the way human bodies are designed and how they function rather than making human bodies conform to workplace tools. The idea is to increase comfort and reduce the possibility of injuries or stress.

FAT16   The original disk file organizational structure used by DOS and Windows 3.1. Maximum partition size is 2048MB.

FAT32   The disk file organizational structure released with Windows 98 (and Windows 95 OSR2 version). Eliminated many of the limitations of FAT16 such as the 2048MB partition size—maximum partition size under FAT32 is two terabytes. It also offers more efficient use of hard disk drive.

Firmware   This is essentially software that has been embedded into certain chips in your computer and that runs automatically without intervention on your part. The distinction is usually made between programs that you can easily change, erase, and delete—software—and programs that you cannot easily alter—firmware.

Gigabyte (GB)   A thousand megabytes or a billion bytes.

A

IDE   Integrated Drive Electronics. An interface that enables up to two devices to be attached to each port. Originally IDE enabled data to pass to its connected devices at the rate of only 2 Mbits/sec, but newer Enhanced IDE Ultra ATA/66 interfaces and devices can transfer data at the rate of 66 Mbits/sec.

ISDN   Integrated Services Digital Network. An early proposal for upgrading the telephone system from analog to digital. Never progressed very far for replacing the telephone system but did make some headway for providing Internet access despite its high costs. It is now being supplanted by ADSL.

Kilobyte (KB)   1024 bytes (2^{10} bytes).

main system board or motherboard   These are often used interchangeably and refer to the same component, the main electronic circuit board in a PC.

Megabyte (MB)   One million bytes.

MHz   The abbreviation for *megahertz* (millions of hertz per second), used as a measurement for the oscillating timing frequency used by processors. In simpler terms, it is an indication of the relative speed of a processor.

MIDI   Musical Instrument Digital Interface. An interface and a file format that enables you to connect a musical instrument to a computer and store musical instrument data. The musical instrument data can then be enhanced, edited, and played back.

MPEG-2   An international graphics standard established by the Motion Picture Entertainment Group (MPEG) for audio and video compression and playback.

Multitasking   This means that several programs or tasks are capable of running simultaneously. In Windows 98 and NT, the operating system controls the amount of CPU time allotted to each running procedure or application.

Optical Character Recognition (OCR)   A means of using your scanner and special software to scan a page of text, such as a newspaper or magazine article, and convert what is being scanned into a text file. Some OCR programs can also convert the scanned document into several popular word-processing formats, such as Microsoft Word and Corel WordPerfect. Keep in mind that several good OCR programs are on the market, and even the best is not 100% perfect.

Plug and Play   A combination hardware and software feature that enables an operating system such as Windows 95/98/2000 to identify and configure hardware you add to your PC. In order to work, the hardware item has to have special chips built in that identify the hardware item. The operating system has to be Plug and Play enabled in order to be able to read those chips and use the information contained within to configure the hardware.

RAM and memory   Often used interchangeably. RAM is short for Random Access Memory and is the electronic memory (chips) that your computer uses for running programs and storing temporary data. RAM is not the permanent storage area for files.

SCSI   Small Computer System Interface. Enables you to connect up to seven devices to the interface. Since the original SCSI standard was released, it has been updated several times and now includes SCSI-2 and SCSI-3, and can achieve data transfer speeds up to 80 Mbits/sec.

SIMMs   Single Inline Memory Modules. SIMMs are electronic modules about 10-1/2 centimeters long that sit in slots, usually located on your main system board.

UNIX   An operating system for mid-sized computers created in the '70s and eventually made available for PCs ranging from PCs to mainframes. It is still in use today and was the design basis for Linux.

Video cards   Also referred to as *video adapters*, *graphic adapters*, and *graphic cards*. These terms all refer to the same device—the interface card installed in your computer that controls and produces video on your monitor. Although the term mostly applies to separate interface cards installed in your PC, the term video card can also refer to video display circuitry built in to the motherboard.

A

APPENDIX B

Manufacturers' Reference

The following is a list of the manufacturers and vendors who make many of the products mentioned in this text and information you need to contact each manufacturer.

BIOS

- **Award BIOS**—http://www.award.com/
- **BIOS Guide**—http://www.pcmech.com/bios/index.htm
- **BIOS Setup Information Guide**—http://www.sysopt.com/bios.html
- **Micro Firmware**—http://www.firmware.com/index.htm

CD-ROM and DVD Drives

- **Creative Labs**—http://www.americas.creative.com/home.html
- **Hewlett Packard**—http://www.hp.com/storage/surestore/

- **NEC**—http://www.nectech.com/cdrom/index.htm
- **Samsung**—http://samsungelectronics.com/products/odd/odd.html
- **Plextor**—http://www.plextor.com/home.html

CPU

- **AMD**—http://www.amd.com/
- **Cyrix**—http://www.cyrix.com/
- **Intel**—http://www.intel.com/

Hard Disk Drives and Peripherals

- **Adaptec**—http://www.adaptec.com/
- **Fujitsu**—http://www.fujitsu.com/harddisk.html
- **IBM**—http://www.storage.ibm.com/
- **Maxtor**—http://www.maxtor.com/
- **NEC**—http://www.nectech.com/storage/index.htm
- **Samsung**—http://samsungelectronics.com/products/hdd/hdd.html
- **Seagate**—http://www.seagate.com/disc/disctop.shtml
- **Western Digital**—http://www.westerndigital.com/

Keyboards and Mice

- **Logitech**—http://www.logitech.com/us/keyboards/index.html
- **Microsoft**—http://www.microsoft.com/catalog/display.
  asp?site=10078&subid=22&pg=1

Memory

- **Crucial**—http://www.crucial.com/
- **Kingston**—http://www.kingston.com/

Modems

- **3-Com**—http://www.3com.com/
- **Creative Labs**—http://www.americas.creative.com/home.html

Monitors

- **Compaq**—http://www.compaq.com/athome/monitors/
- **Fujitsu**—http://www.fujitsu.com/plasma.html
- **Hewlett Packard**—http://www.hp.com/desktops/products/monitors/
- **IBM**—http://www.pc.ibm.com/us/accessories/monitors/index.html
- **Mitsubishi**—http://www.mitsubishi-display.com/default.html
- **NEC**—http://www.nectech.com/monitors/index.htm
- **Nokia**—http://www.nokia.com/americas/displays/index.html
- **Sony**—http://www.ita.sel.sony.com/products/displays/

Motherboards

- **ABIT**—http://www.abit.com.tw/english/index.htm
- **ASUS**—http://www.asus.com/Products/Motherboard/index.html
- **BCM Advanced Research**—http://www.bcmgvc.com/
- **BioStar**—http://www.biostar.com.tw/English02/default.htm
- **FIC**—http://www.fic.com.tw/
- **Gigabyte**—http://www.giga-byte.com/gigabyte-web/newindex.htm
- **Intel**—http://www.intel.com/
- **Soyo**—http://www.soyousa.com/
- **Tyan**—http://www.tyan.com/
- **Motherboard Homeworld Vendor Site**—http://www.motherboards.org/vendors.html

B

PC Cases

- **Addtronics**—http://www.addtronics.com/
- **Antec**—http://www.antec-inc.com/products/enclos/enclos.html
- **Case Outlet**—http://www.caseoutlet.com/case/case.htm

Printers

- **Compaq**—http://www.compaq.com/athome/printers/
- **Epson**—http://www.epson.com/northamerica.html

- **Hewlett Packard**—http://www.pandi.hp.com/pandi-db/home_page.show
- **IBM**—http://www.printers.ibm.com/
- **NEC**—http://www.nectech.com/printers/index.htm
- **Okidata**—http://www.okidata.com/

Scanners & Digital Cameras

- **Agfa**—http://www.agfa.com/
- **Epson**—http://www.epson.com/northamerica.html
- **Fujitsu**—http://www.fujitsu.com/scanners.html
- **Hewlett Packard**—http://www.pandi.hp.com/pandi-db/home_page.show
- **Kodak**—http://www.kodak.com/
- **Nikon**—http://www.nikon.co.jp/main/index_e.htm
- **Sony**—http://www.ita.sel.sony.com/products/imaging/
- **Umax**—http://www.umax.com/

Soundcards and Speakers

- **Altec Lansing**—http://www.altech.com/
- **Bose**—http://www.bose.com/multimedia/
- **Cambridge Soundworks**—http://www.cambridgesoundworks.com/index.htm
- **Sony**—http://www.ita.sel.sony.com/products/av/
- **Creative Labs**—http://www.americas.creative.com/home.html
- **Speechworks**—http://www.altech.com/
- **Turtle Beach**—http://www.voyetra-turtle-beach.com/site/default.asp

Video Cards

- **3dfx Interactive**—http://www.3dfx.com/view.asp
- **ASUS**—http://www.asus.com/Products/Addon/Vga/index.html
- **ATI Technologies**—http://www.ati.com/
- **Creative Labs**—http://www.americas.creative.com/graphics/
- **Diamond Multimedia**—http://www.diamondmm.com/
- **Elsa**—http://www.elsa.com/AMERICA/WELCOME.HTM
- **Matrox**—http://www.matrox.com/

INDEX

Q-R